INTERNATIONAL RIVALRIES IN
MANCHURIA, 1689-1922

INTERNATIONAL RIVALRIES
IN MANCHURIA
1689-1922

(Second Edition Revised)

BY

PAUL HIBBERT CLYDE

1966

OCTAGON BOOKS, INC.
New York

To
PAYSON J. TREAT

PREFACE TO SECOND EDITION

In writing a word of introduction to the second edition of this monograph, the author feels deeply gratified that the reception given the first printing a little more than a year ago seems to justify the present edition.

During recent months a number of books and papers have appeared embodying the use of materials of great importance dealing with the international situation in Manchuria during the years 1894 to 1914. Space will not permit a detailed discussion of these in the text of this edition. A careful reading of a number of these monographs such as Langer's, *The Origin of the Russo-Japanese War,* and Hsu's, *China and Her Political Entity,* has not served to alter materially any of the general conclusions reached by the author in the first edition. These newer contributions, however, are of immense value in that the materials used in them serve to establish as fact much in the story which formerly was based on somewhat superficial evidence.

The author, as was to be expected, has met severe criticism from a number of well known authorities on the subject of his interpretation of the American Open Door policy in the Far East. It has been and still is his purpose to show what status, if any, the American Open Door holds in terms of international law and he has met with no evidence to date warranting any revision of the interpretation that appeared in the first edition.

No attempt has been made to bring the story up to date from 1922. The years succeeding that date have been filled with activity so far as Manchuria is concerned but this story is reserved for a later volume not merely because of limitations of space but because much of the material necessary for an historical treatment of the subject has not yet been made available to the historian. The student who wishes to follow the events of the past five years in Manchuria will find a wealth of journalistic material which is quite informative in such publications as: *The New York Times, Current History, The North China Herald, The Trans-Pacific, Foreign Affairs* and *Japan.*

The bibliography to the first edition has been enlarged by a number of titles of considerable importance.

The author is indebted to Mr. Meiric K. Dutton, director of the Ohio State University Press for many helpful suggestions toward the preparation of this edition.

To his wife, who has ably assisted in reading the proof and in making the index, the author expresses his grateful appreciation.

PAUL HIBBERT CLYDE.

Columbus,
December 14, 1927.

PREFACE TO FIRST EDITION

The story of INTERNATIONAL RIVALRIES IN MAN-
CHURIA is one of the most important elements in what
is generally called the Far Eastern Question. Statesmen and diplomats have wrestled with this question
since the rise of western influence in the Far East during the past and the present centuries, and the Washington Conference of 1921-1922 seemed to foreshadow
a new era in the settlement of international controversies in the Pacific. Yet if one is to judge by the
atmosphere of suspicion and doubt that has characterized much American opinion of Pacific and Far Eastern
questions since 1922, peace in the Pacific is far from
being assured. In a word the Far Eastern Question
has not been solved.

Three years ago one phase of this problem was
called to the attention of the writer by a man who is
a pioneer among American students of the Far East,
Dr. Payson J. Treat, and since that time the author
has devoted his energy to contributing in a small way
to the available literature on Manchuria, that comparatively small northeastern extremity of Chinese territory which has served as a battleground for rival
powers in the Far East.

For more than thirty years, to be precise, since the
outbreak of the Chino-Japanese War in 1894, there has
been a Manchurian question. To be sure this date
did not mark the beginning of Manchurian history, but
events which preceded it did not give rise to the problems which have become so vital in international
affairs since that time. For this reason the writer
has given only a brief and summary treatment to the
early advance of the Russians into Manchuria during

the seventeenth and the middle years of the nineteenth centuries. The writer has also limited the scope of the narrative in respect to the history of the Chinese Eastern Railway, which, after the year 1905, he has touched upon only in the resolutions of the Washington Conference.

In building the story a three-fold purpose has been kept in view. The first was to give an accurate and connected narrative of international diplomacy in Manchuria since 1689 when China signed with Russia the Treaty of Nerchinsk, the first which she contracted with a western power, until the meeting of the Washington Conference in 1921-1922. The second was to co-relate available materials both old and new which might throw a new or clearer light on the subject. And finally to evaluate this material with a view to drawing reasonable and legitimate conclusions.

The controversial nature of the subject has given rise to difficulties and dangers of partisanship, against which the writer has attempted to be constantly on guard. A considerable amount of the secondary literature which treats of Manchurian affairs is the work of writers who have been primarily interested in building a case for one or another of the Powers involved in Far Eastern affairs. Such literature cannot legitimately claim the name, history. The reader is therefore asked to recognize that in the following study the writer's aim has been to define and interpret national motives, for it is only with an understanding of these motives, that have given rise to international rivalries, that we can hope to find the solution of the problem.

In no case has it been the purpose to assess the blame for the wars, jealousies, and hatreds which have arisen out of INTERNATIONAL RIVALRIES IN MAN-CHURIA.

The writer wishes to express his indebtedness to Dr. Payson J. Treat, at whose suggestion he undertook this study and whose guidance has made its completion possible. He is also under obligation to Professors Yamato Ichihashi and F. A. Golder, who have read the manuscript and offered valuable suggestions and criticisms. The manuscript has also been read by Dr. Harry Elmer Barnes. But as for the materials here presented and the conclusions drawn none of the above mentioned authorities is to be held responsible. The writer accepts full responsibility for this interpretation of a phase of Far Eastern diplomacy.

The author is also indebted to Professor Ralph Fanning of the Ohio State University who drew the map of Manchuria which appears at the beginning of this volume, and to Mr. Thornton P. Terhune, M.A., of the Department of History, Ohio State University, who has generously assisted in reading the proof.

PAUL HIBBERT CLYDE.

Columbus,
October 1, 1926

TABLE OF CONTENTS

INTERNATIONAL RIVALRIES IN
MANCHURIA, 1689-1922

INTERNATIONAL RIVALRIES IN MANCHURIA

CHAPTER I

PHYSICAL MANCHURIA AND THE BEGINNING OF FOREIGN INFLUENCE

I. PHYSICAL MANCHURIA

Since the year 1895, when, for a moment, Japan held within her grasp the Liaotung Peninsula and the fortress of Port Arthur, only to see the prize snatched from her by the combined efforts of Russia, France, and Germany, that northeastern section of the Chinese Empire, known to us as Manchuria, has played a major role in the drama of diplomacy. The day on which Japan bowed wisely to the "friendly" advice of these western powers marked the beginning of a fierce and sustained struggle, a struggle of both war and diplomacy, to control the "Three Eastern Provinces."[1] This is the conflict that forms the story of the following pages, which we have called INTERNATIONAL RIVALRIES IN MANCHURIA.

In order that the reader may appreciate the conditions which prevailed in Manchuria at the beginning of our story in 1895, and some of the factors that have drawn Russia and Japan into the turmoil of Manchurian history, it will first be necessary to devote a few words to the country itself and the first advance of the Russians on the Amur.

---

[1] Manchuria consists of three provinces: Fengtien or Mukden, Kirin, and Heilungkiang. Generally speaking these provinces lie to the east of Peking, hence the "Three Eastern Provinces."

In the early years of the 17th century, when the pioneers of our own country were establishing their homes on the Atlantic seaboard of the North American Continent, a remarkable leader, Nurhachu, having united under his banner the scattered tribes of Manchuria, established his capital at Fengtien, the now famous city of Mukden, and entered upon a struggle with China, which in 1644 resulted in the overthrow of the helpless Ming dynasty and the establishment of Manchu power in Peking. From that day until 1912 China was ruled by an alien dynasty, and Manchuria, its ancestral home, became a part of the Empire.

This land was one of the dependencies of the Chinese Empire.[2] It lies to the north and east of the eighteen provinces usually spoken of as China "proper" and together with Mongolia, a similar dependency, forms a vast stretch of territory, separating the Middle Kingdom from Southern Siberia.[3] The area of the three provinces is in the neighborhood of 380,000 or possibly 390,000 square miles, or considerably more than double the area of the State of California. These figures, however, are quoted with all reserve for two reasons. In the first place careful surveys of the entire country have not yet been completed, while in the second, the western boundary against Mongolia has

---

[2] On April 7, 1907, an Imperial decree abolished Manchuria as a dependency under a Tartar General and appointed a viceroy and three governors to rule the country and to administer it on the same basis as the eighteen provinces of the Empire. (Richard, *Comprehensive Geography of the Chinese Empire*, 505.)

[3] The name Manchuria is derived from the term Manchu, designating the people who inhabited the country. The more technical name is Tungsan-Sheng or "Three Eastern Provinces." It is also known as Liaotung or region east of the Liao River. Sometimes it has been called the country of the Eight Banners, a reference to the military organization of the Manchus. The term Kwantung is also applied to designate the country "East of the Barrier." See Richard, *op. cit.*, 486-7.

never been finally determined. To describe Manchuria, therefore, as a definitely fixed territorial unit is not possible at the present time.[4]

The following chapters are in main a study of diplomacy and for this purpose geographical position plays a far greater part than area, for in recent years Manchuria has become a sort of common ground, a no man's land, in which the interests of China, Japan, and Russia have at times been almost hopelessly canfused. It must be remembered that only in the south does Manchuria possess an outlet to the sea, where the city of Dairen and the once impregnable fortress of Port Arthur are washed by the Yellow Sea, and where the Liao, the largest river of southern Manchuria, empties into the Gulf of Liaotung. To the east Manchuria is cut off from the sea by Korea, now a part of the Empire of Japan, and the Maritime Province of Siberia, called Primorsk, which was acquired by Russia in 1860. In the north the Amur or Black Dragon River separates the provinces from Siberia, while to the west Mongolia, over which China has long exercised an uncertain control, forms a barrier with the Transbaikal Province of Russia in the north, and the Chinese Province of Chili in the south.

Within these borders lie the "Three Eastern Provinces": Fengtien, Kirin, and Heilungkiang. In the first, often referred to as Shengkiang or Mukden Province, which comprises the fertile lands of south Manchuria, lie not only the chief cities, the commercial centers of Dairen and Mukden, but the Japanese leased

---

[4] Hoshino, T., *Economic History of Manchuria*, Seoul, 1920, 6. See also Richard, *op. cit.*, 486; *An Official Guide to Eastern Asia, vol.* I Manchuria and Chosen, 1; *The China Year Book* and the *Statesman's Year Book*. Mr. Hoshino has made a valuable contribution and his estimated area of Manchuria, 382,632 square miles, is the most satisfactory figure yet published. See also Adachi, *Manchuria, a Survey*, 13.

territory and the lines of the South Manchuria Railway Company. Here are to be found many places which Manchurian history has made famous: Dairen, called by the Russians Dalny and by the Chinese Talienwan; Mukden, the capital, the ancient and picturesque seat of Manchu power; and Port Arthur, a fortress made immortal by heroic feats of arms. To the north and east the province of Kirin, with its capital of the same name, extends to the Sungari and Amur Rivers on the north and the Ussuri on the east. The last and largest, the Province of Heilungkiang, or the Black Dragon, lies to the west and north where the Khingan Mountains fall away into the boundless plains of Mongolia, and towards the waters of the Amur in the far north. These provinces play the usual part of such territorial divisions in the internal administration of the country, but the reader will meet more frequently with such terms as North and South Manchuria which have come to possess a particular significance since the contact of Russian and Japanese influence. The treaties of 1915 between China and Japan gave further occasion for the use of this terminology, and although geographically the division still remains vague the following suggestion of it is given: starting at Hunchun on the eastern coast, the line takes a northwesterly course passing along the mountain ridges of Laoyeh to Hsiushuitientzu, then follows the course of the Second Sungari, the Nonni and the Taoerho Rivers and ends at the border of the Amur Province.[5]

It is a land of great natural beauty, where mountains and forests, great rivers and fertile plains invite ad-

---

[5] Hoshino, *op. cit.*, 11-12. The best map defining the external boundaries and internal divisions of Manuchuria is that published by the bureau of investigation attached to the president of the South Manchuria Railway.

miration. A land perhaps not so romantically picturesque as its neighbor, the island Empire of Japan, but possessed of the grander dignity of long slowly flowing rivers and wide fields of waving grain. Two great mountain chains traverse the country, the Khingan in the northwest, the Changpai in the southeast, with here and there a peak rising to eight thousand feet. The spurs of these ranges sink into the central plain of South Manchuria, where abound those fertile lands which are its richest endowment. Many of the mountain sides are covered with thick forests of fir, oak, walnut, birch, and pine and present a picture not unlike those with which we are familiar in our own country. Gold and other precious metals have been taken in moderate quantities from the river beds, particularly in the north, and the coal mines of Fushun give promise of wealth well nigh inexhaustible.

During the past two decades the railroad and the steamship have opened the country to a volume of trade not dreamed of in the days when early explorers of Muscovy sailed down the Amur and its branches, the Sungari and Nonni. And even today much of the merchandise is carried by small river boats and pack trains which made their way slowly along ill-kept, often impassible roads. In the south the Liao and Yalu are still popular with the Chinese and Korean boatmen. In ancient times the former river formed the main route of Chinese expeditions against the wild tribes of the north, and along the same course moved the Manchu horsemen gathered under the banner of Nurhachu and his successors in their invasion of the Middle Kingdom.[6]

---

[6] Hoshino, *op. cit.*, 8 ; *Chinese Repository*, vol. 20, 296 ; Fulford, H. E. account of a journey in Manchuria, *Br. Sess. Papers*, C., 1887, vol. XCI, China No. 2 ; and Richard, *op. cit.*, 489 ; Kropotkin's "Russian Explorations in Man-

The climate is both favorable and stimulating, with variations of temperature inevitable in a country reaching from the moderate conditions of lands bordering on the Yellow Sea to the frozen regions of Siberia. Extremes of heat and cold are moderated in the south by the warm current flowing from the southern seas, which makes Dairen an ice-free port the year round. Even the severe winters in the northern sections are tempered somewhat by the Maritime Province, a high protective barrier, warding off the icy current from the Arctic. During the long winter months most of the rivers are icebound and their smooth surfaces provide the best roads of any season of the year. They have been so used for many centuries and are by no means abandoned to this day in a country where roads receive little or no care. Most of the rapid agricultural development of recent years has taken place in the central and southern plains from which the soya bean crops are now finding a world market.

In Manchuria live today some 22,000,000 persons, hardly to be considered a dense population on the basis of any comparison, and in relation to conditions in most parts of China "proper," a mere handful. About 700,000 of these, including more than 100,000 Japanese, reside in the territory leased by Japan in the Kwantung Peninsula and the South Manchuria Railway zone. Large numbers of coolies enter annually from the northern provinces of China to work in the fields and while the majority of these return to their homes in Shantung, many remain as permanent settlers.[7]

---

churia," *Geographical Journal*, vol. XI, 1898, 65 ; and Collin's "Explorations of the Amoor River," Ex. doc. (U. S.) 1857-58, vol. 12, ser. 958, Ex. doc. 98, p. 37.

[7] Population as estimated by the South Manchuria Railway Company in

Before entering upon a discussion of those earliest movements by which Russia first came in contact with China and established her influence in Far Eastern affairs something may be said of Manchurian history in order that the relationship of this country to China may be understood. So far as is known the Manchus do not bear a close blood relationship to the Chinese. They are descendants of a branch of the great Tungus race which at one time spread over the entire regions of Manchuria and the Maritime province. The descendants of this race occupied the "Three Eastern Provinces" in 1644 at the time of the Manchu conquest of China and from its soldiery were dispatched to China the garrisons which held in submission the newly won dominions. Furthermore it was not until a century after the conquest that Chinese emigration to the provinces north of the Great Wall was permitted. Once commenced, however, the influx increased with remarkable rapidity until at the present time the great bulk of the population of Manchuria is Chinese. The Manchu language, never blessed with a great literature, was fostered by the first emperors of the race who ruled in Peking, but despite this patronage it has fallen gradually into disuse. Today it is spoken by only a few of the old Manchu families, while their countrymen, scattered throughout the garrisoned towns of China until the days of the revolution in 1911 and 1912, slowly but surely have been absorbed into the Chinese life and have acquired the dialect of the localities in which they live. Thus while the Chinese

---

1916 was 20,112,100 or 53 persons per square mile. (Hoshino, *op. cit.*, 6.) The Kwantung Government, the administration of the leased territory, gives 19,405.617, while the publications of the Imperial Japanese Government Railways quote 15,834,000. In recent years population has increased rapidly, Richard using the figures 8,500,000 in 1908.

never ceased to look upon the Manchus as an alien and conquering power, much of the national identity of the latter, which was strong in the days of conquest, has been lost.

Prior to the 10th century Manchuria was given over to the warring of numerous branches of the Tungus race, a petty warfare which had little to do with events taking place in China.   These local conflicts resulted in a succession of lesser dynasties, Pechili, Liao, and Kin, which rose and fell in these parts before the conquest of China by the Mongols in 1260; and they further paved the way for the rise of the Aisin-Gioro family, which gave to the race its greatest leader, Nurhachu, whose descendants, as already stated, established their power at Peking in 1644.[8]   Nominally therefore Manchuria became a part of the Chinese Empire governed by officials directly responsible to Peking.   In practice this control was exercised with success so far as the southern province of Fengtien was concerned, but in the north beyond the Sungari on to the Amur as far as the ridge of the Stanovoi Mountains the control was more a matter of theory than of practice.[9]   Annually officials visited these remote regions to collect tribute from the natives, but beyond this Peking had no interest in, and probably very little conception of the economic or startegic value of the Amur basin. This general attitude of disregard might have con-

---

[8] Gowen, *An Outline History of China*, pt. 1, 123 ; pt. 2, 15.

Giles, *China and the Manchus*, 2, 4, and 7.

Boulger, *The History of China*, vol. 1, chapter 36, "The Conquest of China," 534-562.

Cordier, *Histoire Generale de la Chine*, vol. 3, chapter 7, "Les Ming," and chapter 20, "Les Ts'ing" (1644).

Hirth, *The Ancient History of China* may be consulted for the very early phases of Chinese development (sections treating Northern China).

[9] A recent and fairly satisfactory account of the government of Manchuria may be found in Adachi, *op cit.*, chapter 14.

tinued indefinitely but for reports which began to reach
Peking telling of terrible men from the north who
swept down upon peaceful villages where they burned
and plundered, killed the men and carried away their
women. To this problem, the Manchus, already engaged in consolidating their position in China, now
turned their attention, counseled by Jesuit fathers then
living in Peking. This was the condition in Manchuria
in the forties of the 17th century when Poyarkof and
his Cossacks began their devastating career on the
Amur. For a moment therefore we will turn from
China and regard Manchuria from the point of view of
a western power, Russia, which was now pushing steadily toward the Pacific, urged on by a lucrative fur
trade.

II. THE BEGINNING OF FOREIGN INFLUENCE

In the latter years of the 16th and the early years
of the 17th century, explorers, fur traders, and brigands from European Russia began to sweep eastward
across the snow-covered mountains and along the rivers
of Siberia. Their company, composed alike of legitimate adventurers, and fugitives from the law, soon
penetrated from the Urals to the frozen shores of the
Sea of Okhotsk, and in between there sprang into
being the trading posts and towns of Tobolsk, Tomsk,
Yeniseisk, Yakutsk, Nerchinsk, and Okhotsk, all within
the first half of the century.[10] A prosperous fur trade
had drawn these pioneers to the very edge of the Pa-

---

[10] Rambaud, A., *The Expansion of Russia*, 92, published in *The Case of
Russia*, New York, 1915.

    Golder, *Russian Expansion on the Pacific 1641-1850*, chapter 1, "The
Administration of Eastern Siberia in the Seventeenth Century."

    Vladimir, *Russia on the Pacific and the Siberian Railway*, chapter 2,
"The Conquest of Siberia."

cific and with the growth of their rude outposts of empire the problem of supplying the settlements with food presented increasing difficulties. To meet this problem a movement to the south commenced, down and beyond the waters of the Amur into the land of the Manchus, whose armies were then invading China. Shortly after the organization of the Yakutsk district in eastern Siberia, which was fast becoming famous as a center of the fur trade, hunters who followed the Lena to its mountain source were told of great streams beyond the mountains in a land rich with grain and silver. These reports were of such importance that the exploration of the country south of the Stanovoi Mountains was immediately decided upon and undertaken by the energetic administration of Yakutsk. This decision resulted in the barbarous expeditions of Poyarkof, Khabarof, and Stepanof, who in the middle years of the century led their Cossacks down the southern slopes of the mountains to the country of the Amur.[11] Burning and pillaging and striking terror to the native tribes as they advanced these heralds of an expanding Russia soon established themselves at Albasin and other posts on the river, but so great had been their cruelty to the natives that these latter appealed to Peking and armies were ordered to the north to drive out the invaders. An irregular warfare followed, which, while deciding nothing, checked the boldness of the Cossacks who had by 1651 extended their influence over the entire length of the great river. Seven years later the struggle was renewed, and the Cossacks, under the incompetent leadership of Stepanof, fled to the mountains. The Amur was now freed

---

[11] Golder, *op. cit.*, 33-37.
Ravenstein, *Russians on the Amur*, 9-24.
Hsü, *China and Her Political Entity*, 47.

of the Russians as far north as Nerchinsk and more peaceful days were enjoyed by the whole district.[12]

In the meantime Russian adventurers had settled and fortified Albasin on the upper Amur and now attempted to collect tribute from the neighboring tribes who appealed to China for aid. A mission sent from Peking to Nerchinsk accomplished nothing save the dispatch of a return mission to Peking in 1670. Other facts also foreshadowed the coming struggle. The Russians showed a new tendency to expand. Forts were built on the Dseya and its branches in 1681. Frequent disputes arose between the Chinese and the Cossack hunters and traders. Ofttimes there was little or no law to restrain the boldness of the Russians, and the Chinese government, failing after several efforts to induce the Russians to a peaceful settlement, erected forts on the Dseya and in 1685 captured and destroyed Albasin. It was rebuilt almost immediately and a Chinese army was attacking it a second time when an embassy from the Tsar reached Peking asking that the siege be raised and announcing the approach of a plenipotentiary to treat with China concerning the frontier.[13]

The representatives of China and Russia met near Nerchinsk on the Shilka, one of the great branches of the upper Amur, on August 22, 1689. The Chinese were accompanied by Jesuit fathers from Peking and a force of nearly 10,000 soldiers and attendants, a display which, coupled with the tact of the European missionaries, counted for the success of the Chinese in their first diplomatic victory over a western power.

[12] Golder, *op. cit.*, 47-55.
[13] *Ibid.*, 56-63.
Ravenstein, *op. cit.*, 45-53.
Hsü, *op. cit.*, 49-50.

Amid an extravagant show and with much ceremony
the conference was opened.   The Russians proposed
that the Amur form the boundary.   The Chinese, jealous of the northern territory which had been nominally
under their control and in which they had been accus-
tomed to collect tribute, made a counter proposal that
Russia withdraw beyond the Selenga.   The discussions
continued for about two weeks with little indication of
a compromise.   Then the Chinese, taking advantage
of their greater numbers and becoming impatient at the
delay, brought their opponents to a more reasonable
frame of mind through an unmistakable show of force.
The Treaty of Nerchinsk, the first contracted by China
with a western power, was signed on August 27.   By
this settlement the ridge of the Stanovoi Mountains
became the boundary; the Russians were to withdraw
from the country of the Amur, and Albasin, long the
stronghold of outlawed men and a terror to the land
was to be destroyed.[14]

The Treaty of Nerchinsk is notable in two respects.
It was the first which China signed with a nation of
the west and for China it was a diplomatic triumph.
With relatively small effort the Manchu power had
achieved a settlement of its northeastern boundaries
that was to prevail for more than a century and a half.
The eastward and then southerly advance of Russia
toward the Middle Kingdom was effectively checked
and the government of Peking was able to turn to the
internal problems of empire, free from the threatening

---

[14] Ravenstein who has been cited by many writers in connection with the
signing of this treaty gives August 27 as the date of the signing and August 29
for the exchange of ratifications.   August 27 is also given in "Treaties, Conventions, etc., between China and Foreign States" (Maritime Customs).
Cahen, *Relations de la Russie avec la Chine*, 49, gives August 27-September 6.
This is correct, as the difference between the Julian and Gregorian Calendar in
the 17 century would be ten days.

ravages of Cossack adventurers. The treaty by which this settlement was consummated is somewhat baffling. The texts vary widely and employ a vagueness of language which makes conflicting interpretation possible if not inevitable, and more serious consequences might have resulted had either power proceeded to the exploitation of the Amur basin.[15] The full value of the country over which they fought was realized by neither China nor Russia. To be sure, Manchuria was nominally under the government at Peking, but such political control as was exercised was entirely inadequate. Russia on the other hand was primarily interested in these lands because they offered a lucrative fur trade. Political factors which dominated her Far Eastern policy in the middle of the 19th century had not yet arisen and it is therefore not surprising that her program in these early years at Nerchinsk claimed little of the dignity or unity of purpose that might be expected from a great power. Even had there been something worthy the name of policy it is problematical whether Russia could have achieved more than she did, for her leaders sent to the Far East were ill suited to the task before them. They were more concerned with the opportunity to plunder than with the expansion of empire or the opening of new lands. The principal claim of Poyarkof, Khabarof, and Stepanof to distinction was their capacity to use brute force and their unchecked desire to pillage. These

---

[15] The Latin text follows the original Chinese closely and the French varies from it only in a slight degree. The Russian version contains maked differences and the English translations vary according as they are taken from the Chinese and Latin or the Russian text. The question whether the first principles of extraterritoriality were introduced in this treaty arises in connection with the interpretations of the Russian version. Mr. Koo in his *Status of Aliens in China* fails to find support for this view in the Latin text. For the purposes of western readers the French version as given by DuHalde (vol 4, 242-244) is the most satisfactory.

were years when Russia might have done great things, but her leaders were blind and in later times when the opportunities were less favorable to her, the Manchus, now firmly established in Peking, were in a better position to guard their northern frontier. Had the Russian policy been pursued with greater success no one could have questioned her claim to the Amur on the basis of discovery and occupation. If her conquests had been of a decent character there seems to be little doubt that she would have established herself there by 1650. No question could have been raised as to her right of exacting tribute from the native population. Such a right was widely recognized. But she wasted the early years in making enemies of the native inhabitants and their overlords to the south, and after forty years of so-called occupation was forced quietly to accept the terms of the envoys of the Emperor Kang Hsi.

For more than one hundred and fifty years an era of comparative peace ruled between China and the frontier settlements of Russia in eastern Siberia. Russia was content to restrict her colonization to lands lying west of the Amur and China made no more pressing demands on the natives of her northern province than the customary exactions of tribute which they were content to pay; until in 1846 Nicholas I ordered an investigation of the whole Amur question as well as the territory itself and in the following year appointed as governor of Eastern Siberia, Nicholas Muravieff, later known as Muravieff Amursky, a man of capacity and vision.[16]

Russia was fast becoming involved in the diplomatic complications leading to the Crimean War and a long continued agitation for a strengthening of the Far

---

[16] Pasvolsky, *Russia in the Far East*, 12.

Eastern possessions had at last called attention to the interests which might be protected on her Pacific shores. The intervening years since the Treaty of Nerchinsk while generally peaceful, had been disturbed from time to time by minor disputes and bickerings. Although the Russians had been excluded from privileges of navigation on the Amur, the allegiance of tribes inhabiting the border remained a subject of unending dispute. Cossack hunters crossed the border in quest of game and officials demanded tribute from tribes formerly subject to Peking. The Chinese in some places did not claim the full southern slope of the Stanovoi Mountains and in others they were accused of encroaching on Russian lands. Most of these difficulties were due to ignorance of the country and loose interpretation of the treaty. Numerous missions to reach a settlement were exchanged between the powers but nothing came of their proposals.[17]

During the century that preceded the coming of Muravieff to Eastern Siberia a few Russian statesmen advanced the idea that the surrender of the Amur country to China, and especially the right of navigation on the river, was a major blunder of Russian diplomacy. As early as 1741 the desirability of free navigation of the river was brought forward in connection with provisioning the Kamchatka settlements and it was suggested that a post be built at the mouth of the river. Fifty years later a mission was dispatched to Peking to ask for free navigation or consent for a few provision ships to be sent annually down the river; but China would have none of these proposals. Thus while Russia looked with increasing interest on her far eastern lands and China refused any modifica-

[17] Ravenstein, *op. cit.*, 65-71.

tion of the existing arrangement there arrived as governor of Eastern Siberia, in 1848, Nicholas Muravieff. For Russia the choice was a wise one. To the problems which faced him he brought clear vision and an appreciation of great possibilities of the future. The territory he governed stretched from the Yenisei to Bering Strait. His task was to consolidate Russia's position and to further the establishment of a naval base in Pacific waters.[18] In 1849 he visited Kamchatka and confirmed the proposal of a special body appointed by the Tsar that explorations be conducted at the mouth of the Amur, a task which was entrusted to Captain Nevelskoy who started on his mission the same year. Cautioned by the insecurity of Russia's position in Eastern Siberia, Muravieff was determined to avoid serious conflict with China but in spite of this Nevelskoy raised the Russian flag at the mouth of the Amur and proclaimed the whole territory a part of the Russian Empire. It was discovered too that sea-going vessels could penetrate to the mouth of the river without rounding Sakhalin. This discovery was of great importance to the Russians although it was known to the Chinese many years earlier that Sakhalin was an island.[19] Although the report of Nevelskoy's exploit at the mouth of the Amur was at first unfavorably received in St. Petersburg, a decision not to withdraw was reached. Muravieff had won his first victory and Russia was once more established on the Amur.

In 1853, having received imperial sanction, Muravieff ordered the occupation of Sakhalin and thus boldly entered the next phase of the campaign that was to place Russia in possession of the northern bank of the

---

[18] Vladimir, *op. cit.*, 173.
[19] Grossier, *A General Description of China*, vol. 1, 132-133.

Amur and the Pacific coast territory as far south as Korea. He visited St. Petersburg the same year where he urged before the Emperor that a weak China needed the protection of a mighty Russia against the growing power of England on the Pacific. The following year witnessed great activity among the Russians in the Far East. In January the Emperor ordered that all questions relating to the frontier should be settled directly by Muravieff with the Peking government and it was decided to begin navigation on the Amur with or without the consent of China. Accordingly the Peking government was informed that on account of the war between Russia and Great Britain and France, Russia would send troops down the river for the protection of her possessions on the Pacific, and China was asked to appoint a time and place where plenipotentiaries of the two powers might meet to settle questions concerning the frontier. During the summer Muravieff descended the river and proceeded to make military preparations along the seacoast—activities which were favorably received in St. Petersburg. Expeditions down the Amur now became an annual event and in 1856 Muravieff, well acquainted with the visionary claims of the Chinese to sovereignty on the northern bank of the river, was appointed while in St. Petersburg, plenipotentiary to negotiate a new treaty with China.[20]

He returned to Manchuria with plans for colonization along the river. At the same time events in China had attracted the attention of the Russian government. There, relations between the Peking authorities and the foreign powers, especially England and France,

---

[20] Vladimir, *op. cit.*, 197-242.
Ravenstein, *op. cit.*, 117-125.
Hsü, *China and Her Political Entity*, 73-78.

were fast leading to the outbreak of the second European war. Russia, wishing to benefit also should the other foreign powers gain diplomatic representation at Peking, appointed Admiral Putiatin, who had concluded a successful treaty with Japan, as Minister to Peking with instructions to settle the frontier question. At Kiakhta, where he proceeded after an interview with Muravieff, he was refused permission to continue overland to Peking. A further attempt to reach Peking by way of Aigun through Manchuria also failed and a decision to make a third effort by sea followed, but at Tientsin he again encountered obstacles and finally had to content himself with observing the operations of the English and French, then preparing to attack Canton.[21]

Though uncertain as to what Putiatin might accomplish at Tientsin, Muravieff was satisfied with the progress of his policy. He had with great care avoided all unnecessary conflicts with the Chinese. His plan had been one of peaceful absorption well suited to the circumstances then confronting China. By this time her officials well knew the futility of a struggle against the Russians, while the Empire was threatened by the Taiping rebels from within and aggressive foreign powers from without. A peaceful settlement was the only possible solution. This was the situation which Muravieff had most desired and when in the spring of 1858 Chinese officials requested that he confer with Prince T-shan, commander-in-chief of the forces on the Amur, he readily accepted.

On May 11 the first conference was held at Aigun and five days later the convention was signed. Muravieff's decisive action, his ready ability to meet every

---

[21] Vladimir, *op. cit.*, 252-257.

situation, and his unwillingness to be turned aside by
the dilatory methods of the Chinese won for Russia
the entire northern bank of the Amur, a prize which
she had allowed to escape her nearly two centuries
earlier, while the territory between the Ussuri and the
sea was to be held in common by the two powers until
there should be a final settlement of the frontier.[22] In
granting this concession Muravieff probably had in
mind the Treaty of Nerchinsk, which had left undeter-
mined the territory adjacent to the sea, and knew that
the question of the possession of the region which in
1860 became the Russian Maritime province would be
settled with little difficulty after Russia had a firm
hold on the entire northern bank of the Amur. Furthermore navigation of this river, together with the
Ussuri and Sungari, was to be confined to Russian and
Chinese vessels. The trade of all northern Manchuria
was thus thrown open to Russia, and her position in
the Far East immeasurably strengthened. News of
the treaty was received with great satisfaction in St.
Petersburg and Muravieff was created Count of the
Amur. His skill had won the victory for Russia; but
circumstances in China were favorable to his project.
China's military strength such as it was, was occupied
with the troubled internal conditions of the Empire
and the war with the European Allies, and although
more significance was attached to the Amur by Peking
than in 1689, its importance was by no means fully
known. The Aigun Convention was ratified by the
Emperor of China on June 2nd and by the Tsar on
July 8th. In June also China signed the Tientsin
Treaties with British, French, American, and Russian
representatives. The task confronting Putiatin who

---

[22] *Treaties and Conventions, etc., between China and Foreign States*, 81.

signed the Russian Text was comparatively easy. He had the moral support of the English and French forces then in Chinese waters and also the influence that had enabled Muravieff to secure the Aigun Convention a few weeks earlier. He sought no exorbitant demands from China for his instructions were to avoid any action which would threaten the successful conclusion of the Aigun affair.[23]

Russia's next move came the following year. When in January of 1859 it became evident that China was yielding to the pressure of England and France, the Tsar appointed General Ignatieff to proceed to Peking to settle the frontier question on the Manchurian coast. In the meantime Muravieff visited Japan and surveyed the coast of the Ussuri region. The site of Vladivostok was selected for future settlement and the place was occupied by Russia on July 20, 1860. In Peking, Russia was playing a clever and two-faced game. The Allies were marching on the Imperial Capital, and China's extremity was Russia's opportunity to show the sincerity of her long and unbroken friendship. Backed by ample military force the foreigners were come to destroy the dynasty; perhaps to possess themselves of the Empire. Already the court had taken flight. General Ignatieff confirmed the Chinese worst fears and revealed the only way of escape. The intervention of a strong European power was China's only salvation. He had it within his power to make such representations to Lord Elgin and Baron Gros, commanders of the Allied forces, and this intervention China might enjoy for a simple rectification of her Manchurian frontier; for a barren seacoast, a stretch of useless territory. Prince Kung, then in control of

---

[23] The European negotiators at Peking did not know at the time of the Aigun Treaty.

the Peking government, eagerly accepted the offer and so the great Maritime Province, Primorsk, passed to the dominions of the Tsar, and with it China signed away the spot already selected by Russia for the domination of the East—Vladivostok.[24]

In November, 1860, the Treaty of Peking was signed. It corroborated and elucidated the convention concluded two years previous at Aigun and settled many matters not dealt with in that document. By the two treaties Russia, while playing the role of friend and protector, had deprived China of some 343,000 square miles of territory, or more than twice the area of the old empire of Japan. The importance of such territorial acquisitions needs little explanation. After nearly two centuries since the first appearance of the Cossack horsemen on the banks of the Amur, Russian policy had at length assumed something of a definite character. Whereas in her attempts of the 17th century she had blundered blindly and without leadership into a struggle, the object of which was never very clear, she had now found in Muravieff a sagacious and resolute guiding force. Add to this the situation in which a frightened government at Peking was eager to grasp the slightest measure of relief, and the ease with which Russia thus advanced her fortunes in the Far East becomes a natural consequence. For the time being Russia was satisfied. In Vladivostok at the southern tip of the Maritime Province she might build a port for her Pacific squadron. This, her immediate object, had been accomplished while her artful diplomacy had drawn her closer into the confidence of the Chinese government and renewed the Chinese belief in the traditions of perpetual friendship between the two powers.

---

[24] Michie, *The Englishman in China*, vol. 1, 353-359 ; vol. 2, 252.

CHAPTER II

THE CHINO-JAPANESE WAR AND THE TRIPLE INTERVENTION

The history of Japan as a world power had its beginning in the swift and decisive victory of her armies and navy over China in the war of 1894-1895. Following immediately upon that victory, she demanded, among other things, cession by China of the Liaotung Peninsula, the southern promontory of Fengtien or Mukden Province in Manchuria. Thus began a struggle of diplomacy which at times broke into armed conflict, and involved the interests of practically all the great powers of Europe and the United States of America.

The results of the Chino-Japanese war were among the spectacular evidences of the rise of new Japan. Since the July day, 1853, when Commodore Matthew C. Perry sailed into the harbor of Uraga, a small cove in the Bay of Yedo, bearing a letter from the President of the United States, and called to the attention of the Shogun's government the folly of its policy of exclusion and seclusion, a miraculous transformation had been wrought in practically every feature of Japan's national life. Treaties had been concluded with all the great powers of the world, and after more than two hundred years of practical isolation, Japan, step by step, now sought to avail herself of the contributions which western civilization offered. The abolition of the Shogunate and the restoration of the Emperor were only the first steps in the remarkable progress which Japan was to make before the close of the 19th century. How radical, yet how sagacious, that progress was to be, found expression in what is spoken of as the "Charter Oath" taken by the young Mikado on April 6, 1868, the last clause of which stated that "knowledge shall be sought for throughout the world." In 1871 feudalism was abolished and national progress under a strong central government for the first time became possible. During these first years of Meiji many other changes were effected. The feudal levies began to give place to a national army and navy.[1] The development of industry and commerce was facilitated through the building of railways and telegraph lines. Educational reforms laid the foundation that was to open schools capable of caring for every boy and girl in the Empire. The leaders of government were anxious to learn all they could of western ideas and methods, and many of Japan's most brilliant young men were sent to study the western culture. When, therefore, the two greatest powers of the Orient came into armed conflict in 1894, it was not the Japan of the Tokugawas, of feudalism and dual government, of exclusion and seclusion; rather was it a nation reborn to a new life, well started in a new career, perhaps even anxious to test its newly acquired power which was as yet unknown because it was untried, that humbled Manchu power and aroused the apprehension of the three greatest continental nations of Europe. Briefly then, let us consider the causes leading to this struggle.

Mr. J. H. Gubbins has said that "those who are at all familiar with Chinese history will scarcely have failed to notice one persistent feature of it — the suzerainty that China has either exercised, or claimed to exercise, over neighboring states which at one time

---

[1] Treat, *Japan and the United States, 1853-1921*, 99.

or another have fallen under her domination."[2]   Many
states bordering on China had undergone this experience.   In the late years of the 19th century some of
these had recovered their independence, which, however, was not always recognized by China, and in some
cases, Korea for instance, the suzerainty of China had
become almost nominal.[3]   In 1876 Japan concluded a
treaty with Korea, the first article of which declared
that Korea was an independent state.[4] For many years
previous to this, Chinese suzerainty over the Korean
peninsula had ceased to be effective but it was still
asserted by China and acknowledged by Korea.   In
September, 1882, Li Hung-chang issued some trade
regulations for China and Korea which bore no evidence of having received the approval of the king of
Korea.   Among other things they asserted that the
peninsula was a tributary state.[5]   This act strengthened the attitude adopted by Japan in refusing to acknowledge Chinese suzerainty.   In this contradictory
situation lay causes for future trouble.

The growing influence of two powerful nations,
Japan and China, each bent on dominating a kingdom
long since in a state of complete decay, coupled with
the introduction of foreign elements in the intrigues
of contending political factions at the Korean court,

---

[2] Gubbins, *The Making of Modern Japan*, 214-215.

[3] Rockhill, *China's Intercourse with Korea*. This reference gives the background of the subject from the 15th century to 1895.

[4] In 1875 a Japanese ship of war was sent cruising along the coast of
Korea. In December some of her sailors were fired on while on Kianghwa
Island. A naval demonstration was made at Fusan in January, 1876, and a
treaty of amity and friendship was concluded on February 26. (Morse, *Inter-
national Relations of the Chinese Empire*, vol. 3, 8-9. See also *Parliamentary
Papers*, (C) vol. 83, 1876, Japan, No. 1.) The Korean Treaty of 1876 was
modeled on the Perry Treaty which Japan had negotiated with the United
States.

[5] Text in Customs edition of "China Treaties and Conventions," vol.
2, 1521-7.

had already led to internal disorders culminating in antiforeign disturbances and on July 23, 1882, came the first attack upon Japanese in Korea, resulting in the expulsion of the legation and the loss of several Japanese lives.[6] The military clamored for war, but, as in 1876, a settlement was reached by more peaceful methods and despite the dispatch of Chinese ships and men to Korea the latter decided to sign a convention in which it was stipulated that the guilty men should be punished, an indemnity paid, and additional commercial concessions granted. But the luckless Korean administration seemed powerless to control even events in its capital, and Chinese troops were largely responsible for the restoration of order there during 1883. Both Chinese and Japanese garrisons were now maintained at Seoul and for a time affairs were quiet, but further disturbances the following year were the occasion of a second attack on the Japanese legation and this time the Japanese and Chinese troops came into conflict. Despite the extent to which her patience had now been tried by the irresponsible Korean Government and the questionable policy of China, Japan sought an amicable settlement. Inouye was sent to negotiate with Korea and Ito met Li Hung-chang in February, 1885, at Tientsin. Of this latter meeting the Tientsin Convention was the result.[7] Both governments agreed to withdraw their troops, leaving only small legation guards, and to give previous notice "in writing" should the dispatch of troops to Korea by either power become necessary in the future.[8] However, during the ensuing years Yuan Shih-kai asserted China's superior position

---

[6] Treat, *op. cit.*, 149.

[7] The Tientsin Convention, signed at Tientsin, April 18, 1885. *Treaties between China and Foreign States*, (Maritime Customs), vol. 2, 588.

[8] Gubbins, *op. cit.*, 215-216.

at Seoul, where he now resided as Chinese commissioner, and when in March, 1894, a rebellion of the Tong Hak, an antigovernment and to some extent antiforeign sect, broke out, Yuan, after securing a definite request from the Korean king, persuaded Li Hungchang to dispatch Chinese troops to Korea, of which act Li promptly notified Japan. The Mikado's government had also prepared to send troops, and was provoked to prompt action by the use of the clause in the Chinese notification, *"in order to restore the peace of our tributary state."* Japan could not accept such language. The rebellion was suppressed by Korean soldiers before the foreign troops arrived. The Korean king asked the Chinese to leave, but they refused to move until the Japanese did so. The situation now became critical. Japan believed the rebellion was due to official corruption and asked China to cooperate with her in radical reforms. China replied that she could not control the internal affairs of Korea, much less could Japan who had recognized the independence of that state, assert such a privilege. Then Japan decided to act alone and ordered her troops to take possession of the royal palace. Under Japanese pressure Korea abrogated her treaty with China and requested Japan to expel the Chinese forces. On July 25th the Chinese transport *Kowshing* was sunk by Japan. On July 31st China declared war and Japan followed her example on the following day.[9]

The course of the war, which was in all respects disastrous for China, need only be briefly outlined in so

---

[9]Treat, *op. cit.*, 151-152. The writer has refrained from giving a detailed discussion of the causes leading to the Chino-Japanese War for the reason that the causes themselves had nothing to do with Manchuria directly and are introduced merely to make clear the narrative of this period. See Hsü, *op. cit.*, chap. 4.

far as the campaigns touched upon Manchuria.[10] Two
Japanese divisions crossed the Korean border into
Manchuria toward the end of October. Early in November the Chinese were driven from Talienwan by
another Japanese force, and on the 21st the fortress of
Port Arthur was taken. Meanwhile the armies operating from Korea had pushed steadily westward, defeated the Chinese in three engagements near Newchwang and occupied that port, while the Peking forces
retreated northward along the Liao River. Finally the
fall of Weihaiwei in Shantung before Japanese naval
and military forces on March 16th and the continuous
success of the Japanese armies on the Liao brought
home to the Chinese the hopelessness of the struggle.[11]

The overwhelming victory of Japanese arms was a
complete surprise to many foreign observers in the Far
East. In large measure the strength of China was
overestimated, while too few appreciated the progress
effected by Japan in the previous quarter century.[12]
As early as October the British government had invited the United States to join with it, Germany,
France, and Russia in an intervention, on the understanding that Korean independence should be guaranteed by the powers and that an indemnty for the
expense of the war should be paid Japan. Nothing
came of this move and on October 25th Japan rejected
the single offer of Great Britain to mediate. The
Tsungli Yamen, or Chinese Foreign Office, appealed to
the President of the United States on November 2nd,

---

[10] For a general and extensive reference on this subject the reader is
referred to Vladimir, *The China-Japan War*.

[11] Gubbins, *op. cit.*, 211.

[12] Chirol, *The Far Eastern Question*, chapters 2 and 3, presents a picture
of postwar China which explains in part Japan's victory and also some of the
international events which followed in the story of Manchurian affairs. See
also Gerard, *Ma Mission en Chine*, xxiv-xxx (introduction).

asking intervention and basing the claim on the treaty
of 1858, and on the following day the same body requested the ministers of the United States, England,
France, Germany, and Russia to request action of their
governments, agreeing to recognize the independence
of Korea and to pay an indemnity. Before the receipt
of these dispatches the President had offered his good
offices, which Japan refused, desiring that China approach her directly on the subject of peace. There
followed China's first two futile attempts to open peace
negotiations; the visit to Japan of Mr. Detring, a
German and Commissioner of Customs at Tientsin, on
November 26th, who was not received because he was
not properly accredited, and the second mission in February, which failed because the commissioners, Chang
Yen Huan, a minister of the Tsungli Yamen, and Shao
Yu-lien, Governor of the Province of Hunan, did not
possess full powers.[13]   At length in March Li Hung-
chang accepted the unenviable task of suing for peace.
Japan was to be represented by Count Ito, then prime
minister, and Viscount Mutsu, the foreign minister.
Both powers employed American advisers in the peace
negotiations which followed, John W. Foster being
associated with the Chinese and H. W. Denison with
the Japanese.

The situation in which the belligerent powers now
found themselves as they approached the peace conference at Shimonoseki had a significant bearing on
the results of the negotiations. The newly acquired
power of Japanese arms made possible through the
building of a unified national state had brought to her
knees the greatest power of the Orient. Much of this
military and naval strength was due to the energy of

---

[13] Treat, *op. cit.*, 155.

the two clans, Satsuma and Choshiu, which had been a determining factor in the struggle prior to the Restoration, and which had carried the new government through the period of internal strife. The success of their policies, due in no inconsiderable degree to military strength and reinforced by the victory over China, now served the exponents of a militaristic policy, and during the Shimonoseki negotiations the influence of the military group was exerted in an attempt to secure even larger territorial concessions on the mainland than were finally agreed upon. Opposed to this party was the more moderate group represented by Ito.[14]

While, therefore, Japan was urged on toward aggressive tendencies by the warlike elements in her government, China was in no position, either politically or economically, to present a bold front. Her armies had been defeated wherever they took the field and the government at Peking was little better than that of the luckless Korean sovereign to whose assistance it had gone a few years previously. In short, the condition of the country was deplorable. The military was demoralized while the ministers of the Tsungli-Yamen were terrified by the continuous victories of the Japanese. Many of them feared mediation at the hands of the western powers, with the possible exception of the United States, yet they were ready for peace at any price. Utter corruption and complete helplessness pervaded all classes of Chinese officialdom.[15]

Li Hung-chang, accompanied by Mr. Foster and a numerous staff, reached Shimonoseki on the morning

[14] Gubbins, *op. cit.*, 223-224.
[15] Foster, *Diplomatic Memoirs*, vol. 2, 105.

of March 19th and arrangements for the first meeting of the plenipotentiaries were made for the following day. The meeting of the greatest statesman of China, a defeated power, and the prime minister of victorious Japan, was indeed notable. For many years Li had been an outstanding figure in Chinese affairs and was beyond doubt the greatest stateman China produced during the century. He was now 73 years of age. Opposing him was Count Ito, who, as a young man in 1864, had participated in the negotiations that followed the bombardment of Shimonoseki by western powers. In those days he acted on behalf of his defeated and humiliated feudal lord. Now after more than 30 years he negotiated again at Shimonoseki as the first minister of a new and victorious Japan.[16]

The negotiations lasted from March 19th until the signing of the treaty on April 17th. On March 20th, after the exchange of credentials, Li proposed an armistice providing for a complete suspension of hostilities *in statu quo*. The Japanese reply came the following day demanding as a condition of armistice occupation by Japanese forces of strategic points on the road to Peking. These conditions were, from the Chinese point of view, unacceptable and the subject of an armistice was dropped and Li requested that the Japanese present their conditions of peace.[17]

On the same day, March 24th, while he was returning to his residence from the conference, Li was shot and severely wounded by a Japanese fanatic. This unfortunate occurrence, however, proved of great value to China in the hour of her need. The sympathy of all peoples was immediately aroused and nowhere was

---

[16] *Ibid.*, 125-127.
[17] *History of the Peace Negotiations documentary and verbal betweeen China and Japan, March-April, 1895*, 1-4.

this attitude so pronounced as among the Japanese themselves, and three days after the attack upon his person the Viceroy was informed by Viscount Mutsu that the Mikado had commanded his plenipotentiaries to consent to an unconditional armistice. This action was ample evidence of the sincerity of Japanese sympathy and cleared the atmosphere for the future negotiations.[18] At the same time, in view of Li's disability, the Chinese Government conferred joint powers as plenipotentiary upon his son, Li Ching-mai, generally known as Lord Li, who had accompanied him upon his mission.

Japan's first draft of the terms of peace was submitted on April 1st. The terms were severe and humiliating to the Chinese in the extreme. Of the eleven articles in this draft, two, the second and fourth, are of particular significance in our study. By the former Japan demanded cession to her by China "in perpetuity and full sovereignty" of the southern portion of the province of Fengtien or Mukden, and by the latter, a war indemnity of 300,000,000 Kuping taels.[19] China's reply was submitted on April 5th, but this document was largely a recital of the domestic difficulties of the Empire, and it was not until the 9th that the counterproposals of the Chinese were made known. In this draft, Li sought, among other things, to reduce substantially the proposed cession of territory in Manchuria by confining it to a small section

---

[18] *Ibid.*, 9.

[19] *Ibid.*, 11-12. The line of demarkation of the territory demanded by Japan began at the mouth of the river Yalu and ascended that stream as far as San-cha-tsu, thence it ran directly north to Yu-shuti-hsia, and then directly west to the river Liao; it then followed the course of the river south to 41 north latitude, then followed this line westward to 122 east longitude, and then on this line southward to the coast of the Bay of Liaotung. The territory demanded also included all islands belonging to the province in the eastern portion of the Bay of Liaotung and the northern part of the Yellow Sea.

on the eastern coast of the Liaotung Peninsula in the neighborhood of the mouth of the River Yalu, retaining for China such important places as Talienwan, Port Arthur, and Yingkow. He also proposed that the indemnity be reduced to 100,000,000 Kuping taels. Japan replied promptly to China's counterproposals, with reduced demands, on the following day, April 10th. In this statement of her terms Japan sacrificed practically the northern half of the territory originally demanded by her in Manchuria, but retained all the land lying south of a line drawn from a point just north of Antung on the Yalu to Haicheng and thence to Yingkow, thus insuring herself complete control of the important fortress and towns on the southern tip of the peninsula.[20] Japan compromised in the matter of indemnity by fixing her demands at 200,000,000 Kuping taels.

Li now exerted every effort to secure some further modification of the demands but it was soon evident that Ito and Mutsu, hard pressed by the demands of the militarists, had made the last concession of importance that it was in their power to give, and there followed on April 11th, Japan's ultimatum, which declared that the modified demands must be regarded as final and that a reply would be expected within three

---

[20] *History of the Peace Negotiations documentary and verbal between China and Japan, March-April, 1895*, 20-22. In her counterproposal of April 9th the territory offered by China included: the district of Antung, the district of Kung-tien, the prefecture of Feng-hwang, and the subprefecture of Hsiu-yen; the boundaries of which were to be in accordance with the Chinese official surveys.

Japan refused to accept the above settlement and in her counterproposal of April 10th suggested the following modification of her original demand: the line of demarkation to begin at the river Yalu and ascend that stream to An-ping-ho-kou; from thence it was to run to Feng-huang; thence to Haicheng and then to Yingkow where it was to terminate. The islands of the adjacent seas mentioned in the first demands were also included.

days.[21] The text of the treaty as finally modified was telegraphed to Peking and instructions were sent to the Viceroy to sign it, and at ten o'clock on the morning of April 17, 1895, the signature and seals of the plenipotentiaries were affixed to a document which was the forerunner of dramatic events in Far Eastern diplomacy.[22]

By this treaty China ceded to Japan "in perpetuity and full sovereignty" that portion of the Liaotung Peninsula contained within the boundaries submitted by Japan in her counterproposals of April 10th, the Island of Formosa and the Pescadores. China agreed to pay a war indemnity of 200,000,000 Kuping taels and recognized definitely the full and complete independence and autonomy of Korea."[23]

On April 18th, in the evening of the day following the signing of the treaty of Shimonoseki, the Russian minister at Peking, on the order of his government, invited Prince Kung and the ministers of the Tsungli Yamen not to hasten the ratification of the treaty which was to be accomplished by May 8th. At the same time the ministers of Russia, France, and Germany at Peking received information and identical instructions concerning the attitude of their Governments, and the Chinese Government learned from its legations at St. Petersburg, Paris, and Berlin of the instructions forwarded to Peking.[24] The instructions to the ministers were dated April 21 and 22. On the following day, April 23, the Ministers of Russia, France, and Germany at Tokio presented to Baron Hayashi,

---

[21] *Ibid.*, 23.

[22] *Ibid.*, 25. Foster, *op. cit.*, 139.

[23] *Ibid.*, 26-27. Full text of the treaty of peace.

[24] Gerard, *op. cit.*, 41.

acting minister for Foreign Affairs, "in a spirit of cordial friendship," the famous retrocession note which was to deprive Japan of her most coveted fruits of victory.[25] This advice to Japan pointed out that the three powers having examined the terms of peace demanded of China by Japan considered that the contemplated possession of the Liaotung Peninsula by the latter would not only constitute a constant menace to the capital of China, but would render the independence of Korea illusory and thus jeopardize the permanent peace of the Far East.[26] If the world had been surprised by the swift and decisive victory of Japanese arms, it was no less affected by this unexpected turn in the negotiations which followed. But in diplomatic circles intervention was not unlooked for. The Government at Peking believed that in such action rested its only hope of escape from what it considered the excessive demands of the Japanese, while at Tokyo the premier, Count Ito, and Foreign Minister, Viscount Mutsu, anticipated intervention but were unable to determine what direction it would take or the extent to which it would conflict with the terms of the treaty.[27]

The diplomatic background of the situation which gave rise to the Triple Intervention of Russia, France, and Germany is complicated in the extreme, and the pronouncements of statesmen responsible for the intervention and of certain of the diplomats who carried it into effect have not served to solve finally these points of conflict. The origins of the prompt action taken by Russia, France, and Germany, however, are

---

[25] Cordier, *Histoire des Relations de la Chine avec les puissances occidentales 1860-1902*, vol. 3, 289. Hayashi, *Secret Memoirs*, 82.

[26] *Times Weekly Edition*, (London) Feb. 5, 1904, 86. Hayashi, *op. cit.*, 85.

[27] *Ibid.*, 79-80.

to be found in the aims of their so-called Far Eastern policies. And in any attempt to estimate the forces which prompted these powers to action, the reader must constantly bear in mind what interests they already held in Eastern Asia and in what way the holding by Japan of the Liaotung Peninsula, with Port Arthur at its southern extremity, would affect the future development and possible expansion of those interests. The attitude adopted by the Government at St. Petersburg is to be readily understood. It will be recalled that by 1858 Russia had advanced her Far Eastern frontier to the left bank of the Amur and two years later had received from China the Maritime Province stretching southward to Korea. This was with the primary object of strengthening her eastern frontier and providing herself with a base for her Pacific Fleet. In 1891, Russia had commenced the construction of the Transsiberian Railway and with the completion of that line she might look for an even closer relationship and commercial development with her Asiatic neighbor, China, than that which had steadily grown during two centuries of intercourse. There is little evidence that Russia had formulated anything like a definite policy concerning Manchuria at this time. With the possible exception of a very few of her statesmen, those in power at St. Petersburg were woefully ignorant of Far Eastern affairs.[28] But the sudden acquisition by Japan of Liaotung, one of the most strategic positions in all of north China, might have been calculated above anything else to arouse Russian fears in respect to her own future in the Far East.

The explanation for the position taken by France

---

[28] *The Memoirs of Count Witte,* 82.

was to be found in her alliance with Russia, formally announced in June, 1895, and the desire to strengthen her interests in China through an attitude of friendship toward the Peking Government. For several months M. Gabriel Hanotaux at Paris and Prince Lobanof at St. Petersburg had recognized in the possible rise of Japanese power on continental Asia a danger to their interests in China.[29]

The sudden and intimate interest taken by Germany in the results of the Shimonoseki negotiations was not to be explained so readily. Until the nineties of the last century Germany had acted in many respects as a model for institutions of New Japan. Ito had been greatly influenced by German ideas in the formulation of the Japanese constitution and the new national army had been trained under Prussian advisers. Both Prince Bismarck and later Von Bülow saw the danger of strife resulting from conditions of unrest in Russia and hoped that the struggle might take place in Asia rather than Europe. For the time being, therefore, Japanese friendship was not considered too high a price for a practical demonstration of German friendship for Russia.[30] The opportunity for her to rank as a world power in the Far East was at hand. Her action might be calculated to consolidate her political and commercial prestige while at the same time it would lead toward the East her powerful and dangerous eastern neighbor.[31] It was at this time too that the Kaiser was troubled by the specter of the Yellow Peril, so-called.

Japan's victory confronted England with no fears, real or imaginary. The opening of new ports as pro-

---

[29] Gerard, *op cit.*, 41.

[30] Von Bülow, *Imperial Germany*, 48-50.

[31] Gerard, *op. cit.*, 51.

vided in the treaty was in line with British commercial policy, and the position of Japan in Liaotung, presenting a bold front to Russian aggression in Manchuria, was looked upon favorably by Downing Street.[32]   It will be recalled too that Great Britain had led the way in July, 1894, by revising her treaties with Japan and thus strengthened the friendly relations already existing between the two powers.

With this brief statement of the positions of the European powers let us return to a consideration of the origins and course of the intervention itself.   At this point the historian, for the present at least, is confronted with many obstacles.   M. Gerard, who was French minister at Peking from 1893 to 1897, and M. Cordier, the French historian, suggest that the initiative in the intervention came from France; other writers aver that Germany took the first step.   But the best evidence now available indicates that the basis of action, regardless of remote origins, was to be found at St. Petersburg.[33]   This view is in conformity with the revelations of such Russian statesmen as M. Witte and Baron Rosen, and the careful research of such a scholar as Asakawa and many others.[34]

---

[32] *Ibid.,* 43.

[33] Professor Franke declares that in the Triple Intervention Germany was made a cat's-paw and that the affair was handled stupidly by her diplomats. His explanation of the German note to Japan, which he admits was phrased in brusque language, is hardly convincing.   It was intended, he tells us, to impress the Japanese with the clear vision and positive frankness of Germany. Hayashi's account of the conversation when Gutschmid presented the note is not accepted by Franke.   *Die Grossmachte in Ostasien von 1894 bis 1914.* 93.

[34] A similar conclusion has been reached by:

Chirol, *op. cit.,* 65.

Pinon, "La Chine et les Puissances Europeénes 1894-1904," in *Revue des Deux Mondes,* Aug. 1, 1904, 631.

Brown, *The Mastery of the Far East,* 129.

Pasvolsky, *Russia in the Far East,* 24.

Korff, *Russia's Foreign Relations,* etc., 57.

Dawson, *The Cambridge History of British Foreign Policy,* vol. 3, 230.

Denby, "How Peace Was Made between China and Japan," in *The Forum,* August, 1900, 715-716.

At St. Petersburg there was a total absence of any clear conception of what the aims of Russian Far Eastern policy were. Prince Lobanof was entirely ignorant of the Far East when he became minister of foreign affairs; [35] on his own testimony M. Witte was the only man conversant with it,[36] and it was he who was largely responsible for thwarting the peace terms as concluded between Japan and China. After a conference called by the Tsar under the presidency of the Grand Duke Alexandrovich had accomplished nothing, a second conference under the presidency of the Tsar himself assembled, and this special committee on Sino-Japanese affairs decided on April 11th to seek to preserve the *status quo ante bellum* in northern China; to advise Japan to desist from the occupation of southern Manchuria because such an occupation would injure Russian interests and be a constant menace to the peace of the Far East, and finally to issue a statement to the European Powers and to China, that while on her part Russia did not seek any seizures, she deemed it necessary for the protection of her interests to insist upon the retrocession of Liaotung to China.[37]

Under instructions from the Tsar, Prince Lobanof set himself to the execution of this policy, which he carried through with notable success. Playing partly on the jealousy of the French Government and on the desire of the German Emperor for even a temporary *rapprochement* with both Russia and France, he persuaded both powers to join Russia in resisting Japan's demands. His diplomacy is worthy of note for by its success he gained the support of two powers whose rewards for their participation could at best be only of

[35] Rosen, *Forty Years of Diplomacy*, vol. 1, 134.

[36] Witte, *op. cit.*, 82.

[73] *Ibid.*, 83-84. See also Lepsius IX, 253.

a doubtful character.[38]   The participation of three
nations insured a favorable outcome for the intervention and augured well for the future influence of the
intervening powers at Peking.   Of Russia's desire for
a continuance of her favorable relationship with China
there can be little doubt, a circumstance of which Li
Hung-chang availed himself before and during the negotiations at Shimonoseki.

After his appointment as plenipotentiary Li had
spent the days from February 20th to March 5th obtaining his instructions in Peking and visiting ministers of the foreign powers, hoping to interest them in
China's cause.   He pleaded with them that they could
not afford to see the position of their governments
jeopardized through extensive rights acquired by
Japan.   He paid frequent visits to the ministers of
France and Russia, pointing out the danger of allowing
the balance of power in eastern Asia to slip to Japan.[39]

Above all he attempted to encourage on the part of
Russia a dread of the menace which would threaten
her interests in Manchuria and Korea.   As a last effort
he caused telegrams to be sent by the Peking Government to Russia, France, Germany, Great Britain, and
the United States, recommending China's cause and
the mission of her negotiator at Shimonoseki, and
while on his way to the negotiations Li, himself, sent a
telegram from Taku to M. Gerard, making therein a
final appeal to France.[40]   During the course of the negotiations, the western powers were kept informed of
the progress of each conference by the Tsungli Yamen.
On April 10th, it will be recalled, Ito replied to the
Chinese counter-proposal and this reply was commu-

---

[38] Witte, *op. cit.*, 84.   Rosen, *op. cit.*, vol. 1, 137.
[39] Gerard, *op. cit.*, 25.
[40] *Ibid.*, 30.

nicated to the foreign ministers in Peking, by the
Yamen, on April 12th.   At the same time there arrived
from St. Petersburg and Paris a joint indication of the
attitude those governments would observe toward the
demands of Japan, and Gerard and Cassini, the Russian minister, were informed by the Yamen that Li
had been notified Germany would join Russia and
France in this attitude.[41]   In his book, *Ma Mission en
Chine*, Gerard asks whether this presumed attitude on
the part of the three powers caused Japan between
April 5th and 10th to modify her demands.   On this
point it is impossible to make a definite pronouncement.
It may be assumed that in her first statement of demands Japan asked for more than she expected to get,
a view which is borne out by her reception of the
Chinese reply, largely the work of Mr. Foster.[42]   The
fact that Japan's modified demands were presented on
April 10th, following promptly on the Chinese counter
proposals and that word of the attitude of Russia and
France was not communicated to M. Gerard and M.
Cassini until April 12th tends further to weaken the
suggestion of the French minister.   Evidence strength-
ens the belief that Japan was prepared to compromise
to a definite degree and did so the more readily because
of the shooting of Li Hung-chang by one of her nationals.

Further light must be shed on this entire subject
before it will be known what assurance of intervention
by western powers Li had before he sailed for Shimonoseki, and consequently to what degree he was influenced by such assurance during the negotiations.
Mr. Foster asserted that on April 17th, when the treaty

[41] *Ibid.*, 38.
[42] Foster, *op. cit.*, vol. 2, 139.

was signed Li still had no assurance of intervention,[43] yet the Yamen had reported to M. Gerard on April 12th that Li was informed of the attitude of the three powers and Witte had assured him that Japan would not be permitted to keep Liaotung even if it were granted to her by treaty.[44] Probably before he left Peking, Li was satisfied that he had aroused sufficiently the fears of both Russia and France, though he could hardly have anticipated that Germany would join them in definite action against Japan.

To return to the progress of the intervention, it will be remembered that the note of retrocession was presented by the ministers of the three powers in Tokyo, to the vice-minister for foreign affairs, Tadasu Hayashi, on April 23rd, and five days later the Japanese Government, because the honor of the nation was involved, expressed the hope that time would be allowed for reflection. An April 29th, the three ministers having received additional instructions asked that a reply be given before May 8th, the date of expiration of the armistice.[45] Japan's reply of May 1st accepted the advice of the powers to restore Liaotung with the exception of Port Arthur and Kinchow.[46] This response of Japan was declared to be unsatisfactory to the three powers on May 4th, and counseled by England to accept in full the demands, Japan on May 5th, renounced possession of all the territory ceded to her in South Manchuria.[47] Nevertheless, she asked that the Treaty of Shimonoseki should be signed and that the retrocession should be effected by an additional con-

[43] *Ibid.*, vol. 2, 152.
[44] Dillon, *The Eclipse of Russia*, 246.
[45] Cordier, *op. cit.*, 290.
[46] Gerard, *op. cit.*, 47.
[47] Cordier, *op. cit.*, 291.

vention; that the territory in question be occupied by
her until the execution of the terms yet to be concluded,
and that she be paid an additional indemnity as compensation for the territory restored to China.

The ratifications of the treaty were exchanged at
Chefoo on May 8, 1895.[48]   Since the return of Li to
China on April 20th, and the demands for retrocession,
all had been confusion in the Government at Peking.
On April 30th Mr. Foster had a conference with the
cabinet in the office of the Tsungli-Yamen and urged
the ratification of the treaty, which took place the following day, and thus paved the way for the exchange
at Chefoo.[49]   In the harbor where the ratifications
were exchanged Russia had concentrated the most
formidable squadron ever assembled in Chinese waters,
an unmistakable threat to Japan should she fail at the
last moment to ratify the treaty.   Two days later, on
May 10th, the Japanese Government in an Imperial
proclamation announced to the world that the advice
of the powers had been accepted in the interests of the
permanent peace of the Orient.[50]

On May 25th, Russia, France, Germany, and Spain,
who had now joined them, commenced negotiations for
a convention of retrocession in which the following
were the principal points of discussion: an indemnity
to Japan for the retrocession of territory, the evacuation of Liaotung, and the subject of the Pescadores
Islands.   On July 19th, Japan declared that she would
agree to an additional indemnity of 50,000,000 taels
and that she would withdraw her troops to the limits
of the prefecture of Kinchow after the payment of this

---

[48] *Manchuria, Treaties and Agreements*, 5.
[49] Foster, *op. cit.*, 147-150.
[50] *Manchuria, Treaties and Agreements*, 12.

sum and the first payment as stipulated by the treaty of Shimonoseki, and that after the second payment and the exchange of ratifications all Manchurian territory would be evacuated.[51]   This was to be brought about as soon as the indemnity, now reduced to 30,000,000 taels, was paid.   Then, with the receipt of new instructions, the ministers made further overtures to Japan on September 11th asking that a definite time limit be fixed for the evacuation.   Japan's response of October 7th stated that the Government had decided to reduce the indemnity to 30,000,000 taels, not to make the conclusion of a treaty of commerce a condition of evacuation, and to effect the evacuation in three months from the payment of the entire indemnity.   China accepted the condition of retrocession October 16th and three days later an exchange of notes summed up the negotiations resulting from the intervention of the three powers.[52]   The convention was signed on November 8th by Li Hung-chang and Hayashi, and approved the following day by the Emperors of both Japan and China.   The indemnity of 30,000,000 taels was paid at London on November 16th, when the evacuation was already well under way,[53] and the ratifications were exchanged at Peking on November 29th.[54]

Such was the result of the "friendly advice" of the continental powers, tendered Japan in behalf of the "permanent peace" of the Far East.   How effective it was to be, and how far it served their declared purposes, the following chapters will disclose.

---

[51] Cordier, *op. cit.*, vol. 3, 294-295.

[52] *Ibid.*, vol. 3, 296-297.

[53] *Ibid.*, vol. 3, 297 and 300.

[54] See text of the convention of retrocession in *Manchuria, Treaties and Agreements*, 10-12.

CHAPTER III

RUSSIA'S COMPENSATION FOR THE TRIPLE INTERVENTION: THE RUSSO-CHINESE SECRET ALLIANCE OF 1896

The peace of Shimonoseki which would have given Japan a firm foothold on the Asian continent, had her demands not been frustrated by the Triple Intervention, was, as we have seen, regarded with great alarm in Russia, and from this time forward Russian Far Eastern policy commanded greater attention in the councils of St. Petersburg. After her successful thrust toward the East in 1858 and 1860, it seemed that, for the time being, the goal of Russian Far Eastern expansion had been reached. From the signing of the Peking Convention in 1860 until the intervention of the Powers in 1895, Russia had been content to allow a settlement, which had brought peace, to remain unaltered. Nevertheless it could not have escaped the St. Petersburg authorities that Vladivostok, their newly founded Pacific base, was ice-bound for several months of the year, and thus that Russia's ambitions on the Pacific were only partially achieved.

During 1890 Li Hung-chang, who at the time was largely concerned with railway development in North China, had in view the construction of a line traversing the southern part of Manchuria from west to east. The route proposed was from Shanhaikwan through Chinchow to Hsinmintun, thence across the Liao River to Mukden and then in a northeasterly direction through Ninguta to Hunchun on the Tumen River. A survey of this proposed route was commenced in May, 1890, by Mr. Kinder, later engineer-in-chief of the Imperial

Railways of North-China, and reports of these activities which reached St. Petersburg were not received with favor; for what reason will appear later.[1]

It was just at this time that the much debated project of a Transsiberian Railway was receiving more than usual attention at St. Petersburg and on March 17, 1891, the construction of the railway was finally decided upon and announced in an imperial rescript, and two months later the measure was also promulgated from Vladivostok on the Pacific. During the entire 19th century and especially since the exploits of Muravieff on the Amur, the imperfect communication afforded by the Siberian rivers directed public attention to the necessity of constructing railways. Several projects were advanced during the years that Muravieff was on the Amur and also in the later decades preceding 1890. In that year the Russian railways reached toward the east in three lines abruptly stopping at the Urals and when the subject of a transcontinental line was again brought forward it was considered that the time had arrived to launch the project.[2] Although it may never be known to what extent St. Petersburg was influenced by the reported railway schemes of Li Hung-chang in Manchuria, there is little doubt that this knowledge facilitated the schemes of those who favored the construction of the great Russian line.[3]

---

[1] Kent, *Railway Enterprise in China*, 38-41.

[2] Vladimir, *Russia on the Pacific and the Siberian Railway*, 293.

[3] Morse states that until the Japanese war Li had been fearful of Russian designs on Korea, and believed that if Russia got Korea, Manchuria would also go. His tendency, therefore, was to lean toward commercial nations, England and America, to develop Manchuria commercially. But he later realized that the military nations had forced Japan to give back Liaotung. From this time he depended more on Russia. (Morse, *International Relations of the Chinese Empire*, vol. 3, 82.)

Such a railway as would connect European Russia with Vladivostok was one of the most cherished dreams of Alexander III but it had been delayed through the opposition of certain members of the ministry and the Imperial Council, and it was not until Witte, as minister of ways of communication and later as minister of finances, came to a position of influence, that a consistent champion of the railway was secured. Witte's enthusiasm was aided after 1896 by the interest of the young Tsar, Nicholas II, who while his father, Alexander III, was still alive, was appointed head of the Siberian Railroad Committee, which had been formed by Witte to promote the construction of the road.[4] For the successful carrying out of so great a scheme of construction it became necessary to cut the line into a number of sections corresponding to natural divisions, allowing the work to be carried out at different points simultaneously and securing administrative independence for each. The sections of the line which were to be completed after all others were those around Lake Baikal and in the Amur region, where steamers were to operate and serve as connecting links until the last rails were laid.

According to the original plan, including the Amur sections of the railway, approximately 6,000 miles separated Moscow from Vladivostok.[5] Construction of this line was the gigantic task which Russia had set for herself and nowhere were greater difficulties presented than in the Amur sections, where for some 1,300 miles construction would have to be effected through dense forests, across rivers, often far removed from population, where most of the land was uncultivated and the

---

[4] Witte, *Memoirs*, 52-53.

[5] According to Russian measurement the distance is something more than 9000 versts. The verst is 0.6629 miles.

climate most unattractive.[6] It must have been evident
to every Russian engineer, as the eastern sectors of
the line were worked over in detail, that the natural
course was across the northern provinces of Manchuria, which offered a direct route to Vladivostok.
Here was a course which would save 340 miles. By
1896 the Transsiberian Road had reached Transbai-
kalia, and Witte, who was energetically pushing the
venture, claims that it was he who first conceived the
idea of building the road in a direct line across Chinese
territory. Regardless of the origin of this idea, its
conception was not unnatural, for not only would a
course through northern Manchuria eliminate many
engineering difficulties of the Amur route, it would
remove the line from direct competition with the steamship companies operating on the river.[7] The problem
which presented itself therefore was how, through
peaceful means, should the consent of China to this
plan be secured. There was at the time an opposition
group in St. Petersburg which favored a railway from
Kiakhta to Peking; but this was opposed by Witte
because he believed Vladivostok the most desirable terminus and because he feared that a railroad to Peking
would rouse the whole of Europe against Nicholas II.
This fact seems to have been of great importance to the
mind of Witte, for he stresses the fact that Alexander
III, the originator of the Siberian Railroad, had no
political or military designs in connection with it. His
desire was to establish communications by the shortest
possible route between the distant Maritime Province
and Central Russia. On this basis it must be concluded that strategically both Alexander III and his

---

[6] Vladimir, *op. cit.*, 298.
[7] Witte, *op. cit.*, 85.

successor attributed a strictly defensive importance to the road. This policy was in line with Witte's personal view that under no circumstances was the Transsiberian Railroad to serve as a means of territorial expansion.[8]

While Russian policy was thus shaping itself, there broke out the Chino-Japanese War, resulting in Japan's victory and her demand for the cession of the Liaotung Peninsula. Russia saw in this demand not merely the surrender to Japan of territory that would command the approach to China's capital and effectually thwart any influence she might attempt to exert in Korea, but also a definite threat against what Russia even at that time considered as her sphere of influence, and since it was the desire of the Tsar to spread Russian influence in the Far East, Witte set about to create a strong but passive China as neighbor. If this were to be accomplished it was imperative that Japan should be ousted from Liaotung, which was considered a dominating position. This was apparently the extent to which Russian policy had gone at the time.[9] It was another occasion, such as that of 1860, to impress China with the warmth and power of Russian friendship.

The course of the intervention, as already described, was entirely satisfactory from the Russian point of view, and while China was yet rejoicing in escaping from Japanese territorial demands on the mainland, Witte entered into negotiations with the Peking Government, offering it the services of the Russian Government for the conclusion of a large loan needed by China in order to pay the Japanese indemnity.[10] The

---

[8] *Ibid.*, 86.
[9] *Ibid.*, 82.
[10] *Ibid.*, 85.

negotiations for the loan were carried on at St. Petersburg by Witte, in his capacity as Minister of Finance, and by the Chinese Minister. China's credit at the time not being such as to enable her to contract the loan independently, Witte agreed to pledge Russia's resources as security. This proposition, at first, gave rise to the fear of European complications, for the Russian guaranty seemed to place China in a position of dependence on St. Petersburg. But these objections were swept aside and a loan of 400,000,000 francs was floated on the French market.[11] The representatives of the banking houses that participated received Witte's promise of aid in their financial activities in China in return for their services to Russia in connection with the loan.[12] The completion of this loan was Russia's second play in the creation of a neighborly China. The third was equally important, though for the time being its significance was somewhat obscure.

The Russo-Chinese Bank, in which French financiers were the chief shareholders, and which was the progenitor of the Russo-Asiatic Bank, was established by Witte in December, 1895. The object of the bank, as announced in its charter of December 22nd, was to develop commercial relations with East-Asiatic countries.[13] But such a characterization is inadequate to describe its activities. Rather may it be said that the bank was created to take advantage of the more favorable relations created between Russia and China resulting from the intervention and Russia's guaranty of the Chinese loan, and it will be noted that in main

---

[11] Cordier, *Histoire des Relations de la Chine avec les puissances occidentales 1860-1902*, vol. 3, 305-307.

[12] Witte, *op. cit.*, 85.

[13] Charter of the Russo-Chinese Bank, in *Manchuria, Treaties and Agreements*, 19.

the French firms associated with the undertaking were those which had participated in the loan.   Thus it was that among the founders of the Russo-Chinese Bank were such houses as: La Banque de Paris et des Pays-Bas, Le Comptoir National d'escompte de Paris, Le Credit Lyonnais, and MM. Hottinger et Cie.[14]   At the outset the Chinese Government and the Russian Treasury invested heavily in the institution.[15]   The capital of the bank, which was to play such an important part in the history of Manchuria, was originally fixed at 6,000,000 gold rubles and the years following its establishment witnessed striking progress.   Its business expanded as the power of Russia expanded, and a network of its branches covered Siberia and the Far East, and extended to India and Persia.   But the Russo-Japanese War was to strike a blow at its power from which it did not recover until 1910, when it was amalgamated with the Banque du Nord and renamed the Russo-Asiatic Bank.[16]   The part which this bank was to play in the affairs of Manchuria will appear presently.

In the spring of 1896, Li Hung-chang, the negotiator of the Treaty of Shimonoseki, was sent to Russia as China's Ambassador Extraordinary, to attend the coronation ceremonies of Tsar Nicholas II.   The selection of such a dignitary was significant in the extreme.   At the time of the appointment, Li occupied the post of First Chancellor, the position of greatest esteem in the Empire.   It was evident, therefore, that in sending this statesman, as emissary to the Moscow coronation, China wished to express her gratitude for the favors

---

[14] Cordier, *op. cit.*, vol. 3, 311.

[15] Witte, *op. cit.*, 85.

[16] *Manchuria, Treaties and Agreements*, 17.

Russia had bestowed upon her.[17] Li made the journey to Russia by way of the Indian Ocean, was met at the Suez Canal by representatives of the Tsar's Government, and reached St. Petersburg on April 30th. By this time Russia had decided that the presence of Li would be taken advantage of to pursue negotiations for a Russian railway across the northern provinces of Manchuria and as Prince Lobanof, the Russian Minister of Foreign Affairs, was none too well versed in the affairs of the Far East, the Tsar entrusted Witte with the conduct of the negotiations.[18] Circumstances pointed to a successful conclusion of Russia's schemes. It was known that Li was favorably disposed toward Russia, an attitude which had been strengthened by his close associations with Count Cassini and M. Gerard, the Russian and French Ministers at Peking. He had been drawn still closer to Russian and French interests by what he considered Japan's aggressive attitude and the timely intervention of the three powers. And to strengthen all this, had not Witte contracted the loan specially guaranteed by Russia, by which China was enabled to meet the indemnity? It was, therefore, natural that the first meeting of Li and the astute Minister of Finance should find the former attentive if not enthusiastic toward Russia's proposals.

For many years following these negotiations between China and Russia in 1896 the whole subject of their relationship at this time remained a matter of dispute, and it was not until the publication of the Memoirs of Count Witte himself that the world learned what

---

[17] Asakawa, *Russo-Japanese Conflict*, 87, suggests that China had resolved to send Wang Tsz-chun to St. Petersburg but that Count Cassini, Russian Minister at Peking, was reported to have intimated that no one but Li Hung-chang was acceptable to Russia, as the representative of the Chinese Emperor.

[18] Witte, *op. cit.*, 87.

actually took place at St. Petersburg and Moscow. To Witte then we must turn for this story, corroborated by the evidence of M. Gerard in his book *Ma Mission en Chine*.[19]

The first visits between Li and Witte in St. Petersburg were of a very formal character and no attempt was made by the latter to enter upon negotiations of a diplomatic character. Witte recounts in his characteristic manner how he had been told that in conducting negotiations with Chinese officials it was necessary, above all, not to show any haste, for they considered that very bad taste. Business, in fact, was to be transacted slowly and with every attention to ceremony. This type of procedure characterized the first interviews, but it soon gave place to a less formal intercourse and the conversations of the diplomats became outspoken and business-like.[20]

Russia's case as it was then presented by her Finance Minister was well calculated to appeal not merely to Li, but to his Government in Peking. Witte lost no time in stressing the services which Russia had recently rendered the Middle Kingdom. On this point he dwelt throughout the negotiations. Nor was the Viceroy permitted to forget that Russia, having proclaimed the principle of the territorial integrity of the Chinese Empire, intended to adhere to that principle in the future. But if Russia were to uphold that principle she must, so Witte argued, be in a position to render armed assistance to China. It was pointed out to Li that although during the Chino-Japanese War detachments were moved by Russia from Vladivostok

---

[19] A critical analysis of the sources used in this chapter will be found to support the case presented by M. Gerard.

[20] Witte, *op. cit.*, 88.

to Kirin, their progress was so slow, due to the absence of railroad communication, that the war was over when they reached their destination. Russia therefore believed that if she were to uphold the territorial integrity of the Chinese Empire it would be necessary for her to have a railway following the shortest route to Vladivostok across the northern part of Mongolia and Manchuria, and argued further that such a line would not only raise the productivity of the territories through which it passed, but also be favorably considered by Japan.[21]

Despite the fact that China had accepted Russia as her natural friend, from which a favorable attitude toward Russian proposals might be expected, Li raised objections to Witte's arguments. Nor was this wholly surprising, for the scheme as outlined opened wide the door of northern Manchuria to Russian economic and political penetration, and it was not until the Tsar expressed to Li personally his wish that the negotiations be brought to a successful conclusion that the envoy agreed to three major provisions of a secret pact which was to be concluded between the two powers.[22] By the first of these China granted Russia permission to build a railroad through northern Manchuria in a straight course from Chita to Vladivostok. This road was to be in the hands of a private corporation. Witte had urged that the road be constructed and owned by the Russian Treasury Department, but Li would not hear of this. By the second, China was to cede to Russia a strip of land sufficient for the construction and operation of the railway and in which the private corporation was to exercise untrammelled authority. And finally the two

---

[21] *Ibid.*, 89.
[22] *Ibid.*, 89-90.

countries were to come to the defense of each other should Japan threaten the territory of China or the Far Eastern maritime possessions of Russia.

The course of the negotiations was reported to the Tsar and the Foreign Minister, by the Minister of Finance, and the text of a treaty was drafted by Lobanof and approved by Witte. Later after it had been submitted to the Tsar, Witte noticed that the words *par le Japon* were missing from the clause dealing with the Russo-Chinese union against Japan. In this altered version the pact provided for the mutual defense of the two countries in the event of an attack on either of them not merely by Japan but by any other power.[23] Fearing should he do so that his action would appear as an affront to the Foreign Minister, Witte did not call Lobanof's attention to this error, but requested the Tsar to order that the phrase *par le Japon* be used in the final draft. When the day for signing the document arrived and the envoys gathered in the offices of the Foreign Ministry, Witte, in glancing over the texts to be signed, observed that the words limiting the alliance to a defensive one against Japan had not been inserted. The situation required prompt action. Prince Lobanof was informed immediately and with fine composure he requested the envoys to take lunch with him as it was then past noon. During this interval Russian secretaries substituted new copies of the treaty in which the words *par le Japon* were plainly visible. When the negotiators returned, the document was duly

[23] On page 91 of his Memoirs Witte writes: "I was actually frightened. The alteration was of momentous importance. A defensive alliance against all the other powers was quite different from such an alliance against Japan. Several European Powers, including France, our ally, and England, have interests in China, and to obligate ourselves to defend China from all those countries meant to arouse them all against us and to invite no end of trouble."

signed by Li Hung-chang for China and Prince Lobanof and Witte for Russia.[24] The agreement was ratified by both powers without delay, and by September 8th a railway contract between Russia (in reality the Russo-Chinese Bank) and China, for the construction and operation of the Chinese Eastern Railway across northern Manchuria, had been agreed upon. Before entering upon a discussion of this agreement, however, some phases of the secret compact remain to be considered.

The announcement of a railway concession was the only news which the outside world gained for many years of the 1896 negotiations, but it was long persistently rumored that the concession for the Chinese Eastern Railway was a first fruit of a secret political agreement supposed to have been signed in Peking by Count Cassini, the Russian Minister, which was to attain notoriety under the name of "The Cassini Convention." It is now well established that this convention was never a reality. But in its issue of October 30, 1896, the *North China Herald* published what purported to be a translation of the convention. In explanation of the text, so published, the *Herald* stated that Count Cassini did not leave for St. Petersburg on September 30th until he could take with him signed and sealed an important agreement supposed to be the right of way for the Siberian Railway across northern Manchuria.[25]

The form in which "The Cassini Convention" was phrased was, however, sufficient to discredit it,[26] and

---

[24] Witte, *op. cit.*, 93. The treaty was signed June 3 (May 22, Russian style), 1896, memorandum of Mr. MacMurray to Professor Treat.

[25] *Manchuria, Treaties and Agreements*, 28.

[26] Cordier, *op. cit.*, vol. 3, 347.

According to the *Herald* translation of "The Cassini Convention" it provided for the following:

it is now known that it was the definite ratification of the railway contract of September 8th for which Count Cassini delayed his departure from Peking.[27]

1. Right to construct the Siberian Railway across Northern Manchuria.

2. China should be permitted to redeem the railway after thirty years.

3. If China extended her railways from Shanhaikwan to Mukden and Kirin she was to allow Russia to provide the funds for construction.

4. Any railway extensions in Manchuria by China were to follow Russian railway regulations in order to facilitate commercial intercourse.

5. Russia was to be permitted to maintain railway guards along the Chinese Eastern Railway.

6. Customs duties were to be regulated by the treaty of February 20, 1862 O. S.

7. Russia to be permitted to exploit mines in Manchuria.

8. Should China wish to reform her Manchurian army she would be permitted to secure Russian advisers.

9. China states that she is willing to lease to Russia the port of Kiaochow for fifteen years.

10. China agrees to properly fortify Port Arthur and Talienwan and Russia promises not to allow any foreign power to encroach upon them. China will permit Russia to use these ports for military purposes in time of war.

11. Russia is not to interfere with these ports in any way except in case of war.

12. Treaty to go into effect as soon as signed, and with the exception of the articles regarding Port Arthur, Talienwan, and Kiaochow the various clauses shall be notified to the authorities of the two empires.

[27] Gerard, *Ma Mission en Chine*, 146-148.

M. Gerard's comments in this connection seem of sufficient importance to warrant inclusion here:

"Although the treaty was intended to remain secret, I one day had in my hands for a few minutes, during a visit which I made in the spring of 1897 to Li Hung-chang at his residence in Peking, the copy of the document which he had signed the previous year with Prince Lobanof . . . . The English translation of this text was published fifteen years later, when the treaty itself had expired, in the London *Daily Telegraph*, by the son of Li Hung-chang, Li Ching-mai, who was then Chinese Minister at the Court of St. James, and who sought to defend his father's memory against unjust attacks. The treaty was in fact a treaty of alliance, concluded for a period of fifteen years, by which the Chinese Government obligated itself, in the event of an aggression by Japan, to place at the disposal of the Russian Government its ports and all means of defense. The principal clause of the treaty was the assent given by the Chinese Government to the construction and operation in the Manchurian provinces of Amur (Heilungkiang) and Kirin, of a line of railway connecting with the Russian Siberian lines, the concession for which was made to the Russo-Chinese Bank by a contract to be signed by the Chinese Minister at St. Petersburg and the delegate of the Bank (art. 4). It was stipulated in article 6 that the treaty should come into force on the day on which the contract for the construction and operation of the railway should have been approved and ratified by the Emperor of China. . . . .

Not until the publication of an article entitled *Manchuria—A Chinese View of the Situation,* by An Admirer of Li Hung-chang[28] in the London *Daily Telegraph* of February 15, 1910, was the world informed that while attending the coronation ceremonies of the Tsar Nicholas II in 1896 Li had concluded with Russia a secret treaty of alliance, the text of which was now published for the first time.[29] The substantial accuracy of this disclosure was adequately confirmed by the publication in 1918 of M. Gerard's *Ma Mission en Chine;* the appearance of Count Witte's Memoirs in 1921, and finally by the submission to the conference on limitation of armament at the Washington Conference of 1921 by the Chinese Delegation of a telegraphic summary of the text of the secret treaty, made possible by the clever diplomacy of Witte.[30]

Looking back over the entire period of the negotiations of 1896 it now appears how essential to the Russian scheme of things the Transmanchurian line had become. This is not to say that the men who were

---

"The English newspapers at Shanghai had published, long before it was signed, the alleged text of the treaty and of the contract. They published another so-called version in the month of October, 1896, some days after the ratification at Peking of the contract in regard to the railway. These various texts, to which the English press gave the name of the "Cassini Convention," were apocryphal. They confused the treaty of alliance, properly so called, with the railway contract. . . . . The true facts as here outlined establish that there never was, properly speaking, any 'Cassini Convention'; that the treaty of alliance was concluded at St. Petersburg in the month of May, 1896, between Li Hung-chang and Prince Lobanof; that the railway contract was signed on September 8th following, also at St. Petersburg, by the Chinese Minister, Shu Ching Cheng, and the delegates of the Russo-Asiatic Bank; and that it was this contract for whose definite ratification at Peking on September 30th Count Cassini waited before proceeding on his way to Russia."

[28] The writer, as explained by Gerard, was Li Ching-mai, son of Li Hung-chang, who was at that time Chinese Minister to the Court of St. James and who sought to defend his father's memory against unjust attacks.

[29] *Manchuria, Treaties and Agreements,* 30.

[30] *Conference on the Limitation of Armament,* 1414.

molding Russia's Far Eastern policy had seen far in advance or determined the course and manner of their policy. Probably little thought had been given to it. Nevertheless, to the mind of Witte and those who sympathized with his aspirations, it now appeared that the Transmanchurian line would provide the most natural and effective instrument for the development of Russian influence in northern China. The concession, it was felt, was not too much to ask of China in return for Russia's part in the Triple Intervention and the matter of a defensive alliance might well be thrown in by St. Petersburg for good measure. The alliance was one that was assuredly welcome to Peking though it would have been as difficult then as now to conceive in what material way Russia could benefit by the armed assistance of such an impotent fighting power as China. Nevertheless, it assured the most amiable of relationships and by throwing open Chinese ports to Russian vessels in case of hostilities added a further bait to Russian aspirations. How fortunate it was for China that Japan remained in ignorance of this secret pact until after the Russo-Japanese War will appear after a consideration of the negotiations which terminated that conflict.

In his *Forty Years of Diplomacy* Baron Rosen after speaking of the compensating concession acquired by Russia refers to "another concession" granted by China which was permission for Russia to use in case of emergency the port of Kiaochow as a naval base in Far Eastern waters. If such an agreement were reached in the form of a separate convention, the document has never been revealed. Rosen believed the arrangement to be an aimless one meant to satisfy the claims to consideration of the Russian naval General Staff, "possibly occupied with the elaboration of some vague strategical plans and combinations."[31]

The terms of the railroad concession by which China had agreed to grant to the Russo-Chinese Bank the right for the construction and operation of the Chinese Eastern Railway were drawn up under Witte's instructions by the Assistant Minister of Finance, Piotr Mikhailovich Romanof, in consultation with the Chinese Minister in St. Petersburg, who was also China's envoy to Berlin, and it was in the latter capital that the terms of the concession were drafted and finally signed, as stated, on September 8, 1896.[32] The terms of this concession were very favorable for Russia, and in them is found the origin of an organization for many years destined to play an important part in Manchurian history, the Chinese Eastern Railway Company.[33]

By the first clause of the railway contract of September 8th it was provided that the Russo-Chinese Bank will establish for the construction and operation of a railway from the city of Chita to the Russian South Ussuri Railway, a company under the name of the Chinese Eastern Railway Company. The company possessed absolute and exclusive right of administration of its lands. Only Russian and Chinese subjects might become shareholders in the company; China possessed the right at the expiration of 36 years to redeem the railway but under such burdensome terms that it was highly improbable she would be able to do so, and finally at the end of 80 years the railway and

[31] Rosen, *Forty Years of Diplomacy*, vol. 1, 140. Witte records in this connection that in 1895 the Chinese Government agreed to open to Russia the port of Kiaochow, but adds that Russia did not take advantage of this privilege because she found the harbor inconvenient, and the question of a harbor for Russian warships remained open until late in 1897. (*Memoirs*, 98.)

[32] Witte, *op. cit.*, 94-95.

[33] *Manchuria, Treaties and Agreements*, 13-14.

all its property was to pass without payment to the Chinese government.[34]   The statutes of the company were given imperial sanction on December 16, 1896. In many respects it was a unique organization.   It was free from the control of the Russian Minister of Communications under whose charge all the other railways were placed, and it was not subject to the supervision of the Board of Auditors.   It was controlled directly by the Russian Ministry of Finance.

The President of the company was to be a Chinese, and only Chinese and Russians would be permitted to own stock.   The Chinese government was to assume responsibility for the protection of the road and criminal cases were to be settled by the local authorities and not through extraterritorial jurisdiction.   The lands, however, necessary for the construction, operation, and protection of the line were to be turned over to the company with an absolute and exclusive right of administration.   The clause providing for the return of the railway in 80 years and granting China the right of purchase in 36 years caused Russia no anxiety.   Before the expiration of either period St. Petersburg hoped to dominate completely, if she had not actually acquired, the "Three Eastern Provinces."[35]   Later as will be seen the company undertook other activities in addition to the operation of the line itself.   Notwithstanding that the road was nominally in the hands of a private corporation, an examination of the statutes is convincing proof that the Chinese Eastern Railway Company was firmly in the grip of the Russian government.

---

[34] *Ibid.*, 13-17.   See also *Charter of the Russo-Chinese Bank*, 17-27, and *Statutes of the Chinese Eastern Railway Company*, 34-39.

[35] *Manchuria, Treaties and Agreements*, 15-17.   Article 12 of the Railway Contract reads: The Chinese Government transfers to the Company the com-

The railway concession was not the only stake for which Russia was playing at the coronation ceremonies, for during these proceedings another treaty was signed by Russia, and to which Japan was a party. This document sanctioned Russia's dominating position in Korea and determined Japan's sphere of influence in that country. Russia was to be permitted to keep military instructors in Korea and acquired the right to appoint the financial councillor to the Korean Emperor while Japan on her part was granted certain commercial and industrial privileges.[36] In these activities were plainly visible a beginning of encroachment on the independence of Korea which had been guaranteed by the Peace of Shimonoseki less than a year previously.

In fact the period following the Shimonoseki Treaty down to the acquiring of the railway concession in northern Manchuria the following year was only the beginning of a feverish activity on the part of the Russian Departments of War and Foreign Affairs in the working out of a Far Eastern policy. The alleged concession of Kiaochow as a naval base, already referred to is but one evidence of this spirit. Rosen suggests that it was not inconceivable the War Department had likewise, unknown perhaps to the Minister of Foreign

---

plete and exclusive right to operate the line on its own account and risk, so that the Chinese Government will in no case be responsible for any deficit whatsoever of the Company, during the time allotted for the work and thereafter for a further eighty years from the day on which the line is finished and traffic is in operation. This period having elapsed, the line with all its appurtenances, will pass free of charge to the Chinese Government.

At the expiration of thirty-six years from the day on which the entire line is finished and traffic is in operation the Chinese Government will have the right to buy back this line upon repaying in full all the capital involved, as well as all the debts contracted for this line, plus accrued interest.

[36] Witte, *op. cit.*, 97-98. The Yamagata-Lobanof protocol to which reference is made does not bear out in fact the statement of Witte. It did not sanction Russia's dominating position in Korea. (British and Foreign State Papers, 1895-1896, vol. LXXXVIII. 471-473.)

Affairs, conceived some plan of action in another direction. This utter lack of co-ordination in the working of Russia's state affairs was, as we shall have occasion to see frequently, the rule, not the exception. At all events, further proof of Russia's growing interest in east Asia was seen in the dispatch to Korea of a Colonel of the Grand General Staff who returned to Russia with an elaborate plan for the organization of the Korean army which was to be effected by a special military mission of officers of all arms of the Russian army.[37]

Rosen, who was much interested in Far Eastern affairs, learned at this time also that the Russian Naval Department was in search of an ice-free port in Korea, "and was entertaining vague plans for a future acquisition of one of them, preferably the port of Mazampo, on the southern extremity of the Korean Peninsula, as a permanent naval station" for the Russian fleet in Far Eastern waters. Rosen closes this comment with the suggestion that these plans may have been inspired by the knowledge that some kind of a protectorate had been promised to the King of Korea even as early as 1896.[38] In fact, the events of 1895 and 1896 had assumed such a character that already there were not lacking in Russia statesmen firmly convinced that St. Petersburg was pushing a policy which could only end in armed conflict with Japan.[39]

---

[37] Rosen, *op. cit.*, vol. 1, 140-141.

[38] *Ibid.*, vol. 1, 141.

[39] *Ibid*, 142.

CHAPTER IV
RUSSIA IN MANCHURIA 1898-1902
THE LEASE OF PORT ARTHUR

The story of Russian influence in Manchuria finds no more interesting or complicated period than that on which we are now entering. The reader will recall the part played by St. Petersburg in the intervention of 1895 which forced Japan to restore to China the Liaotung Peninsula, and also the compensation that Russia secured in the right to build her Siberian Railway across the northern provinces of Manchuria. The route of this road, as it was conceived by its originators, was not, according to Witte, associated in any way with political or military designs, and even the construction of the road across Chinese territory might, under other circumstances, have been accomplished while a nonaggressive policy was maintained. But most of Russia's statesmen at this time were in no position to judge intelligently of her questions of Far Eastern Empire and arrived at their conclusions on a no more substantial basis than a personal preference for Japan or China. Alexander III and Nicholas II were unfamiliar with the Far East and were easily swayed by fantastic schemes and arguments of political adventurers, while their statesmen, as we shall see, were, with few exceptions, in no position to advise the Tsar on the subject of a Far Eastern policy.[1]

Under a more responsible form of government than that of St. Petersburg, the policy which had its first manifestation in the secret diplomacy which gave to

---

[1] Witte, *Memoirs*, 82.

Russia the right to build her Siberian Railway across northern Manchuria, might have retained something of a legitimate character. But this was far from being the case, and in order that the development of Russia's Asiatic policy may be the more readily understood a word should be said concerning the methods by which that policy was formed.

The organization of Russia's autocratic government made anything approaching an efficient administration impossible. Each of the ministers of state worked independently and received authority for his acts from the Emperor personally. Occasionally the Tsar presided over a council of ministers for the consideration of some grave question of policy, but these occasions were rare. Thus there was no ground of common understanding, and Nicholas II convoked a council of ministers even less frequently than his father.[2] This situation must be borne constantly in mind in any consideration of the developments attending Russian activities in the Far East during the years now under review.

It was this absurd state of affairs in Russia which in part at least made it possible for Witte to exert the influence he wielded so well in the negotiations with China in 1896; but his success in that move was a decided factor in the failure which was to follow. Iswolsky tells how Witte, as Minister of Finance, gave evidence of a tendency to dominate all other members of the so-called cabinet, and to become *de facto*, if not *de jure*, the real head of the Russian government. His

---

[2] Iswolsky, *Recollections of a Foreign Minister*, 111-112.

Witte, *Memoirs*, chapter 4, gives numerous examples of the unsystematic working of the Russian administration.

Alexinsky, *Modern Russia*, 175.

Dillon, *The Eclipse of Russia*, 151, stresses the incompetency of the bureaucratic administration.

control of the treasury, of course, aided him in this ambition. Further than this, the Minister of Finance developed a state within a state by creating and super-imposing on the existing organs of government others which derived their powers directly and solely from his ministry. In this manner he controlled an innumerable host of functionaries, and it would appear that the forces Witte thus wielded were better organized and performed greater service than the corresponding government services.[3] But they involved great national waste and their existence could continue only so long as they were controlled and guided by the will of Witte, himself.

So it was that in the working out of Russia's Far Eastern schemes, Witte brought to the task an influence entirely out of proportion to that of the other ministers of state. But his power was a thing dependent on the sovereign will, and might fade as rapidly as the Emperor's favor. These points are of great importance, for in them lies not only the explanation of the skill with which Witte carried out the first stages of his policy, the building of the Siberian road across Manchuria, but also the confusion which overtook Russian affairs there in later years when Witte's influence was no longer supreme and when the favor of Tsar Nicholas II was bestowed upon a group of adventurers whose chief contribution to Russian history was a disgraceful and costly war. Witte's control in Far Eastern affairs was secure until the events of 1898. He had played a considerable part in the intervention of 1895; he had negotiated successfully with Li Hung-chang at St. Petersburg the following year; he had been instrumental in the formation of the Russo-Chi-

---

[3] Iswolsky, *op. cit.*, 113.

nese Bank and the Chinese Eastern Railway Company which was to carry the new road across the Chinese lands. All this had been accomplished with remarkable success. The relationship between China and Russia had been strengthened. Some questions may have arisen in the minds of the ministers at Tokyo, but as later events showed they would not have assumed a serious tenor, had Russian policy stopped there, with the Chinese Eastern Railway firmly under Witte's control. Unhappily, however, these indications of an economic development as the outstanding feature of St. Petersburg's program were blasted when in 1898 Russia seized Liaotung, the very prize she had forced Japan to return to China three years previously.[4]

It is sufficient to note at this point how in 1897, prior to his departure to Tokyo, Baron Rosen, in a secret memorandum on the subject of Russian Far Eastern policy, with particular reference to Japan, felt that this policy was acquiring dangerous features and warned his government against "all such vague aims as hegemony, predominant influence, or similar imponderabilia of more than doubtful value, the pursuit of which could only excite rivalry, suspicion, and general hostility, and might at any moment embroil us in most dangerous complications."[5] The memorandum attacked vigorously all ideas of an aggressive Far Eastern policy and advocated a friendly understanding with Japan as well as with China, as "the best guarantee of a solid and lasting peace."[6]

Dramatic events in the Far East were heralded when in November, 1897, Germany seized Kiaochow in the Chinese province of Shantung. Ever since the in-

---

[4] Iswolsky, op. cit., 118-119.

[5] Rosen, op. cit., vol. 1, 143.

[6] Ibid., 146.

tervention of 1895 she had been looking for a port on
the coast of China which would serve as a naval base
and a center for German trade. Her warships had
surveyed the coast and the conclusion was reached that
Kiaochow was the port which Germany must have.
But it will be recalled that Witte in 1895 had secured
from the Chinese government the right to use the harbor of Kiaochow.[7] No action was taken by Russia at
the time and in 1897 the Kaiser personally secured the
promise of the Tsar not to oppose the German occupation of the harbor, despite Russia's apparent prior
claim to it.[8] Probably Nicholas II would not have
consented so readily to the Kaiser's request had he
been less ignorant of Far Eastern affairs,[9] and this
turn taken by events allowed the question of a harbor
for the Russian fleet to remain an open one until Germany's seizure of the port. This, according to Witte,
was not altogether surprising to the Russian Foreign
Minister, Count Muravieff, who received immediately
a request from the Chinese government for a detach-
ment of Russian warships to be sent to the seized port
to observe Germany's actions there. The Russian
chargé at Peking was notified the ships would be sent
but this order was immediately canceled and Li Hung-
chang was informed that negotiations were doubtless
being carried on between Berlin and St. Petersburg.[10]

First indications of a grave change in Russia's policy in China now made their appearance. Early in
November several ministers of the Russian government, including Witte, received a memorandum drawn
up by Count Muravieff, pointing out that the occupa-

[7] Witte, *op. cit.*, 98.

[8] *Ibid.*, 100.

[9] Dillon, *op. cit.*, 248.

[10] Witte, *op. cit.*, 98.

tion of Kiaochow by the Germans offered an auspicious occasion for Russia to secure a Chinese port, notably Port Arthur or Talienwan, as a base for the Pacific navy; and a council of ministers to consider this scheme was called under the presidency of the Tsar. Muravieff advanced the plea that Russia needed a Pacific port and that the moment was opportune for the seizure of Port Arthur and Talienwan. This proposition met with an indignant protest from several of the ministers, including Witte and the Minister of the Navy, Admiral Tirtoff, who felt it to be an adventurous undertaking that could only lead to serious consequences to the relations then existing with Japan.[1] Witte too forsaw disastrous results to his far-reaching policy of peaceful, economic penetration into Manchuria. He recalled to the ministers that Russia had declared herself a champion of the territorial integrity of the Chinese Empire, and on that ground had forced Japan to withdraw from Liaotung in 1895; that it would be treachery for Russia to seize the territory of a country with whom she had a defensive alliance, and finally that such action would be injurious to Russian interests which depended largely on the development of the most favorable relationship with China. As against Witte and Tirtoff, the scheme found its principal support in the Foreign Minister and the Minister of War, Vannovski.[12] Emperor Nicholas, impressed with the grave consequences suggested by Witte, refused to sanction Muravieff's measure, but several days later astonished his Minister of Finance

---

[11] Rosen, op. cit., vol. 1, 197.

[12] Witte, op. cit., 99. The support of the naval ministry was given to Witte largely because this ministry favored the establishment of a naval port not in Manchuria but in Korea, where it may be presumed it was to serve as a more effective weapon against Japan.

in a private audience by announcing, "I have decided to occupy Port Arthur and Talienwan. Our ships with troops are already on their way there." The Tsar had sanctioned the occupation because he was informed by Muravieff that British ships were in the waters of north China and would take Port Arthur if Russia did not act first. This rumor, according to information received later by Witte from the British ambassador at St. Petersburg, was false, and he now attempted to secure the consent of the Kaiser to withdraw from Kiaochow in order that Russia's pretext for action might vanish. This attempt, of course, failed and it was only at this time that Witte learned of the promise the Tsar had made to William II respecting Kiaochow during his visit in 1897.[13]

Early in December, accordingly, a squadron of Russian warships occupied Port Arthur and Talienwan. Meanwhile, Witte, who with the ministers of war, the navy, and of foreign affairs, was most intimately concerned with the progress of Russia's Far Eastern policy, continued to advocate withdrawal. These efforts were in vain because, as Witte believed, "it was natural for the young emperor to follow the advice of his Foreign Minister and Minister of War, which was in agreement with his own thirst for military glory and conquest."[14] Trusting in Russian assurances that St. Petersburg had no intention of seizing Chinese territory and that the occupation of Port Arthur was merely a protective measure against Germany at Kiaochow, the Chinese were at first reassured, and offered to supply coal for the Russian warships. In January, 1898, General Alexey Kuropatkin was appointed Min-

---

ister of War and immediately assumed a policy as aggressive if not more so than that of his predecessor, Vannovski, and advocated that the demand upon China include not merely Port Arthur and Talienwan but also the southern portion of the peninsula.[15]

Being in complete disagreement with the policy from which there now seemed to be no escape, Witte affirms that he requested permission to retire from the Ministry of Finance. This was refused and he was asked to continue as head of the ministry and to assist in carrying out the new policy. China now became reluctant to comply with Russian demands, and the signing of the agreement of March 15, 1898, by which, among other things, Russia secured a lease of Port Arthur was accomplished only after bribery had been resorted to on the part of Russian officials.[16] Russian policy, as manifested in this act, was, as Witte himself said, a violation of traditional relations with China, a fatal step which finally resulted in the Russo-Japanese War.

While these events were happening in the Far East, European governments other than Russia began to realize the full significance of Russian policy in Manchuria and the British government urged China to open Talienwan to trade and foreign settlement on the same terms as other treaty ports, feeling that this would insure British trading privileges in north China and tend to preserve the principle of the "Open Door."

---

[15] Witte, *op. cit.*, 101.

[16] *Ibid.*, 102-103. With reference to the charge of bribery Witte writes that under the influence of English and Japanese diplomats China at first refused to make any concessions. Whereupon Witte wired to the agent of his ministry in Peking to see Li Hung-chang and other officials and to advise them to come to terms. The agent was instructed to offer Li a present of 500,000 rubles. Witte adds that this was the first time he resorted to bribery in negotiations with Chinese.

This move was firmly opposed by Russia while her ships were arriving in considerable numbers both at Talienwan and Port Arthur, and when in March the final agreement for the lease was signed Russia declared that she had no intention of infringing the treaty rights of other powers in China. Expressing the view of the British government, however, Lord Salisbury stated while the negotiations between Russia and China were in progress that Her Majesty's government would not regard with any dissatisfaction the lease by Russia of an ice-free commercial port, connected by rail with the Transsiberian Railway, but he held that questions of an entirely different kind were raised by the occupation of Porth Arthur, a position useless for commercial purposes but of great military strength and strategic importance. Russia defended her action on the ground that Talienwan was useless without Port Arthur and consented that the former should be thrown open to foreign trade but declined to alter the status of Port Arthur as a closed and primarily a military and naval port.[17]

Beginning, therefore, with the convention for the lease of the Liaotung Peninsula with Port Arthur and Talienwan, Russia now concluded with China a series of agreements which indicated beyond doubt the skill with which Russian diplomacy had worked at Peking and the power which it now exerted over the Chinese government. Article I of the agreement of March 27th stated that for the purpose of insuring Russian naval forces an entirely secure base on the littoral of north China, Port Arthur and Talienwan were placed at the disposal of the Russian government and added: "This act of lease, however, in no way violates the sovereign

---

[17] *The London Times*, Weekly Edition, Jan. 29, 1904, 70.

rights of H. M. the Emperor of China to the above-mentioned territory." The limits of the territory to be leased in addition to the ports were to be determined by a separate Procotol to be concluded at St. Petersburg. In the previous year Germany had leased Kiaochow in the Province of Shantung for 99 years, but by Article 3 of her March agreement Russia merely acquired a 25-year lease. Subsequent events were to show why Russia satisfied herself with this brief period.[18] Article 8 was of signal importance for by it China agreed that the concessions granted by her in 1896 to the Chinese Eastern Railway Company should be extended by branch lines which were now to be built to Talienwan and to In-tzu, the second of which was never constructed. Here again the final sentence of the article is significant for Russia affirmed that consent for the construction of this railway "shall never, under any form, serve as a pretext for the seizure of Chinese territory or for an encroachment on the sovereign rights of China."[19]

On May 7th of the same year Russia concluded an additional agreement with China defining the boundaries of the leased and neutralized territory.[20] Russia agreed that the terminus of the branch line which was to connect the transsiberian road with Liaotung should be at Port Arthur and Talienwan. Railway privileges in the district traversed by this line were not to

---

[18] See exchange of notes between China and Japan concerning the extension of this term, May 25, 1915. (*The Sino-Japanese Negotiations of 1915*, published by the Carnegie Endowment for International Peace.)

[19] Text of Convention in *Manchuria, Treaties and Agreements*, 41-44.

[20] The line marking the leased territory commences from the north side of Ya Tang Bay on the west coast of Liaotung passing through the ridge of Ya Tang Mountain, (the mountain ridge being included in the leased ground) and continuing to the east coast of Liaotung near the north side of P'i-tzu-wo Bay. North of this line there was to be a zone of neutral territory defined in article 2 of the agreement.

be given to other powers. Within the leased territory the administration of Russia was supreme, while in the neutral zone nothing could be done by China without the consent of Russia, either as regards the opening of ports, the granting of railroad and mining concessions, or industrial and mercantile privileges.[21]

Finally, on July 6, 1898, was signed the third agreement between Russia (in reality the Chinese Eastern Railway Company) and China concerning the southern branch of the railway now to be constructed. This contract was to be drawn up in accordance with provisions of the Chino-Russian Treaty of March 27th and the supplementary agreement of May 7th. The name of the new road was to be the Southern Manchurian Branch of the Chinese Eastern Railway and in accordance with permission granted to the company in 1897 to cut timber and mine coal for the use of the railway, it was agreed to allow the company to fell timber on government lands, and in the regions traversed by the line to mine such coal as would be needed for the construction and operation of the road. Within the leased territory Russia was to fix the customs tariff while China retained the right to levy and collect duties at the boundaries on goods moving between the leased territory and the interior of China. It was further provided that China might arrange with Russia for the latter government to establish the customs at Talienwan (now named Dalny by Russia) and from the date of opening of the port to international trade to appoint the Chinese Eastern Railway Company to act as the agent of the Chinese Imperial Board of Revenue to manage the customs in its behalf.[22] Having decided,

---

[21] Text of Agreement in *Manchuria, Treaties and Agreements*, 46-47.

[22] Text of Agreement in *Ibid.*, 47. With Russia possessing the right to fix the tariff, the United States was given a legitimate cause for asking for the maintenance of the principle of the "Open Door."

however, to make Dalny a free commercial port no Chinese customs were established by Russia nor did the Chinese Customs transact business in the leased territory while under Russian administration.[23]

Such were then the main points of Russia's fast growing policy in the Far East as it developed between the months of March and July, 1898. In its official statement which appeared at St. Petersburg on March 29th, setting forth to other governments that the lease of Liaotung had been secured, the Russian government termed the agreement of March 27th a "direct and natural outcome of the friendly relations between great neighboring empires, all of whose endeavors should be directed toward the preservation of tranquillity along the vast extent of their neighboring possessions . . ." To this was attached another avowal of the sacred light in which Russia regarded the sovereign rights of China and the privileges enjoyed through treaty by other powers.[24]

The pursuance of Russia's openly aggressive policy was of course not opposed by France, the power that had ably seconded her in 1895, and the Manchurian activities were a welcome sign to Germany. Of the European powers, Great Britain alone was seriously affected as clearly indicated on April 2, 1898, when the British Minister at Berlin, Sir F. Lascelles, received telegraphic instructions to inform the German government that Great Britain's sole object in asking China to lease Weihaiwei was "to maintain the balance of power in the Gulf of Pechili, which is menaced by Russia's occupation of Port Arthur."[25] That such was

---

[23] Memorandum of research department of the South Manchuria Railway Company, 5.

[24] *Parliamentary Papers*, CIX, 1899, China, No. 1, Incl. No. 1.

[25] *Ibid.*, China, No. 2.

the attitude of Great Britain was well known in Russia not merely in diplomatic circles but generally as evidenced by press statements.[26]

Public opinion in Japan was much excited by the events which placed Russia in possession of the very position from which she had compelled the Japanese to withdraw. Japanese diplomacy took no prominent part in the controversy, but facilitated the Anglo-Chinese Agreement by which Great Britain leased Weihaiwei, and thus strengthened the already excellent relations between the two countries.[27] Yet while the Japanese government avoided anything resembling an aggressive attitude toward Russia, the occupation of Port Arthur was "a grievous hurt to the Japanese national feeling," and one that might easily lead to serious consequences. This fact was fully recognized too in St. Petersburg by all the ministers with the exception of Count Muravieff and the Emperor. A sane statesmanship, however, was in control at Tokyo and Baron Rosen who had arrived there the previous year as Russia's Ambassador reported in a private letter to Admiral Tirtoff, head of the Russian Naval Department, that while popular feeling in Japan was aroused, the Japanese government took a less sentimental and more practical view of the situation, reasoning apparently that since Russia had now secured an ice-free port in Manchuria she would cease her designs in Korea where Japan could never permit her to establish herself. It was shortly after this that Japan suggested to St. Petersburg through Baron Rosen, a reciprocal agreement to refrain from inter-

---

[26] *Ibid.*, No. 14, Incl. 1. Great Britain was granted a lease of Weihaiwei in July, the terms of the lease being the same as those secured by Russia at Port Arthur. The lease was to continue so long as Russia occupied Liaotung.

[27] *The London Times,* Weekly Edition, Jan. 29, 1904, 70.

ference in each other's policy, Russia's in Manchuria and Japan's in Korea. Russia failed to acquiesce in this proposal and the matter was dropped.[28]

Evidence of the jealousy with which Russia regarded any seeming encroachment on her sphere of influence in north China was given in July, 1898, when she entered a protest at Peking against a concession to British capitalists for the extension of the railways of north China to Newchwang, which, until the opening of Dalny, was the only Manchurian port at which foreign trade might be conducted. The Russian opposition was ultimately withdrawn after important alterations had been made in the concession, the negotiations attending which culminated in an Anglo-Russian railway agreement of April 28, 1899.[29] By this agreement, which was in reality an exchange of notes between Count Muravieff, the Russian Foreign Minister, and Sir C. Scott, the British Ambassador, the two powers defined the spheres in which they might seek railway concessions in China. Great Britain engaged not to seek for her own account or on behalf of British subjects or of others, any railway concessions to the north of the Great Wall of China and not to obstruct applications for railway concessions in that region supported by the Russian government, while Russia engaged not to seek on her account or on behalf of Russian subjects or of others any railway concessions in the basin of the Yangtze, and not to obstruct applications for such concessions there supported by the British government.[30]

---

[28] Rosen, *op. cit.*, vol. 1, 156-157.

[29] *The London Times,* Weekly Edition, Jan. 29, 1904, 70.

[30] Full text of exchange of notes between Sir C. Scott and Count Muravieff in *Manchuria Treaties and Agreements,* 53-54.

The attitude of the Russian Government as expressed on August 12, 1898, to Mr. Balfour at the Foreign Office by M. Lessar was that Russia would

With the establishment of this understanding respecting railways with Great Britain, Russia further
consolidated her position in Manchuria by an exchange
of notes with Peking. The first of these from the
Tsungli Yamen to the Russian Minister reinforced a
previous understanding that China reserved the right
to construct all railways which might be built from
Peking to the north or northeast, with Chinese capital
and under Chinese supervision. If, however, it was
proposed to have such construction undertaken by any
other power, the proposal should first be made to the
Russian government. Furthermore, on no consideration was any other government to be allowed to construct such railways. The reply of the Russian Minister, M. de Giers, was delivered on June 17th. This
note referred to a communication between Peking and
St. Petersburg of July 31, 1898, and stated that while
the Russian government would not at once ask for the
construction of a road connecting the main line of the
Manchurian Railway with Peking, the demand of
Russia for the construction of this road was based on
the responsibility assumed by the Chinese government
in the above-mentioned communication.[31] Thus far
Russian policy in Manchuria had encountered few obstacles. Japan's attitude was anything but aggressive.
Great Britain still appeared to be Russia's greatest
rival, and any danger to Russian interests from this
source was disposed of by the Scott-Muravieff ex-

welcome investment of British capital, in Manchuria, but that British control
of an important line of communication which might mean rivalry with the
Manchurian railway, could not be permitted. (*Parliamentary Papers*, CIX,
1899, China, No. 2.)

[31] Full text of notes in *Manchuria, Treaties and Agreements*, 54-55. The
note of the Chinese Government of July 31, 1898, here referred to, has not
been discovered.

change of notes and the later communications between St. Petersburg and Peking.

While she was thus disposing of the international problem confronting her in Manchuria, Russia did not neglect to strengthen her position in the leased territory and to prepare for the expansion of her interests there. Witte, it will be recalled, was opposed to the whole scheme of the lease but once the step was taken he began to expand his program of action there. Russia now had three things to accomplish to give practical value to the concessions she had acquired: the construction of a railway line connecting Harbin on the Chinese Eastern Railroad with Port Arthur; the fortification of Port Arthur, which was to be the base of the Pacific Fleet, and the building of a commercial port at Talienwan, to be known as Dalny.[32]

Under Witte's direction construction was commenced on the new line along which the rule of his ministry was supreme and as the policy was molded to meet the needs of the situation as they arose he was soon to acquire a veritable army under his command in the form of a guard for the protection of the railway, as well as a river and an ocean fleet.[33]   At the same time the number of Russian troops in the Far East was increased, supply depots were established and the fortification of Port Arthur and Vladivostok was undertaken hastily.   In fact one quarter of the total sum allotted to all fortress construction and maintenance from 1898 to 1902 was spent upon these Far Eastern strongholds.[34]   It soon became evident, therefore, that it was not merely an ice-free port, but in reality a fortress that Russia desired to acquire on the Pacific.

---

[32] *Economic Development of Korea and Manchuria,* 157.

[33] Iswolsky, *op. cit.,* 120-121.

[34] Kuropatkin, *The Russian Army and the Japanese War,* vol. 1, 126.

For this purpose Port Arthur was admirably situated. So far as Russian desires in Liaotung were concerned no further development would have taken place on the coast, had it not been, as Witte affirms, that the occupation of the peninsula so alarmed the powers having vested interests in China that Russia, in order to pacify these nations, forced herself to build an ice-free commercial port, Dalny, in the vicinity of Port Arthur.[35] This port which has been referred to as Talienwan was, when the Russians acquired their lease in 1898, merely a desolate fishing hamlet on the shores of Talien Bay and it was there that Russia laid out and built the nucleus of one of the finest cities in the Orient.[36] When later the Japanese acquired it, the name of Dalny was changed to Dairen. The city continued to increase in size until in a few years the original town built by the Russians became but a small section of it.

In August, 1899, Dalny was declared an open port by Imperial ukase[37] and later in the year Russia replied reluctantly though in a manner generally favorable to the "Open Door" note of Secretary of State Hay of the United States government.[38] Nevertheless, Russian military strength in Manchuria was being constantly increased. By the close of 1899 Russia had 20,000 men at Port Arthur and Dalny and Cossack guards patrolled the railway line then under construction.[39]

---

[35] Witte, *op. cit.*, 105.

[36] *Economic Development of Korea and Manchuria*, 157, 246. Russia, however, was not permitted to possess the City of Dalny in its full splendor for it was only partially built when the Russo-Japanese War broke out. The early work of construction was delayed somewhat under the Russian regime, but by the end of 1902 when through traffic between Harbin and Port Arthur was opened, it had become quite an important town.

[37] *The London Times*, Weekly Edition, Jan. 29, 1904, 70.

[38] United States *Foreign Relations*, 1899, 141-142.

[39] *The London Times, loc. cit.*, 70.

From many points of view the Manchurian venture was harmul of itself but from the standpoint of Russian foreign relations it was soon to prove fatal, and, as it will appear later, may be considered one of, if not the main cause, of the Russo-Japanese War. Had Russia been content to use Port Arthur as a naval base, refraining scrupulously from extending her influence throughout the interior of the peninsula, it is conceivable that in time Japan might have accommodated herself to the situation, for evidence is not lacking of the passive attitude of the Japanese government at the time and its desire to come to a friendly understanding with Russia on the Manchurian and Korean question. This latter question will be referred to in detail in a subsequent chapter. When, however, to the Manchurian blunder was added the mad adventure of a group of royal favorites, Bezobrazoff, Abaza and their following in Korea and on the Yalu, the reckoning between the two powers was hastened. As we shall see both Witte and Lamsdorff, who succeeded Count Muravieff as Russian Foreign Minister, opposed the band of courtiers and schemers who succeeded in drawing the Tsar into these Far Eastern adventures, and who for the time ousted the Foreign Minister and Minister of Finance from the control of Far Eastern affairs. Yet these facts alone will not serve to absolve them from all responsibility for the events which followed. On Witte's part, at least, a desire to remain in power seemed to overbalance all other considerations and this in itself prevented him from giving that vigorous opposition to a policy which he knew must end in catastrophe.[40]

---

[40] Iswolsky, *op. cit.*, 122-123.

CHAPTER V

RUSSIA IN MANCHURIA, 1898-1902

THE OCCUPATION OF MANCHURIA

The years following Russia's occupation of Port Arthur and the Liaotung Peninsula were troubled ones for China. With the seizure of Kiaochow by Germany in 1897 and the subsequent scramble of the European powers for leaseholds and concessions both the sovereignty and integrity of the Chinese Empire appeared to be in imminent danger. The creation of the so-called "spheres of influence" had produced a grave national problem for Peking and an acute international problem affecting all the powers possessing interests in that kingdom. It was this situation that occasioned the announcement of the "Open Door" policy, as proposed by the government of the United States; but this was not the only result of the wretched policy of the powers toward Peking during the previous years. During the months that the "Open Door" notes were being considered by the powers addressed, there was perfected in north China an organization whose purpose was the expulsion of the troublesome foreigner. It is impossible here to enter into a full discussion of the origin of this revolutionary body. Suffice it to say that in 1898 the Emperor of China, in a belated effort to rehabilitate a thoroughly corrupt and incapable administration, had agreed to far-reaching reform measures, but these had lasted only one hundred days, and reaction, represented by the Empress Dowager, again seized control.[1]

---

[1] Morse, *The International Relations of the Chinese Empire*, vol. 3, 137-154

Results of this action were soon seen in the provinces, especially in Shantung, where the Governor made no attempt to suppress a secret society later known as the Boxers. At first the society had been anti-Manchu. Its chief feature now was a strong antiforeign sentiment; its main purpose to drive out the foreigners and all Chinese affiliated with them, and in particular the Christians. The situation was serious by May, 1900; in June the siege of the legations in Peking began, and while these events were taking place the powers whose nationals were thus endangered made hasty preparations for relief. The relief expedition entered Peking on August 14th. With the negotiations which ensued and the final protocol which was signed on September 7, 1901,[2] between China and the Powers we are not concerned, but it has been deemed necessary to speak briefly of the general aspects of the Boxer rising that the part played by Russia in events that were soon to take place in Manchuria may be more readily understood.

Russia was one of the principal powers represented in the expedition that relieved the Peking legations, and in the subsequent negotiations. There were 4,500 Russian troops participating in the march on the Imperial capital, and M. de Giers, representing the St. Petersburg government at Peking, was soon to interpret a role not unlike that which Ignatieff, it will be recalled, had played in connection with the Peking convention of 1860.[3]

When the Boxer uprising first became menacing to foreign interests in China, opinion in St. Petersburg had been divided as to what action Russia should take. General Kuropatkin, the Minister of War, favored

---

[2] Treat, *Japan and the United States, 1853-1921*, 172-176.

[3] See chapter I.

at this time an active, aggressive participation by Russia in the concerted action of the Powers against China. On the other hand, Witte, controlling the Ministry of Finance, seeing a further threat to the success of his policy of peaceful penetration and absorption, vigorously opposed this.[4] Unfortunately the Boxer movement spread to Manchuria and thus changed the entire complexion of the situation. It is probably true that the Chinese inhabitants had received the Russians favorably at first, when their activities were confined to the main line of the Chinese Eastern Railway in North Manchuria, but after the occupation of Port Arthur considerable hostility was manifested by the native population. There had been armed attacks on the southern branch of the railway, then under construction, and in 1899 the Governor of Mukden had issued a proclamation to the people of his province, accusing the Russians of oppressive measures and of occupying land illegally for the construction of Talienwan or Dalny.[5] Yet despite these conditions Russia had not expected that the Boxer uprising would spread to Manchuria, and relying on her close association with the reactionary party at Peking, under the Empress Dowager and her clique, St. Petersburg believed its interests there would not be greatly affected. But in July when anxiety with regard to the fate of the legations was at its height news reached St. Petersburg of an organized outbreak against the Russians in Northern Manchuria. Large forces were moved into the area of the disturbance and order was restored in drastic manner. At Blagovestchensk on the Russian side of the Amur repression took the form of a

---

[4] Witte, *op. cit.*, 107-108, and Kuropatkin, *op. cit.*, vol. 1, 158.
[5] Witte, *op. cit.*, 109-110.

massacre of Chinese, many of whom probably had not participated in the rising.[6] Russian forces were soon in control of all Manchuria. The administration of the Chinese Eastern Railway Company was anxious for a peaceful understanding with China, but the Ministry of War was opposed to anything so compromising to the dignity of a great power. The Russian army behaved in Manchuria as in a conquered country. The forces of the Boxers were insignificant and were easily defeated wherever a conflict occurred, yet the Russian troops remained throughout the "Three Eastern Provinces" and thus provoked the trouble that was to follow. On the one hand this policy created a division of opinion in the Russian Government itself and on the other an international situation which the powers concerned with Far Eastern affairs considered with just alarm.[7]

Progress of Russia's policy of complete occupation of Manchuria was now rapid. In spite of official and public assurances that her intention was only the restoration of order, General Grodekof, Commander-in-Chief and Governor-General of the Amur Province, declared on August 14th that Russia had annexed the right bank of the Amur. For this action the Emperor extended his thanks and the news was published to the world. Then followed seizure of the highly important harbor of Newchang, where, after hoisting the Russian flag, Russian administration was estab-

---

[6] *The London Times*, Weekly Edition, Feb. 5, 1904, 84.

[7] Witte, *op. cit.*, 109-110. In reference to the continued occupation of Manchuria by the Russian forces Witte says: "For a year and a half this was a cause of difference between the Ministry of Finance, the administration of the Eastern Chinese Railway, and the agents of the Foreign Office on one side, and the War Ministry on the other. His Majesty vacillated and rendered inconsistent decisions. He did not definitely condemn the view held by the Ministers of Finance and Foreign Affairs. On the other hand he seemed to countenance General Kuropatkin and his group."

lished. Similar action was taken at Harbin.[8] Naturally enough the result, Witte asserted at the time, was
distrust on the part of the Chinese, jealousy and malevolence in Europe, and alarm in Japan. By this time
the Peking legations had been relieved, and with the
major portion of Manchuria reduced under a military
occupation by Russia a new stage in the development
of the Manchurian question commenced. The "Three
Eastern Provinces" were no longer a mere "sphere"
of Russian influence. They had been occupied by armed
forces and were still occupied by these forces. The
question which now confronted Russia was how this
temporary occupation was to be made permanent. As
Witte had predicted, the suspicion and jealousy of certain of the powers, Great Britain and Japan in particular, had been aroused by the occupation. To counteract the fears of these nations Russia now began to
issue a series of "assurances," which were designed
to convince the world of the sincerity of Russia's oft
expressed policy regarding the territorial integrity of
the Chinese Empire.[9] While, therefore, we are following the course of Russian secret diplomacy as it
affected Manchuria from 1900 to 1902 and are observing on the other hand how this diplomacy might be
reconciled with Russia's repeated assurances to the
Powers, it will be remembered that Russia was represented in Peking by M. de Giers, who was negotiating
as one of the allies adjusting the Boxer trouble.

Russia had already declared her intention to cooperate with the other powers at Peking and claimed

---

[8] Witte, op. cit., 113, letter to Minister of Interior Sipyagin dated at St.
Petersburg, August 10, 1900. (See also reports of the British Consuls Hosie
and Fulford and the American Consul Miller, in China, No. 5, 1900, 47 ; No. 2,
1904, 29-33 and 57th Cong. 2nd sess. HD, vol. 1, 147.)

[9] Asakawa, The Russo-Japanese Conflict, 140-147.

to have put forward certain "fundamental principles" as a basis of common action, such as harmony among the powers, preservation of the *status quo* in China prior to the rebellion, and the elimination of everything that might tend to a partition of China.[10] This pronouncement of the Russian Government was probably deemed expedient by reason of the impression which the declaration of General Grodekof, relative to annexation of the Amur, had produced. It was this communication to the Powers, too, which contained the first of the famous Russian "assurances." This opening chapter of what was to prove one of the most astonishing periods of Russian diplomatic history declared that as soon as order had been established in Manchuria and all means had been taken for the protection of the railway, Russia would not fail to recall her troops from these territories, provided the other powers did not place obstacles in her way.[11] But military operations in Manchuria did not cease. Russia withdrew her troops from Peking after the relief of the legations and concentrated them in the "Three Eastern Provinces" and a proclamation to the inhabitants was issued by General Gribsky reminding them of the massacre of Blagovestchensk and placing the territory of occupation under Russian law. Orders for a partial demobilization were reported in October but, being qualified by many reservations and exceptions, were of little effect. This action was promptly followed by the ordinance which created a military force of "railway guards" numbering 12,000 men, who were to police the zone of the Chinese Eastern Railway.[12]

---

[10] *Ibid.*, 147.

[11] *The London Times*, Weekly Edition, Feb. 5, 1904, 84.

[12] *Ibid.*

Early in November large naval reinforcements were
dispatched by Russia to the Far East and at the same
time it became apparent that while Russia was negotiating with the Allies in Peking for the settlement
of the Boxer troubles throughout China, she considered
Manchuria as a special field not affected by the Peking
negotiations in which she might carry on independent
negotiations, of a secret nature, with China. On December 31, 1900, the Peking correspondent of *The
London Times* reported that an agreement had been
concluded between Russia and China regarding the
Russian military occupation of Fengtien or Mukden
Province in Manchuria, and the resumption of the
Chinese civil administration there. The Agreement
was signed at Port Arthur by a representative of
Tseng, the Tartar general at Mukden, and General
Korostovetz, representing Admiral Alexieff, the Russian Commander-in-Chief. By the agreement Russia
was said to have consented to allow the Tartar general
and the Chinese officials to resume the civil government at Mukden, which had been disrupted by the occupation by Russian troops but only on certain stipulated conditions. All forts in Fengtien not accupied
by Russians were to be dismantled, Newchwang and
other places occupied by the invaders were not to be
restored until the pacification of the province was complete, and a Russian political resident with general
powers of control was to be stationed at Mukden,
where he was to be kept closely informed of all important measures enacted by the Tartar general.[13]

---

[13] *Parliamentary Papers*, (1904) CX. China No. 2, Incl. in No. 3. The
text of the preliminary Russo-Chinese Arrangement regarding Manchuria
which came to be known as the Alexieff-Tseng Agreement is also published in
Manchuria, Treaties and Agreements, 68. In Rockhill the agreement is given
under the title, "Signed at Port Arthur, January 30, 1901," and with a foot-
note stating that "the original convention bears date November 11, 1900."

News of this agreement between Russia and China at a time when St. Petersburg was negotiating with the Allies in Peking was more than sufficient to arouse alarm concerning Russia's intentions in North China. There was an evident conflict in the purposes of the Powers. The British Government, as was to be expected, kept itself as minutely informed on the progress of Russia's negotiations as possible. The question had already been raised as to whether China would confirm the Alexieff-Tseng Agreement and by February 7, 1901, the British Government was informed that Russia was pressing for ratification, while on the other hand China was ready to repudiate the Agreement, it was understood, and to punish the Tartar general who concluded it, if she were sufficiently encouraged in this attitude by the other foreign powers. The Japanese Government also proposed at this time to inform the Chinese Minister at Tokyo that the conclusion of any such Agreement as the Alexieff-Tseng affair, or any arrangement affecting territorial rights in China ought not to be made by the Chinese Government and any one of the powers. The British Government was in complete accord with this view.[14]

Although for some years the authenticity of the reported Alexieff-Tseng Agreement was a subject of debate, there now remains no doubt that an arrangement of some kind was reached. Russia's explanation of her actions in Manchuria was given by Count Lamsdorff, the Foreign Minister, to Sir C. Scott, the British Ambassador, on February 6th. The Foreign Minister denied that Russia had concluded an agreement which gave her a virtual protectorate over South Manchuria.

---

[14] *Parliamentary Papers*, (1904) CX, China No. 2, Memorandum given to Baron Eckardstein by the Marquess of Lansdowne, February 7, 1901.

However, the rumors concerning Russian action, he said, probably found their basis in the fact that the Russian military authorities who had been engaged in the "temporary" occupation and pacification of that province, had been directed when reinstating the Chinese authorities in their former posts to arrange with the local civil authorities the terms of a *modus vivendi* for the duration of the simultaneous presence of Russian and Chinese authorities in South Manchuria. The object of this, Count Lamsdorff explained, was to prevent the recurrence of disturbances in the vicinity of the Russian frontier and to protect the railway from the Russian frontier to Port Arthur. It might be confidently stated, he added, that no convention or arrangement with the Central Government of China of a permanent character had been concluded, nor had the Emperor any intention of departing in any way from the assurances which had been publicly given that Manchuria would be restored to China as soon as circumstances permitted it. The Foreign Minister made the position of his government quite clear, in that, when the question of final evacuation of Manchuria should be considered Russia would be obliged to obtain from China an effective guarantee against the recurrence of attacks on her frontier and the destruction of her railway, but had no intention of seeking this guarantee in the acquisition of territory or an actual or virtual protectorate over Manchuria.[15]

On February 27th, Sir E. Satow, the British Minister at Peking, forwarded to his Government the full text of an agreement which the Russian Government was said to be pressing on the Chinese Minister at

---

[15] *Parliamentary Papers*, (1901) XCI, China No. 2, Sir C. Scott to the Marquess of Lansdowne, St. Petersburg, February 6, 1901.

St. Petersburg and which was more far-reaching than the arrangement signed at Port Arthur.[16]   On March 1st, the Chinese Ministers to England, Germany, Japan, and the United States requested joint mediation of these powers on the subject of the Russo-Chinese impasse in Manchuria. Great Britain replied immediately that when an official text of the alleged agreement was received the British Government would confer with the other powers whose mediation had been invited.[17] The Government of the United States had already during February warned the Peking Government of the danger of coming to a separate agreement without the full knowledge of the powers then engaged in negotiations.[18] On March 4th, the Marquess Lansdowne telegraphed Sir C. Scott to inform Count Lamsdorff that though the presentation of his explanation of the Alexieff-Tseng Agreement to Parliament would somewhat allay, it would not dispel the apprehensions created by the publication of numerous versions of the agreement, for by the terms of these it appeared that much more was involved than a purely temporary measure.[19] Sir E. Satow forwarded to his Government on March 6th what was claimed as the Chinese text of the agreement and three days later the British Ambassador at St. Petersburg was instructed to inform Count Lamsdorff that it was impossible to describe the contract as of a temporary and provisional nature and that the treaty rights of Great Britain in China were

---

[16] *Parliamentary Papers*, (1904) CX, China No. 2, Sir E. Satow to the Marquess of Lansdowne, Peking, February 27, 1901. In *Shina Kankei Tokushu Joyaki Isan*, 109, is printed a Japanese version of what purports to be a "Secret Treaty between Russia and China," concluded in February, 1901. (*Manchuria, Treaties and Agreements*, 68.)

[17] *Parliamentary Papers* (1904) CX, China No. 2 (17).

[18] *Ibid.*, Incl. in (19).

[19] *Ibid.*, (20).

certainly affected by it.[20]   This pronouncement had an almost immediate effect on St. Petersburg for on March 19th the Viceroy at Nanking expressed to Sir E. Satow his gratitude for the exertions of the British Government which had caused Russia to modify her demands.[21]

The attitude of Germany toward the Manchuria question at this period is of particular interest because of the Anglo-German convention of October, 1900, and Germany's interpretation of it.   By Article 3 of the convention it was provided that "in case another power should take advantage of complications in China to obtain territorial advantages in any form whatsoever the two contracting parties bind themselves to conclude a preliminary agreement with respect to measures eventually to be taken for the protection of their respective interests in China."   The whole situation which had existed in Manchuria since the military occupation by Russia in 1900 seemed to suggest the very contingency referred to in Article 3 just quoted. Before lodging its protest at St. Petersburg on March 9th, the British Government had hoped to be joined by the Wilhelmstrasse in a joint formal protest against these proceedings.   But Count von Bülow stated in the Reichstag on March 15th that "the agreement had no reference to Manchuria" and that Germany had "no important national interest" there.   Germany maintained further that the negotiations attending the signing of the Anglo-German convention left no doubt that Manchuria was in no way involved, while Lord Lansdowne replied that the agreement was certainly intended to refer to Manchuria as well as the Eighteen

---

[20] *Parliamentary Papers*, (1904) CX. China No. 2, 25 and 26.
[21] *Ibid.*, No. 27.

Provinces of China proper.[22] Mr. Schmitt in *England and Germany 1740-1914* says that "in British eyes, Germany was deliberately encouraging Russia in a line of action detrimental to British commercial interests in order that German diplomacy might have a freer hand in the Near East, where British interests were already suffering from German competition; and Germany was once more able to argue that British diplomacy was playing its favorite game of using a Continental power to exert pressure on Russia."[23]

During March, 1901, the British and Japanese Governments discussed the Manchurian question, and Baron Hayashi informed the Marquess of Lansdowne that in the view of his Government a special convention such as was being negotiated separately by Russia was contrary to the principle of solidarity which then united the Powers and would materially lessen China's capacity to meet her obligations to the Powers. For these reasons the Japanese Government was ready to join Her Majesty's Government in again advising the Chinese Government not to sign the amended draft of the convention. The British Government immediately expressed its hearty accord.[24]

Three of the powers then again exerted their influence upon China. The Japanese Minister at Peking brought strong pressure to bear upon the Chinese Government to reject the proposed convention, while the British and American Governments warned Peking of the danger of the situation. Further than this, some of the highest officials of the provinces, including the Viceroys of the Yangtze, memorialized the throne in

[22] Schmitt, *England and Germany, 1740-1914*, 150-151.
[23] *Ibid.*, 151.
[24] *Parliamentary Papers* (1904) CX, China No. 2, (No. 28).

terms of the utmost urgency.[25] With such a combination of pressure being exerted against her, Russia now
for the first time apparently began to realize that she
had overstepped the mark of safety so far as her Far
Eastern problem was concerned. The strong protest
of the British Government, followed by one equally
pointed from Tokyo, indicated clearly that these powers
would not be content to see Russia pursue a type of
action such as had characterized her advance in Man-
rhuria in 1898. Her reply to Japan, however, stated
that she was unwilling to discuss the terms of the
agreement with a third power, that it was only a temporary arrangement and would not impair the sovereignty of China or injure the interests of other states
there.[26] The Chinese Government on its part had not
ventured to disregard the remonstrances of the Viceroys nor the advice of the Powers and finally during the
last days of March refused to sanction the agreement.

Realizing now that she had carried her game of
double diplomacy too far Russia on April 6, 1901, presented her view of the Manchurian question in the
"Official Messenger." In a lengthy and detailed survey
the Government stated that without in any way dis-
associating herself from the other powers in their
common action with regard to the Chinese question,
Russia was nevertheless obliged by reason of her special relations with China "to reserve a certain liberty
of action" and not to bind herself by engagements contrary to her interests and historical traditions. Russia's immediate political aims were stated to be two in
number. First, the preservation of the Russian mis-

---

[25] *The London Times,* Weekly Edition, February 5, 1904, 85.
    Parliamentary Papers (1904) CX, China No. 2, (No. 33).
[26] *The London Times, loc cit.,* 85.
    Parliamentary Papers 1904 CX, China No. 2, (No. 34).

sion at Peking, and the protection of Russian subjects against the criminal intentions of the Chinese insurgents, and secondly, the offer of assistance to the Chinese Government in its struggle against the insurrection with a view to a speedy restoration of normal conditions within the Empire. The statement then called attention to Russia's repeated assurances that her occupation of Manchuria was only a temporary measure. However, a following paragraph drew a careful distinction between those questions which concerned all the Powers in China and those which were matters solely between China and an individual power and a clear impression was conveyed that Russia was seeking to be liberal in all that concerned the Powers generally while she attempted to pursue a policy of secret and aggressive demands on China with respect to Manchuria, a question which, of course, concerned only Russia.[27]

Once again Russia announced that her occupation of Manchuria was merely an expedient necessary to bring about the restoration of order. However, she was careful to include a paragraph declaring the question of the complete and final restitution of Manchuria to China could only be accomplished after a normal state of affairs had been established, with a central government at Peking sufficiently strong to guarantee Russia against the renewal of the disturbances of 1900. Three days prior to the publication of this important statement a circular addressed to the Russian diplomatic officials abroad had announced that Russia would not insist on the signature of the convention.[28]   This seemed to indicate a favorable solution of the question,

---

[27] *Parliamentary Papers*, (1904) CX, China No. 2, (Incl. in No. 37).

[28] *The London Times, loc. cit.*, 85.

but only a few months had passed when on August 14th it was reported by Sir E. Satow, the British Minister at Peking, that Russia, although she persistently denied it, was resuming her negotiations with China to bring about the signature of a Manchurian agreement.[29]   The text of the agreement was at first reported to be the same as that which had already been forwarded to the British Foreign Office.   Later in the month other texts of the proposed Agreement were forwarded to the British Government by Satow, giving the original terms proposed by the Russian Minister, the first alterations of March, 1901, and the further concessions made by Russia in August.   These demands were less excessive but the United States Government, supported by Great Britain and Japan, entered a protest against a clause in the new agreement which was intended to secure special privileges for the Russo-Chinese Bank.   This protest stated that an arrangement by which China gave any corporation or company exclusive rights in the industrial development of the province of Manchuria would be viewed "with concern" by the United States Government as a "distinct breach" of the treaties between China and other foreign powers.   This, it was added, would seriously affect the rights of American citizens and tend toward impairing the sovereign rights of China.[30]

Russia had now been in practically undisputed control of Manchuria and the important treaty port of Newchwang since July, 1900.   At Newchwang the outward signs of Russian rule were everywhere apparent. The Russian flag flew from the forts and public build-

---

[29] *Parliamentary Papers*, (1904) CX, China No. 2 (40), Sir E. Satow to the Marquess Lansdowne.

[30] *The London Times, loc. cit.*, 85, and United States *Foreign Relations*, 1902, 275.

ings, the Russian customs flag was hoisted on the Imperial Maritime Customs Building and the native customs were administered by the Russians, assisted by a staff lent to them by Sir Robert Hart.[31]   Some time previous to November 27th Sir Robert stated that he would take an early opportunity of urging the Chinese Government to demand from the Russian Minister the restoration of the customs revenues of Newchwang in order that they might be devoted to the service of the indemnity bonds in the terms of the final protocol signed by China at the demand of the Powers.[32]

Now a new factor was to make itself felt in the Manchurian question, and indeed with such force as to cause for the time being at least a much saner attitude on the part of the Russian Government.   During the troubled years since Russia's occupation of Port Arthur in 1898 the United States, Great Britain, and Japan had worked in harmony.   All believed in the "Open Door" policy and the territorial integrity of China. On the other hand it was apparent by this time that Russia, while she had given a half-hearted assent to Secretary Hay's "Open Door" note, was nevertheless acting in a purely aggressive manner in which she could rely upon support, moral, if not material, from France, and perhaps Germany, as indicated in the latter's attitude toward the Anglo-German Convention of 1900.   This situation, in which an aggressive Russia was advancing to a complete control of Manchuria, which would mean eventually complete control of Korea also, was quite intolerable from the Japanese point of view.   For now Japan's position in the Far East was menaced by the same combination of powers

[31] *Parliamentary Papers*, (1904) CX, China No. 2 (Incl. in 43).
[32] *Ibid.*, No. 46.

that had humbled her in 1895. It was natural, therefore, for Japan to seek support. An alliance with the United States seemed out of the question in view of the traditional policy of the American government, which at that time could not be counted upon to maintain by force the principles that it had enunciated.[33]

With Great Britain the case was different. She had long been fearful of a Russian advance toward India, and now this threat was directed at China and Korea, where large British commercial interests would be jeopardized. Therefore Downing Street did not regard with disfavor the proposals first advanced by Baron Hayashi. At first these were merely tentatively presented as personal views regarding the possible future relations of Japan and England, but they met at once a favorable response from Lord Lansdowne. While progress was thus being made toward an Anglo-Japanese understanding, there was also a strong party in Japan favorable to an accord with Russia, and during the time that Hayashi was opening the way for an alliance in London, Count Ito was sent to St. Petersburg to formulate if possible an agreement with Russia. Ito's visit, however, accomplished nothing of value and only disclosed the existence of divided opinion within the inner circle of the Japanese Government and laid the Government open to a charge of double dealing.[34] With a condition of affairs such as that existing at St. Petersburg nothing short of a powerful alliance, appearing at least to be a safeguard against further aggression in Manchuria, would have been sufficient to turn Russia from her wild scheme to control

---

[33] Treat, *op. cit.*, 178.
[34] Rosen, *op. cit.*, vol. 1, 165
    Hayashi, *Secret Memoirs*, 140-162.

the "Three Eastern Provinces." And so, on January 30, 1902, the Anglo-Japanese Alliance was signed in London. The two high contracting parties recognized the independence of China and Korea and added that they had no aggressive tendencies in either country. Both powers were stated to have special interests in China, while Japan was held to have political, commercial, and industrial interests in Korea. If either power in defense of the interests thus defined should become involved in war with another power, the other signatory to the alliance would observe a strict neutrality, but if other powers joined the conflict against one of the allies, the second power would come to its support, conduct the war in common, and make peace in mutual agreement with it. The alliance was to be effective for five years.[35]

In reality this alliance, so far as the Manchurian question was concerned, meant that if war broke out between Japan and Russia, Great Britain, as Japan's ally, would be able to restrain Russia's associates, France and possibly Germany, from entering the struggle and overwhelming the Mikado's Empire. Russia and France replied to the statement of the Alliance on March 19th by affirming that they had many times declared their adherence to the principles contained in the Anglo-Japanese agreement, and then added that as they too were obliged to take into account aggressive action of third powers, or new trouble in China threatening its territorial integrity or its free development, all of which might become a menace to their own interests, they reserved the right to discuss the means of securing their safety.[36] In this manner the Franco-Russian

---

[35] Text of alliance in United States *Foreign Relations*, 1902, 514.
[36] *Parliamentary Papers*, (1904) CX, China No. 2 (50).

Alliance was extended to the Far East,[37] but it was noticeable that the Russo-Chinese negotiations now progressed with greater rapidity and smoothness and on April 8th resulted in the signing of what has come to be known as the Manchurian Convention of Evacuation.[38] By this most important agreement, Chinese authority in Manchuria was to be re-established. China agreed to observe strictly the stipulations of the Contract concluded with the Russo-Chinese Bank on September 8, 1896, and assumed the obligation to protect the railway and all Russian subjects. Russia agreed, provided that new disturbances did not arise and the action of other powers did not prevent it, to withdraw all its forces from Manchuria in the following manner: within six months from the signature of the agreement to clear the southern portion of the Province of Mukden up to the River Liao of Russian troops, and to hand the railways over to China; within the following six months to clear the remainder of the Province of Mukden and of Kirin of Imperial troops; and within the next six months to remove the remainder of the Imperial troops from the Province of Heilungkiang. Of particular interest, too, was the second clause of Article 3 which stated that "after the complete evacuation of Manchuria by Russian troops the Chinese Government shall have the right to increase or diminish the number of its troops in Manchuria, but of this must duly notify the Russian Government, as it is natural that the maintenance in the above-mentioned district of an overlarge number of troops must necessarily lead to a reinforcement of the Russian military force in the neighboring districts, and thus would bring about an increase of

---

[37] Treat, *op. cit.*, 180.
[38] Text of convention in *Manchuria, Treaties and Agreements*, 65-67.

expenditure on military requirements undesirable for both states." [39]

Four days later the announcement was made that M. Lessar at the time of signing the Manchurian Agreement had handed a note to the Chinese Plenipotentiaries which declared that the surrender of the civil government of Newchwang into the hands of the Chinese Administration would take place only upon the withdrawal from that port of foreign forces and the restoration to the Chinese of Tientsin which at the time was under international administration. [40]

The terms of the Agreement itself proved to be satisfactory in general to the British and Japanese Governments although Marquess Lansdowne expressed the view to the Russian Ambassador, M. de Staal, that although "it was generally recognized that the new agreement was in many respects an improvement on the earlier versions, which had obtained publicity . . . . there were several points which were a good deal criticized in this country, notably those provisions which limited the right of China to dispose of her military forces and to construct railway extensions within her own territory." In the meantime Count Lamsdorff had made it quite clear to Sir C. Scott, the British Ambassador at St. Petersburg, that Russia would insist on the qualification freeing her from all engagements and obligations under the Convention of Evacuation should there be a renewal of disturbances in China. [41]

Despite this fact, it appeared that the greatest danger point in the Manchurian crisis had been passed.

[39] The convention of evacuation was signed by M. Paul Lessar, Envoy Extraordinary and Minister Plenipotentiary of Russia to China, on the part of Russia and by Prince Ching and Wang Wen-shao, on the part of China.

[40] *Parliamentary Papers*, (1904) CX, China No. 2 (Incl. in No. 51).

[41] *Ibid.*, No. 2 (53).

Russia had at length consented to withdraw her troops under a definite time limit and for this reason Great Britain and Japan, who were most intimately concerned with the execution of the Agreement, were content not to examine too minutely some of the less satisfactory provisions. They shared a hope that the Agreement would be loyally interpreted and that by the expiration of eighteen months the last of Russia's battalions would have retired from the "Three Eastern Provinces."[42]

---

[42] *Parliamentary Papers,* (1904) CX, China No. 2, 52.

CHAPTER VI

MANCHURIAN FACTORS IN THE CAUSES OF THE RUSSO-JAPANESE WAR

Although the signing of the Manchurian Convention of April 8, 1902, seemed to indicate that the danger point in the Far Eastern crisis had been passed and that the powers most interested in China might look for a peaceful settlement, fear still lurked in diplomatic circles that the intentions of Russia were not to be reconciled with the high principles of Chinese sovereignty she had so often expressed during the preceding two years. And thus the agents of Great Britain, Japan, and the United States, in China, kept their Governments fully informed of events in Manchuria as the time approached for the final and complete evacuation of the provinces by the Russian troops. It will be recalled that the Convention of Evacuation itself, while being a material improvement over those former agreements which Russia had attempted to force upon China, was, nevertheless, favorable to Russian ascendency in Manchuria and contained restrictions on the freedom of Chinese action there, which were not pleasing to Great Britain, Japan, and the United States. These powers then, it may be assumed, could only be satisfied with a complete fulfillment of the Convention. Anything less than this would merely increase their dissatisfaction and lead to further complications.

The first hopes of the Powers that Russia would carry out in letter and spirit the terms of the Convention were strengthened by October 8, 1902, the close of the first period of six months; for the restoration to China of the Shan-hai-kwan-Newchwang-Hsinmintun

Railway had been carried out in September and all
Russian troops were withdrawn from the southern portion of Mukden Province, although this evacuation simply meant the movement of the troops to points in the
railway zone, where they remained to guard the line.[1]
April 8, 1903, was the term fixed in the convention for
the second stage of the evacuation, but this date passed
without further withdrawal of Russian forces. Furthermore, a reversal of Russian policy immediately became evident.   Mukden Province was reoccupied and
troops were moved into portions of Southern Manchuria, which prior to this time had not been occupied.[2]
This proceeding, from the point of view of the interested powers, was highly arbitrary and calculated to
cast grave doubts on the good faith of the Russian
Government, and when in the course of a few weeks
it was announced that St. Petersburg was making
evacuation conditional upon further concessions from
China, some of which directly affected the treaty rights
of the Powers at the port of Newchwang, which was
included in the area to be evacuated by Russia before
April 8th, representations were again made at St.
Petersburg by the governments chiefly interested. The
new demands, in seven articles, of a highly exclusive
nature, had been lodged at the Peking Foreign Office
by the Russian *Chargé d' Affaires* on April 5, 1903,[3]
and the news of this action, which soon leaked out, was
confirmed by Prince Ching.[4]   The further evacuation

---

[1] *Parliamentary Papers*, (1904) CX, China No. 2 (Incl. in N. 66). The
number of military guards of the Russian Railways in Manchuria had been
fixed at 30,000 by this time and this number included 300 men for the protection of the railway coal mines to the northeast of Liao-yang.   Incl. in
No. 63.)

[2] Kuropatkin, *Military and Political Memoirs*, (Kennan translation) in
McClure's, September, 1908, 486-487.

[3] Asakawa, *op. cit.*, 242.

[4] *Parliamentary Papers*, (1904) CX, China No. 2 (81).

of Manchuria was probably implied, if not declared, to be dependent upon the acceptance of these demands.[5] These new requirements are of sufficient importance to be summarized from the most authentic version available.[6]

1. No portion of the territory restored to China by Russia, especially at Newchwang and in the valley of the Liao, shall be leased or sold to any other power under any circumstances; if such sale or lease to another power be concluded, Russia will take decisive steps in order to safeguard her own interests, as she considers such sale or lease to be a menace to her.

2. The system of government actually existing throughout Mongolia shall not be altered, as such alteration will tend to produce a regrettable state of affairs, such as the uprising of the people and the disturbances along the Russian frontier.

3. China shall engage herself not to open, of her own accord, new ports or towns in Manchuria, without giving previous notice to the Russian government, nor shall she permit foreign consuls to reside in those towns or ports.

4. The authority of foreigners who may be engaged by China for the administration of any affairs whatever shall not be permitted to extend over any affairs in Northern Provinces (including Chili), where Russia has the predominant interests. In case China desires to engage foreigners for the administration of affairs in Northern Provinces, special offices shall be established for the control of Russians: for instance, no authority over the mining affairs of Mongolia and Manchuria shall be given to foreigners who may be engaged by China for the administration of mining affairs; such authority shall be left entirely in the hands of Russian experts.

5. As long as there exists a telegraph line at Newchwang and Port Arthur, the Newchwang-Peking line shall be maintained, as the telegraph line at Newchwang and Port Arthur and throughout Sheng-king Province is under Russian control, and its connection with her line on the Chinese telegraph poles at Newchwang, Port Arthur, and Peking is of the utmost importance.

---

[5] Asakawa, *op. cit.*, 242-243.
[6] *Parliamentary Papers, loc. cit.*, Incl. in No. 94.

6. After restoring Newchwang to the Chinese local authorities, the customs receipts there shall, as at present, be deposited with the Russo-Chinese Bank.

7. After the evacuation of Manchuria, the rights which have been acquired in Manchuria by Russian subjects and foreign companies during Russian occupation shall remain unaffected; moreover, as Russia is in duty bound to insure life of the people residing in all the regions traversed by the railway, it is necessary, in order to provide against the spread of epidemic diseases in the Northern Provinces . . . . to establish at Newchwang a quarantine office after the restoration of the place to China; the Russian civil administrators will consider the best means to attain that end. Russians only shall be employed at the posts of Commissioner of Customs and Customs Physician and they shall be placed under the control of the Inspector-General of the Imperial Maritime Customs . . .

These demands including, as they did, provision for the non-alienation of Manchuria and the *status quo* in Mongolia and practically closing the former territory against the economic enterprise of all nations save Russia had a far graver significance than the numerous secret engagements Russia had attempted to secure from China prior to April 8, 1902. On that day Russia had definitely stipulated the course of action she would follow, in the evacuation of the provinces. Now, without apparent pretext save her ill-concealed desire to annex the "Three Eastern Provinces," the execution of that convention was made conditional on the acceptance by China of these seven additional stipulations.[7] Prince Ching, now controlling the affairs of the Chinese Foreign Office, not only considered these Russian terms quite unacceptable but failed to discover any reason or right which Russia could advance for the additional demands. Accordingly during the latter days of April he refused to entertain the conditions.[8]

---

[7] Witte, *op.cit.*, 118.
[8] *Parliamentary Papers*, (1904) CX, China No. 2 (78, 81, 127).

A firm protest had already been entered at Peking by the Japanese government and was followed by that of the British government,[9] and before the British protest reached him Mr. Townley, the British *Chargé*, had assured Prince Ching that he would receive from Great Britain similar support to that which had been given him by the British government during the negotiations which attended the signing of the Convention of Evacuation.[10]

By April 26th the United States government had instructed Mr. Conger to urge on the Chinese Foreign Office to refuse certain of the conditions demanded by Russia, and also made direct inquiries in a friendly spirit at St. Petersburg pointing out at the same time to the Russian government that the conditions laid down by it in the seven additional articles were not in accord with the proposed stipulations contained in the new draft treaty between China and the United States.[11] This courteous but firm protest of the American government was followed immediately by Great Britain whose government instructed its ambassador at St. Petersburg to address the Foreign Minister in language similar to that used by the American representative.[12] And it may be inferred that the Japanese government took similar action.[13] Thus the relations of the three governments were drawn closer by their unity of opinion regarding Russia's policy. As a result of further instructions, Mr. MacCormick, the United States Ambassador, had an interview with

[9] Asakawa, *op. cit.*, 245. *Parliamentary Papers*, (1904) CX, China No. 2 (79, 80).

[10] *Parliamentary Papers*, (1904) China No. 2 (81, 82).

[11] *Ibid.*, Nos. 83 and 85.

[12] *Ibid*, No. 89.

[13] Asakawa, *op. cit.*, 246.

Count Lamsdorff on the evening of April 28th. Count Lamsdorff denied in a positive manner that such demands as were rumored had been made by the Russian government. He expressed surprise that his government should have been suspected of not wishing to observe the published conditions of evacuation and gave the ambassador the most positive assurance that no such demands had been made by the Imperial Government.[14]

After stressing this assurance to the full limit of his ability Count Lamsdorff stated that American capital and commerce were what Russia most desired for the development of Manchuria and he concluded by adding that any delay in carrying out the evacuation was due to the natural necessity of obtaining assurance that the Chinese government was fulfilling its obligations which could be better ascertained by the Russian Minister, who was about to return to Peking, than by a secretary, temporarily in charge of the legation. It will be observed that while this interview denied the fact that the reported demands had been made by Russia, it did not establish that no demands whatsoever had been made by her.

This positive stand of the Russian government was strengthened, in part at least, by a statement made on April 29th by Count Cassini, the Russian Ambassador at Washington, which appeared in the New York *Tribune* of May 1st. Count Cassini stated that he had been instructed to assure the Secretary of State not only that American interests in Manchuria would be safeguarded, but also that the American Minister in Peking had been entirely misinformed concerning Russia's actions and purposes in the provinces. Here, however,

---

[14] *Parliamentary Papers*, (1904) CX, China No. 2 (91).

Count Cassini added a very significant remark when he declared that "of the opening of new treaty ports in Manchuria it is impossible for me to speak at present, but it is the earnest conviction of those best acquainted with the state of affairs there that such a move will not be to the best interests of the territory."[15]

Count Cassini's remarks were clearly designed with the purpose of courting a favorable attitude on the part of the United States government. He stated that both the Russian and American governments desired peace in Manchuria and he found grounds, although he did not state them, for concluding that the American government might exert a powerful influence for the preservation of that peace. The Russian Ambassador went further. He said that it was because of the long standing and genuine friendliness which without exception had characterized the relations of these two great countries, as well as in recognition of the frankness with which the American Secretary of State had dealt with the Russian government in all diplomatic matters, that the latter took pleasure in assuring the United States regarding negotiations pending with another power "even though in so doing all diplomatic precedent was broken." Cassini's reference to the question of opening new ports in Manchuria was virtually a contradiction of what Count Lamsdorff had said, and subsequently was contradicted by the latter.

In the meantime the negotiations at Peking on which Lamsdorff had been silent but to which Cassini had referred were continued by M. Plancon and Prince Ching. The former wished specific assurances on the first three of the original demands. These were whether China contemplated a territorial cession to

---

[15] *Parliamentary Papers*, (1904) CX, China No. 2 (91 incl. in 112).

another power in the Liao Valley; whether there was an intention to assimilate the administration of Mongolia to that of China proper; and whether China would permit the appointment of foreign consuls in Manchuria in other places than Newchwang. Prince Ching replied there had never been any question of ceding territory in the Liao Valley; that the administrative system of Mongolia had been discussed but a change had been disapproved by the throne and was not now under discussion and that the appointment of new consuls depended upon the opening of new ports which would be decided upon a basis of the commercial development of the provinces.[16] Shortly after this the United States government instructed its commissioners at Shanghai to insist upon the opening of new Manchurian ports,[17] and against this plea of the American government the Russian Minister continued during May to exert opposition.[18] There followed the attempt of the American government to secure the co-operation of the Russian Minister at Peking in asking China for further treaty ports in Manchuria,[19] and the reports of Russia's further attempts to secure China's consent to the seven articles continued; but finally, on June 19th, Mr. Townley, the British *Chargé d' Affaires,* was informed by Prince Ching that an agreement would soon be arrived at with Russia whereby Manchuria would be preserved to China without loss of sovereign rights and that China would open treaty ports in Manchuria after the evacuation if she saw fit.[20] The significant facts remained, however, that the Russian

---

[16] *Parliamentary Papers,* (1904) CX, China No. 2 (95).

[17] *Ibid.,* No. 98.

[18] *Ibid.,* Nos. 110, 114, 117.

[19] *Ibid.,* Nos. 119, 120.

[20] *Ibid.,* No. 126. Asakawa, *op. cit.,* 254-255.

evacuation was entirely uncertain despite the assurances of Counts Lamsdorff and Cassini, and as to the opening of certain cities such as Mukden, Harbin, Antung, and Tatungkao, the commercial motive was not the sole question involved. The whole situation indicated that Russian influence was gaining in the counsels of Peking. Nevertheless, during October, 1903, on the day on which the withdrawal of Russian troops, provided for by the Convention of Evacuation, should have been completed, two treaties of commerce and navigation, the one between China and Japan, the other between China and the United States, were signed at Peking, providing for the opening of three Manchurian towns, Mukden, Antung and Tatungkao, as treaty ports and for foreign settlement.[21]   These treaties were signed in the face of severe opposition from Russia, but with their ratification in January, 1904, the Government at St. Petersburg deemed it expedient to accept the situation and reiterated its usual assurance to the powers in a circular dispatched to its representatives abroad.[22]

Although the Chino-Japanese War of 1894-1895 had been fought to settle the Korean question, that ill fated country did not cease to be a storm center of Far Eastern diplomacy. Japan had learned from her own past history that the Hermit Kingdom was a convenient bridge for invaders from the continent and she rightly viewed with suspicion, not to say apprehension, the attempt of any power, whose relationships with Japan were not of the most cordial kind, to gain a foothold there. It will be remembered that Japan had undertaken to bring about reforms in Korea by herself,

[21] MacMurray, *Treaties*, vol. 1, 411-433.

[22] *The London Times*, Weekly Edition, February 5, 1904, 85.

having failed to secure the aid of China in the undertaking. The result was the growth of a strong pro-
Japanese party in the government, opposed by a group
headed by the Korean Queen. In the course of court
intrigues brought about by this situation the Queen
was murdered and it appeared that the Japanese Minister Viscount Goro Miura was involved in the crime.
Mr. (later Baron) Komura, who succeeded to the ministry at Seoul, reversed the policy of his predecessors
and abstained from active interference, and all this
while the influence of the Russian party steadily increased. In January, 1896, during a rising in northern
Korea, Russian marines entered Seoul and the Korean
King fled in disguise to the Russian legation where he
remained until February 20th, of the following year.
The growth of Russian prestige was now seen everywhere. Russian interests secured a great timber concession on the northern frontier (of which more will
be said later in this chapter) and mining rights along
the Tumen River.[23]

While these rapid developments were taking place
Japan seemed to have forsaken her traditional policy
of safeguarding Korea's independence and sent Field-
Marshal Yamagata to St. Petersburg for the coronation
of Nicholas II and to negotiate respecting the position
of the two powers in Korea. The result was the Yamagata-Lobanof Protocol, signed on June 9, 1896, in which
the two powers engaged to cooperate in supporting the
Korean administration and if further questions arose
to discuss them in an amiable spirit.[24] Regardless of
what her intentions were, Russia did not observe the

---

[23] Asakawa, op. cit., 257-263.

[24] Ibid., 264.

Rosen, op. cit., vol. 1, 125, tells how at the coronation ceremonies the
Tsar received in private audience a special ambassador of the King of Korea

terms of the protocol. Russian influence was extended to all branches of the Korean army and attempts were made to control taxation and the customs. Then followed another agreement between Japan and Russia, the Nishi-Rosen Protocol of April 25, 1898. This step was distinctly in Japan's favor. It gave an explicit recognition of the independence of Korea, it incorporated the best principles of the previous agreement and recognized special economic interests of Japan in the peninsula.[25] During 1900 and 1901 Russia made a number of unsuccessful attempts to lease ground in south Korea, in particular the port of Mazampo, as a naval harbor, in which attempts she was frustrated by the persistent support given the Korean Government by Mr. Hayashi, the Japanese Minister. Attempts were also made by Russia in 1901 and 1902 to place a Russian in control of the Korean customs and to put the country under financial obligation to St. Petersburg by means of a large loan. Both efforts failed, but they are of interest as indicative of the constant pressure now being exerted on the Korean Government.[26] While the course of Russian diplomacy, thus briefly outlined, had met practically complete failure at the capital and in southern Korea, its efforts in the north were attended with greater success, in the matter of whaling concessions and the construction of telegraph lines.[27] It has been necessary to mention these facts

---

who submitted a request of his sovereign to be taken under the protectorate of Russia. The request was immediately granted by Nicholas through his astonishing ignorance of Far Eastern affairs, and called forth just indignation from Lobanof when informed by the Tsar of what he had done. Every possible precaution was taken by Russia to guard the secret, but Rosen believes that Japan did not remain long in ignorance of a matter which so vitally affected

[25] Asakawa, *op. cit.*, 271.

[26] *Ibid.*, 278-279.

[27] *Ibid.*, 282-285.

her interests in Korea.

with respect to Korea, for they formed an integral part of Russia's aggressive policy and cannot be held as distinct and independent of the events which were taking place in Manchuria.

Inseparably bound on the one hand with Russian intrigues at Seoul, and on the other with her secret diplomacy as manifested concerning the occupation of Manchuria, were the activities of an organization which came to be known as the Yalu Timber Company. In the year 1898 a Vladivostok merchant named Briner received from the Government of Korea, on extremely favorable terms, a concession for a timber company which should have authority to exploit the great forest wealth of the upper Yalu River, which forms a section of the boundary between Manchuria and Korea.[28] Briner was unable to organize a company and in 1902 sold his concession to Alexander Mikhailovich Bezobrazoff, a mysterious Russian promoter and speculator, who had held the rank of State Councillor in the Tsar's civil service and who was in high favor with many of the court nobility. Bezobrazoff was not long in arousing the interest of his Grand Ducal friends in the untold wealth of the Far East in general and his timber concession on the Yalu in particular. Many of them took stock in the company. Soon after this Bezo-

---

[28] The details here presented concerning the Yalu Timber Company are taken primarily from the article of Mr. George Kennan which appeared as an editorial note attached to Mr. Kennan's translation of certain sections of General Kuropatkin's Memoirs which appeared in *McClure's Magazine*, September, 1908, 497-499. The story of the timber company as told by Mr. Kennan was reprinted with the permission of the editor of *McClure's* in the Lindsay translation of the Memoirs which appeared as a two-volume work entitled "The Russian Army and the Japanese War."

It should be noted that Asakawa says the original contract for the timber company's concession dated as far back as August 26, 1896, when the Korean king was living at the Russian Legation in Seoul. (*Russo-Japanese Conflict*, 289.)

brazoff created a remarkably favorable impression on the mind of Tsar Nicholas II, and acquired an influence over him which was to have far-reaching and disastrous results, and Mr. George Kennan declares that it is now certain that the Tsar himself was financially interested in the timber company. Bezobrazoff's organization in fact seems to have consisted of the Tsar, the Grand Dukes, certain favored noblemen of the court, and Admiral Alexieff, the negotiator of the alleged Alexieff-Tseng agreement, of which mention has already been made.

It will be recalled that between October 8, 1902, and April 8, 1903, there occurred a most regrettable reversal of Russian policy. The first period of evacuation which was to clear the southern portion of Mukden Province of Russian troops had been completed, the second period of withdrawal had commenced, when suddenly and without warning Russian troops swarmed back into the evacuated regions and even occupied territories not previously penetrated. This change had caused grave apprehensions on the part of the powers, but the Japanese Minister at St. Petersburg, Mr. Kurino, had been able to ascertain during April, 1903, that neither Count Lamsdorff the Foreign Minister, General Kuropatkin, the Minister of War, nor M. de Witte, had any knowledge of the movement of troops which was alleged to be in the direction of the Yalu River and the Korean border.[29]

Prior to the signing of the Convention of Evacuation in April, 1902, there had been a differenece of opinion between Admiral Alexieff, commander of the Russian forces in the Far East, and the Minister of War, General Kuropatkin. The latter had by this time

---

[29] *Parliamentary Papers*, (1904) CX, China No. 2 (No. 57).

swung over from his aggressive attitude and together with Witte and Lamsdorff believed that Russia's only safe course was to evacuate the Chinese Provinces in accordance with the terms of the Convention.[30]   The signing of the Convention of Evacuation therefore was a settlement for which Kuropatkin stated he was eager, and his department made energetic preparations for carrying it into effect. Then without warning, and after Mukden itself had been evacuated, the retirement of the forces was stopped by order of Admiral Alexieff in his capacity of commander-in-chief of Kwantung. The reasons for this action have never been perfectly clear. It is significant, however, that the change in policy which stopped the withdrawal of troops from South Manchuria corresponded in time with the first visit to the Far East of Bezobrazoff.[31]

It was in November, 1902, that Bezobrazoff, having by this time enlisted the sympathies of the Tsar, was sent to the Far East to study possibilities of exploiting its wealth of natural resources. Witte was instructed by the Tsar to place 2,000,000 rubles at Bezobrazoff's disposal in the Russo-Chinese Bank, and to keep the transaction secret. In the Far East, where he remained two months, he declared himself to be the personal representative of the Emperor, but his presence introduced confusion into the administration and he advocated a policy of industrial aggression backed by military force. Thus two distinct factors arose in the Russian policy; one phase of it was official, moderate in character and represented by the Ministers of State; the other was secret, was inspired by Bezobrazoff, and

[30] Kuropatkin, "The Military and Political Memoirs," *McClure's Magazine*, Sept., 1908, 486.
[31] *Ibid.*, 486-487.

supported, it would appear, by Emperor Nicholas. That the influence of the favorite grew to a prodigious degree there can be no doubt, for in May Bezobrazoff was promoted in rank. At the same time the Yalu timber enterprise assumed broader proportions and in order to lend support to it and Russia's other undertakings in northern Korea Admiral Alexieff sent a force of cavalry with field guns to Feng-wang-cheng, a town on the road from Mukden to the mouth of the Yalu.[32]

By June and July of 1903 the situation in the Far East was thoroughly complicated. The construction and equipment of the Chinese Eastern Railway with its southern branch to Port Arthur and Dalny was well advanced; vast sums of money were being expended by the Minister of Finance; an army corps of railway guards protected the line and was directly under the control of the Ministry of Finance; Vladivostok was fast losing its importance as the terminus of the main line of the Siberian Railway while energetic efforts were being made to construct Dalny as a suitable seaport, and through all these activities the Russo-Chinese Bank, the financial agent of Russian expansion, was extending and broadening the scope of its interests. At the same time, and amid this seeming successful exploitation, it is difficult to conceive of the utter confusion, the secrecy, and deception and the all-pervading atmosphere of suspicion which characterized the Manchurian question during the summer months of 1903. Bezobrazoff journeyed again to the Far East at this time where Kuropatkin was already reviewing the entire military situation and a number of conferences

---

[32] Kuropatkin, "The Military and Political Memoirs," *McClure's Magazine,* Sept., 1908, 487.

took place at Port Arthur. The decisions arrived at did not differ materially from those which had been reached in the spring at St. Petersburg. The idea of annexing Manchurian territory was abandoned, but guarantees were to be demanded of the Peking Government to safeguard Russia's interests in the provinces.[33]

Both Kuropatkin and Witte submitted reports to the Tsar on the subject of Far Eastern affairs immediately upon their return from the Port Arthur Council. Kuropatkin advised that the Yalu concession be sold to foreigners that Russia might avoid the danger of further friction with Japan, while Witte, feeling that Russian action would soon bring the powers generally into conflict in China, again urged that "absorption take place naturally, without precipitating events, without taking premature steps, without seizing territory.[34] Nor is it too much to say that the matter of a settlement was now a necessity, for in July Japan again approached

---

[33] Witte, *op. cit.*, 120-121.

In his *Memoirs* Kuropatkin tells that there were present at the Port Arthur Council, in addition to himself and Admiral Alexieff, State Councillor Lessar, Russian Minister in China; Chamberlain Pavloff, Russian Minister at Seoul; Major General Vogak; State Councillor Bezobrazoff; and M. Plancon, an officer of the diplomatic service.

On the Manchurian question the council came to the conclusion that in view of the extraordinary difficulties and enormous administrative expenses that the annexation of Manchuria would involve it was in principle undesirable, and this decision applied not only to southern but to northern Manchuria. As to the Korean question it was decided that the occupation of all or part of Korea was undesirable. The council also inquired into the affairs of the Yalu Timber Company and came to the decision that although the enterprise appeared to be a commercial organization its employment of officers of the active military service to do work that had military importance undoubtedly gave to the company a politico-military aspect. The council therefore acknowledged the necessity of taking measures at once to give the enterprise an exclusively commercial character, to exclude from it officers of the regular army and to commit the management of the timber business to persons not employed in the service of the Empire. On July 7th, these conclusions were signed by all the members of the council including Bezobrazoff. (Kuropatkin, "The Military and Political Memoirs," *McClure's Magazine*, Sept., 1908, 491.)

[34] Witte, *op. cit.*, 121-122.

St. Petersburg seeking for a mutual understanding on the Manchurian and Korean problems. Despite this no decision was reached by Russia. Just at the moment, in fact, when a Russian acceptance of the Japanese proposals would have cleared the entire situation there occurred another of those startling events, contrived by Russian diplomacy, which stirred anew all the jealousies and fears which Japan had experienced since the Russians seized Port Arthur in 1898. On August 13th the territories of the Amur and Kwantung were created a viceroyalty with Admiral Alexieff, Governor of the Kwantung Peninsula, as viceroy.[35] The change was brought about without any intimation of it having been given to the Ministers of War, Finance, or Foreign Affairs, who had previously been in charge of Far Eastern affairs, and shortly after this Witte, having realized he could no longer remain a member of the government, was dismissed from the Ministry.[36]

The creation of this Far Eastern viceroyalty meant inreality that Bezobrazoff and Alexieff took into their own hands the direction of the Manchurian policy. At the Port Arthur Council Alexieff had repeately assured Kuropatkin of his opposition to the schemes of Bezobrazoff and his clique, but the Admiral was evidently playing a double game. While pretending to be sympathetic to Kuropatkin in opposing the Yalu affair he was secretly supporting the enterprise. The events which advanced his efforts so well can only be explained by the fact that now the Tsar was completely under the influence of a group composed of Bezobrazoff, Alexieff, Admiral Abaza, a personal adviser, and the powerful

---

[35] *Parliamentary Papers,* (1904) **CX,** China No. 2 (No. 144).
[36] Witte, *op. cit.,* 123.

Minister of the Interior von Plehve, who, it seems, at this time had formed an alliance with Bezobrazoff and together with him brought about the dismissal of Witte who ceased to be Minister of Finance on August 29, 1903.[37]

Kuropatkin refers many times to the Tsar's desire that war should be avoided and it is probable that Nicholas did wish to avoid open hostilities if he could do so without impairing all the vague conceptions which he entertained concerning expansion in the Far East and the profitable returns which were to be expected from the Yalu Timber Company. But on the other hand it is equally true that late in November, 1903, the Tsar was disregarding the advice of Kuropatkin, was expressing full confidence in Bezobrazoff, and was ordering further reinforcements to the Far East.[38] This is doubly significant, for in October the Minister of War had submitted another special report to the Tsar on the Manchurian question in which it was pointed out that Russian military occupation of South Manchuria would lead to Japanese occupation of southern Korea.[39] In December Kuropatkin pro-

---

[37] Kuropatkin, "The Military and Political Memoirs," *McClure's Magazine*, Sept., 1908, 499.

Mr. Kennan, the translator of the *Memoirs*, in an appendix on the activities of the Yalu Timber Company, produces a number of documents found in the archives of Port Arthur and published after the close of the war. The document that shows most clearly the interest of the Tsar in the Yalu Timber enterprise is a telegram sent to Bezobrazoff at Port Arthur in November, 1903, by Rear Admiral Abaza, who was then director of the special committee on Far Eastern affairs and who acted as the Tsar's personal representative in all dealings with Bezobrazoff and the timber company. This telegram stated that "Witte has told the Emperor that you have already spent the whole of the two millions. Your telegram with regard to expenditures has made it possible for me to report on this disgusting slander and at the same time contradit it . . . . Immediately upon receipt of the Admiral's statement arrangements will be made with regard to the reinforcements of the garrison . . . . The Emperor expressed the fullest confidence in you."

[38] *Ibid.*, 499.

[39] *Ibid.*, 494.

posed to the Tsar that Russia return Port Arthur and Kwantung to China, and secure in return certain special rights in north Manchuria, but this suggestion was not approved and meanwhile negotiations which were being carried on between Tokyo and St. Petersburg became more and more involved. The correspondence regarding these negotiations, which was presented to the Imperial Diet in March, 1904, and later published in an English version by the Japanese Government merits close attention.

How serious the whole situation in the Far East had become by the close of July, 1903, and how apprehensive was the Japanese Government[40] finds expression in the note which Baron Komura addressed to Mr. Kurino at St. Petersburg on July 28th. The note called attention to the fact that "the Japanese Government have observed with close attention the development of affairs in Manchuria, and they view with grave concern the present situation there. So long as there were grounds for hope that Russia would carry out her engagement to China and her assurances to other powers on the subject of the evacuation of Manchuria, the Japanese Government maintained an attitude of watchful reserve. But the recent action of Russia in formulating new demands in Peking and in consolidating rather than in relaxing her hold on Manchuria compels belief that she has abandoned the intention of retiring from Manchuria, while her increased activity along the Korean frontier is such as to raise doubts regarding the limits of her ambition. The unre-

---

[40] On June 23rd the four principal members of the Japanese Cabinet, Viscount Katsura, Baron Komura, General Terauchi, and Admiral Yamamoto, and five privy Councillors met before the Throne and decided upon the principles upon which the negotiations with Russia should be opened. (*Asakawa, op. cit.*, 296.)

strained permanent occupation of Manchuria by Russia would create a condition of things prejudicial to the security and interest of Japan. Such occupation would be destructive of the principle of equal opportunity and in impairment of the territorial integrity of China. . . ." The note further sets forth the danger to Japan of a Korea dominated by Russia. For these reasons the Japanese Government had resolved to approach the Russian Government with a view to the conclusion of an undertaking designed to settle these questions of controversy. Mr. Kurino was therefore instructed to present to Count Lamsdorff a *note verbale* suggesting that the powers come together for this purpose.[41] The persistency of Russia in maintaining her grip on the Manchurian provinces had not of itself been sufficient to provoke the Japanese Government to action. Rosen tells how the early summer of 1903 witnessed, on the surface, at least, a perfect calm in the Japanese national life. This was completely changed, however, and an undercurrent of alarm became evident as a result of the two events in Russia, which have already been mentioned: the fall from power of Witte, as Minister of Finance, and the creation of the Viceroyalty of the Far East with Admiral Alexieff as Viceroy.[42]

The fall of Witte meant to Japan the triumph of an aggressive policy in the Far East. Beyond this it was evident that the creation of the new viceroyalty and of the special "Committee of Far Eastern Affairs" with extensive powers that conflicted not only with each

---

[41] *Correspondence regarding the Negotiations between Japan and Russia, 1903-1904*, No. 1, Baron Komura to Mr. Kurino, Tokyo, July 28, 1903. Japan at this time was beginning to realize the value of publicity. The correspondence cited here was published in English translation in Washington at the outbreak of the Russo-Japanese War and exerted much influence in swinging American opinion to the side of Japan.

[42] Rosen, *op. cit.*, vol. 1, 219.

other but with those of the Foreign Office, could only complicate an already delicate situation. In this situation Japan opened her negotiations with Russia. Her policy was clearly defined. She felt assured of the support of her ally, Great Britain, and also of the United States, both of which powers had been aroused by Russia's threat against the territorial integrity of China and the principles of the "Open Door."

Against the clearly defined policy of Japan, which will be discussed presently, was that of Russia, undefined, ill suited to her national needs, a vague collection of absurd aspirations to domination and hegemony, in which the Ministry of Foreign Affairs, the Viceroy of the Far East and the Committee of Far Eastern Affairs all contended for the supreme power.[43]   Japan therefore found herself confronted by a situation which left no alternative save the opening of direct negotiations seeking a friendly solution, and it should be noted that in Baron Komura's first instructions to Mr. Kurino it was the continued occupation of Manchuria and the new demands upon China which were uppermost in the Japanese mind.   It was these things which were to lead to war.

Count Lamsdorff's reply was of the most friendly character.   He expressed full accord with the views of

---

[43] *Correspondence*, 222-223.   The Committee of Far Eastern Affairs, under the nominal presidency of the Emperor was designed to be the ruling power in Russia's Far Eastern Policy.   The conduct of this policy by 1903 was divided among three separate authorities, more or less independent of each other and never in full agreement on any subject.   The first was the Ministry of Foreign Affairs, which was at the same time the weakest because it was distrusted by the Tsar.   In the second place there was the Viceroy, who Rosen believes was the most enlightened although hampered by considerations of loyalty to the Throne.   Finally there was the Committee of Far Eastern Affairs, holding the greatest power because of its intimate connection with the supreme authority. The Ministers of Foreign Affairs, Finance, War, and Marine were ex-officio members of this committee but its activities were directed primarily by Rear Admiral Abaza, who enjoyed the Emperor's special confidence.

the Japanese Government but delayed an official answer until he should see the Tsar.[44]   On August 3rd Japan proposed six articles as the basis of an understanding with Russia.   These included a mutual engagement to respect the independence and territorial integrity of China and Korea and to maintain the principle of equal opportunity for the commerce of all nations there;[45] reciprocal recognition of Japan's predominating interests in Korea and of Russia's special interests in railway enterprises in Manchuria; neither power was to impede such commercial development of these interests as was in keeping with Article 1; if either power found it necessary to dispatch troops to protect its interests, they were not to exceed the actual number required and were to be withdrawn as soon as their mission was accomplished; Russia was to recognize Japan's exclusive right to give advice and assistance in the interests of reform and good government in Korea; and this engagement was to supplant all others existing between Japan and Russia respecting Korea.[46]   These proposals which Mr. Kurino was not able to present to Count Lamsdorff until August 12th, in no way, save perhaps in the matter of Korean railway extension, affected Russia's legitimate interests in Manchuria.[47]   But Russia's real objection was to the

---

[44] *Correspondence,* No. 2, Mr. Kurino to Baron Komura, St. Petersburg, July 31, 1903.

[45] Japan had agreed to this in the Anglo-Japanese alliance.   Russia's agreement to the principle had only been informal up to this time.

[46] *Correspondence,* No. 3, Baron Komura to Mr. Kurino, Tokyo, August 3, 1903.   Article 3 included a provision that the extension of the Korean railway from Korea into Manchuria was not to be impeded.   The provision respecting the number of troops which either power might send to affected areas was in the nature of a delicate reminder to Russia that her concentration of forces in Manchuria was unnecessary.

[47] It was at this point that the course of the negotiations began to take a less favorable turn.   Japan's first approach and Lamsdorff's reply had opened the way for an amicable interchange of views.   But that auspicious beginning

principle of the territorial integrity of China which she had half-heartedly agreed to in response to the Hay note.[48] That agreement, however, was one which Russia would hardly accept too seriously and she had no intention of signing an agreement that might bring her into conflict with a power on the subject of China's integrity. Lamsdorff now proposed that the negotiations be transferred to Tokyo, a suggestion that was generally interpreted as an expedient to cause delay. Doubtless St. Petersburg felt that the Japanese Government would not be in a position to press its proposals so effectively at Tokyo as would be the case if carried on through Mr. Kurino and the Foreign Office in St. Petersburg. Furthermore, every week of delay added to the strength of those sections of the Siberian railway then being constructed around Lake Baikal.[49] Accordingly after prolonged correspondence extending to September 9th, the Japanese Government found no alternative but to consent that the negotiations be transferred to Tokyo.[50]

On October 3rd the counterproposals of Russia were presented in Tokyo by Baron Rosen. These called for a mutual engagement to respect the independence and

---

stood in marked contrast to their disastrous end. This was due, of course, to the political situation at St. Petersburg which was probably quite beyond the control of Count Lamsdorff. (Asakawa, *op. cit.*, 300.)

[48] At this time when Russia was negotiating with both Japan and China, she also intimated through her Ambassador in London that she desired an accord with Great Britain respecting their interests in China. Russia, it appears, wished Britain to declare Manchuria as outside her sphere, in return for a similar declaration by Russia regarding the Yangtze Valley. Lord Lansdowne's reply stated the readiness of his Government to conclude an agreement, but insisted it must include the Manchurian question. (China, No. 2 [1904], No. 142, August 12).

[49] On September 9th Sir E. Satow had informed Lord Lansdowne that Prince Ching had informed him of fresh proposals made by the Russian Government. These demands came in the midst of the Russo-Japanese negotiations at Tokyo and on the eve of the period of Manchurian evacuation. (China No. 2, 1904, Nos. 147, 148, 149, 156.)

[50] *Correspondence*, Nos. 7 to 14.

territorial integrity of Korea; Russia agreed to recognize Japan's predominating interests in Korea; there
was to be a mutual engagement that neither power
would use Korea for strategical purposes, and the
northern part of Korea was to be a neutral zone into
which neither of the contracting parties would send
troops; Japan was to recognize Manchuria as entirely
outside her sphere of interest.[51] The positions thus
taken by the two powers indicated clearly their approach to the Far Eastern problem. Japan had set
forth proposals which in main should have been satisfactory to any power having and desiring to maintain
legitimate rights in China. Russia's counterproposals
on the other hand made equally emphatic that St.
Petersburg's aspirations could not be reconciled with
the policies of Great Britain and the United States,
much less with that of Japan.

Japan replied to Russia's counterproposals, making
certain concessions, but insisted that Russia engage
to respect China's sovereignty, the territorial integrity
of Manchuria and not to interfere with Japan's commercial freedom there, while the latter would recog-

---

[51] *Correspondence*, No. 17. It should be observed in connection with these
counter-proposals that Russia avoids in Article 1 any mention of observing
the territorial integrity of China. In Articles 2, 3, and 4, she carefully avoided
mention of Manchuria. By Article 6, the neutral zone thus proposed included
about half of the kingdom of Korea and in Article 7 Russia disposed of the
entire Manchuria question by suggesting that Japan cease to consider those
provinces as a sphere in which she had any interest whatsoever. A comparison
of this counter note with the original note of Japan reveals at once that
Russia seriously reduced Japan's demands concerning Korea, by excluding her
right of rendering advice and assistance to Korea in the latter's military
affairs and also by quietly suppressing the important clause providing for
mutual recognition of the principle of equal economic opportunity for all
nations in Korea. The date fixed in the convention of April, 1902, for the
final evacuation of Manchuria arrived on October 8th, five days after the
Russian counter note was received by Japan, but the day came and passed
with no sign of evacuation. On the contrary, the Russian Minister at Peking
was engaged, regardless of the negotiations at Tokyo, in urging Prince Ching
to change the terms of the convention. (Asakawa, *op. cit.*, 311-312.)

nize Russia's special interests.[52]   This suggestion was followed on October 30th by the presentation of Japan's definite amendments.   In these Japan reiterated what she conceived as her rights in Korea and suggested the establishment of a neutral zone on the Korean-Manchurian frontier extending for fifty kilometers on either side of the line.   Japan agreed to recognize Manchuria as outside her sphere of interest and asked Russia to make a similar avowal concerning Korea. Japan further agreed not to interfere with the commercial and residential rights of Russia in virtue of her treaty engagements with Korea and requested Russia to give a like guarantee with respect to Japan's treaty rights in China.[53]

On November 12th, in the course of an interview between Count Lamsdorff and Mr. Kurino, the former stated for the first time that the Manchurian question was the actual issue between the two powers, and added that from the very beginning the Russian Government had considered this question as one pertaining exclusively to Russia and China, to which Mr. Kurino replied that his country was ready to recognize the special interests which Russia had in Manchuria, and had no intention of trespassing upon them but affirmed that Japan had a perfect right to demand that the independence and territorial integrity of China should be respected and the interests of Japan formally guaranteed.[54]   Another interview followed on November 22nd in which Count Lamsdorff made the signifi-

---

[52] *Correspondence*, No. 19, Baron Komura to Mr. Kurino, Tokyo, October 16, 1903.

[53] *Correspondence*, No. 22, Baron Komura to Mr. Kurino, Tokyo, October 30, 1903.   In Article 5 Japan engaged not to undertake on the coasts of Korea any miitary works capabe of menacing the freedom of navigation in the Straits of Korea.   Article 10 called for a mutual engagement not to impede the connection of the Korean Railway and the East-China Railway when these had been extended to the Yalu River.

cant statement that his government was ready to enter into immediate agreement with Japan regarding Korea, but as for Manchuria, Russia had taken it by right of conquest, was ready to restore it to China but only with certain guarantees which would protect her enormous interests there. While China refused to give these guarantees it was impossible for Russia to come to an agreement with a third power.[55]

Baron Rosen presented Russia's counterproposals to Japan's definite amendments at Tokyo on December 11th. These consisted of eight articles in which Russia agreed not to impede the connection of the Korean and East China Railways but failed to discuss at all Japan's contentions respecting Manchuria.[56] Japan replied calling attention to this grave omission. Finally on January 7th, Russia attempted to appear ready for a

[54] *Correspondence*, No. 25, Mr. Kurino to Baron Komura, St. Petersburg, November 13, 1903.

[55] *Ibid.*, No. 27, Mr. Kurino to Baron Komura, St. Petersburg, November 22, 1903. Mr. Kurino concluded this dispatch with the statement: "I judge from the tone of Count Lamsdorff's conversation that the modifications proposed by Admiral Alexieff will not be favorable to our proposition regarding China and Manchuria."

[56] *Ibid.*, No. 34, Baron Komura to Mr. Kurino, Tokyo, December 12, 1903.

It has not infrequently been said that Germany pushed Russia into the mad scramble of the Russo-Japanese War to free her own frontier from the pressure of Russian troops and to weaken the combination between France and Russia. This statement requires careful qualification, for there was difference of opinion between the German Foreign Office and the Kaiser. Holstein drew up a memorandum in July, 1902, to the effect that encouragement must not be given to Russia to expect German protection in Russia's frontier in Europe if Japan and Russia became involved over affairs in Manchuria. It was the opinion of the German Foreign Office that such support, if given, might lead to a general conflict, fought largely upon the sea, and promising much loss and little gain to Germany. This was the policy then of the Wilhelmstrasse. (Die Grosse Politik XIX. i, 5-7.)

The Kaiser on the other hand was worried by his favorite spectre of the "Yellow Peril," and therefore believed that it was Russia's duty to check Japan. "This is the greatest danger that threatens the white race, Christianity, and European civiization," he told Bülow. "If the Russians yield further to the Japanese, in twenty years the Yellow Race wil be in Moscow and Posen . . . . We must call the Tsar's attention to the greatness of the Yellow Peril which he does not understand." (Die Grosse Politik, XIX, i, 63.)

Bülow was in agreement with Holstein and wished to avoid action which would antagonize England. On the eve of the war, Bülow discovered January

settlement by making a slight concession. In this she agreed not to impede Japan, or other powers, in the enjoyment of rights and privileges acquired by them in Manchuria under existing treaties with China, "exclusive of the establishment of settlements."[57]   Six days later Mr. Kurino was instructed, among other things, to inform Russia that Japan considered the following modifications concerning Manchuria as necessary: recognition by Japan of Manchuria and its littoral as being outside her sphere of interest and an engagement on the part of Russia to respect the territorial integrity of China in Manchuria.[58]. The negotiations now dragged on while Japan attempted in vain to get a definite reply to her proposals.[59]   This regrettable state of affairs was aggravated too by reports that Japan was sending troops to Korea and that Russia was moving forces to the Yalu, both of which reports were denied.[60]

On the evening of January 31st Count Lamsdorff informed Mr. Kurino that it was impossible for him to

---

4, 1904, that the Kaiser had written the Tsar a letter lacking the caution of the draft prepared by the Foreign Office. It contained, among other things for the Tsar's encouragement: "It is evident to every unbiased mind that Korea must and will be Russian." Bülow remonstrated and advised stopping delivery of the letter, but the Kaiser refused. (Die Grosse Politik, XIX, i, 89.)

[57] *Correspondence*, No. 38, Baron Komura to Mr. Kurino, Tokyo, January 7, 1904. A "settlement" is a district under extraterritorial jurisdiction of a treaty power.

[58] *Correspondence*, No. 39, Baron Komura to Mr. Kurino, Tokyo, January 13, 1904.

[59] A new factor had now entered the situation. The Chiro-American and Chino-Japanese commercial treaties which had been concluded on October 8, 1903, the date appointed for the final evacuation of Manchuria, were ratified on January 11, 1904, the former opening to the world's trade Mukden and Antung, and the latter Mukden and Tatung-kao, thus not only increasing treaty rights, including rights of foreign settlement of Japan and the United States in Manchuria, but reinstating the sovereign rights of China in the territory and directly reversing the exclusive claims of Russia therein. (Asakawa, *op. cit.*, 335.)

[60] *Correspondence*, No. 44, Baron Komura to Mr. Kurino, Tokyo, January 28, 1904; No. 45, Mr. Kurino to Baron Komura, St. Petersburg, January 28, 1904.

state the exact date on which Russia's reply would be given. He said that the seriousness of the situation was fully realized but that final decision rested with the Emperor.[61] This was the last attempt at evasion and delay on the part of Russia, for an February 5th at 2:15 in the afternoon Baron Komura dispatched two telegrams to Mr. Kurino in St. Petersburg. In the first of these Japan terminated the negotiations and stated that she would take such independent action as was necessary to defend her "menaced position" and to protect her rights and interests. Attention was called to "the successive rejections by the Imperial Russian Government by means of inadmissible amendments of Japan's proposals respecting Korea, the adoption of which the Imperial Government regarded as indispensable to assure the independence and territorial integrity of the Korean Empire and to safeguard Japan's preponderating interests in the Peninsula, coupled with the successive refusals of the Imperial Russian Government to enter into engagements to respect China's territorial integrity in Manchuria which is seriously menaced by their continued occupation of the province, notwithstanding their treaty engagements with China and their repeated assurances to other powers possessing interests in those regions . . ."[62] By the second telegram which was to be presented simultaneously, Japan severed diplomatic relations, since in the belief of the government every means of conciliation had been exhausted in vain.[63] On February 10th Japan declared war.[64]

---

[61] *Correspondence*, No. 47, Mr. Kurino to Baron Komura, St. Petersburg, February 1, 1904.

[62] *Ibid.*, No. 48, Baron Komura to Mr. Kurino, Tokyo, February 5, 1904.

[63] *Ibid.*, No. 49, Baron Komura to Mr. Kurino, Tokyo, February 5, 1904.

[64] *Manchuria, Treaties and Agreements*, 75-76, for text of Japan's declaration of war. (For a much fuller discussion of the subject treated here than this chapter will permit the reader is referred to Langer, Wm. L., *The Origin of the Russo-Japanese War* in *Europäische Gespräche*, Hamburg, 1926.)

CHAPTER VII

THE PORTSMOUTH TREATY AND THE TREATY OF PEKING

The Russo-Japanese War and the settlements arising out of the treaty which concluded it form one of the most interesting and at the same time significant episodes in the history of Far Eastern diplomacy, for it was on the basis of the treaty of Portsmouth between Russia and Japan which ended the war, and the later Treaty of Peking between Japan and China, that a solution of Manchurian problems was to be found in the years following. The campaigns of the war itself cannot concern us in a study of this kind. Suffice it to say that generally speaking from a military and naval point of view Japanese arms met with a success greater than might reasonably have been expected. In the battles of Liao-yang, Shao, and Mukden the Russian armies under General Kuropatkin were defeated and driven northward in Manchuria. Port Arthur had fallen in January, 1905, after a siege which cost the Japanese between thirty and forty thousand casualties and two months after the battle of Mukden, which ended on March 16th, the Russian Baltic Fleet, which had sailed from European waters for the Far East on October 15, 1904, was met in the Straits of Tsushima by a Japanese fleet under Admiral Togo and completely defeated, only two vessels escaping.[1]

By the summer of 1905 both combatants were exhausted. The Japanese campaigns had been characterized by aggressive tactics throughout, but each victory

---

[1] Gubbins, *op. cit.*, 258-263.

carried them further from their base, while the Russians, as they retired, found it easier to maintain their position. Though she had been successful on land and sea, the military reserves of Japan were seriously depleted and the nation generally was tired of the war and the burden it involved. In Russia the problem had not been one of finding reserves but rather of transporting them to the front. Each month that the war dragged on made this the easier, for the work of completing the final units of the Siberian Railway around Lake Baikal was now progressing. Thus while the maintenance of her armies in the field presented a problem of ever increasing difficulty to Japan, Russia could view a situation in which the worst elements seemed to be eliminated. Nevertheless, the internal conditions of the Tsar's Empire were beset by difficulties which threatened grave trouble were the war prolonged.[2]

The course of the war had been closely watched by both the European powers and the United States. Great Britain and France were, of course, intimately concerned with the progress of events, the former as the ally of Japan, and the latter as the ally of Russia. Early in 1905, when news of the frightful sacrifices made by Japan in the siege of Port Arthur, and of the casualties occasioned by both armies from strenuous winter campaigns, reached the outside world, President Roosevelt of the United States grew strongly to believe that a further continuation of the struggle

---

2. Gubbins, *op. cit.,* 263.

It is also true that the Kaiser and his miitary advisers believed that the Russians would win in a war with Japan. After Japan's first victories and when President Roosevelt privately suggested peace terms which America and Germany should attempt to bring about, the Kaiser still believed that the Russians would be victorious. "One should not begin to divide the bear's skin before he has been shot." (Die Grosse Politik, XIX, ii, 537.)

would be a bad thing for Japan and perhaps even worse for Russia.[3]   As early as January, 1905, Mr. Roosevelt, privately and unofficially advised the Russian Government to make peace, and during the weeks which followed both Cassini and Takahira, the Russian and Japanese ambassadors at Washington called on Mr. Roosevelt to discuss peace negotiations, but little progress was made as neither side was willing to make the first move.[4]

During the last week of April the Japanese Ambassador in Washington approved a suggestion made by Mr. Roosevelt that he attempt to bring the warring powers together for direct negotiations.[5]   It is probable, too, that the Japanese Foreign Office approved Mr. Roosevelt's suggestion, but the war party, including the army and navy, was clamoring for indemnity and the cession of territory.[6]   On May 27th came the news of Japan's great naval victory and four days later the first overtures for peace reached the President from Japan.[7]   On June 5th, Mr. Roosevelt wired to Ambassador Meyer in St. Petersburg the plan which he desired to be placed before the Tsar.   By this plan Mr. Roosevelt proposed to ask both powers, on his own initiative and with absolute secrecy, whether they would not consent to meet without intermediaries, in order to discuss the whole peace question.   If Russia would consent the President would try to get Japan's

[3] *Theodore Roosevelt, An Autobiography*, 540.

[4] Bishop, *Theodore Roosevelt and His Time* . . . ., vol. 1, 375.   The Japanese maintained at the time that they could only treat for peace directly on the word of the Tsar for it was evident that no other minister had power to bind the Russian Government.   Cassini informed Mr. Roosevelt at the time that his government was bent upon war, but that privately he would welcome peace.

[5] *Ibid.*, 378-379.   The Ambassador submitted to Secretary Taft at this time a statement of Japan's terms of peace.

[6] *Ibid.*, 380.

[7] *Ibid.*, 382.

consent, not saying that Russia had consented. To this plan the Tsar, after much clever persuasion on the part of Ambassador Meyer, consented, and the world was informed of President Roosevelt's action which was to bring Russia and Japan together.[8] On June 8th, having privately secured the consent of both belligerents, Mr. Roosevelt sent an identical note to each of them stating that the "President feels that the time has come when in the interest of mankind he must endeavor to see if it is not possible to bring to an end the terrible and lamentable conflict now being waged . . . ."[9] Japan accepted this invitation on June 10th and two days later Russia followed her example. Then came a difficult period of negotiations to reach a decision for a common meeting place, which was finally settled with the selection of Portsmouth in New Hampshire.[10]

Russia's acceptance of President Roosevelt's invitation received the support of a few Russian statesmen such as Witte, who, however, was now removed from the Government; but the majority of high officials, naval, military, and civil, did not think the moment opportune for a settlement.[11] It may be said in fact that the whole official hierarchy of St. Petersburg regarded with intense suspicion the proposal of the American President. The success which attended

---

[8] Howe, *George von Lengerke Meyer*, 154-162.

[9] Bishop, *op. cit.*, vol. 1, 382 *et seq.*

[10] *Theodore Roosevelt, An Autobiography*, 540-541.

[11] Dillon, *The Eclipse of Russia*, 299. Generals Linievitch and Kuropatkin and the Minister of War, Sakharoff, all advised the Tsar to continue the struggle. Thus on the eve of the Portsmouth Conference the great body of Russian official opinion believed that Russia's increasing armies were about to redeem the disgrace of Liaoyang, Shao, and Mukden, and regardless of the facts in the military and naval situation it was natural that the generals should hope for an opportunity to re-establish the prestige of their forces. Witte believed, however, that both Linievitch and Kuropatkin hoped for the success of the peace mission. (*Memoirs*, 135.)

Ambassador Meyer's interview with the Tsar on June 7th increased the apprehension of the bureaucracy, involved in its own games of intrigue at court. The clique which had fostered the war in the first place and which now advocated a continuing of the struggle frowned upon any influence which aided the Tsar in adopting an independent course of action. The absurd position of the ministers, which in part accounted for Count Lamsdorff's inability to deal in a straightforward manner with Ambassador Meyer, added to the complications,[12] and created in the mind of Mr. Roosevelt grave fears concerning the success of his venture in the role of peace-maker.[13]

The two nations as a part of Mr. Roosevelt's plan were to meet on terms of equality, but by reason of her military and naval victories Japan naturally approached the conference with the sentiments of a victor. Manifestations of this spirit, however, were well controlled and it was a Government knowing well

---

[12] Howe, *op. cit.*, 168-169.

[13] Bishop, *op. cit.*, vol. 1, 394. Witte had favored, consistently, a peaceful settlement of the Manchurian question and when the American proposal of the peace conference was put forward by Mr. Roosevelt he advocated heartily its adoption. His mind, which saw more clearly than Kuropatkin and Linievitch the economic and in particular the financial phases of the crisis, was impressed by the fact that Russia had exhausted her resources at home and her credit abroad. There was, as he believed, not the slightest chance of floating either a domestic or a foreign loan. A continuation of the war would mean resorting to further issues of paper money, which with the vast quantities that already existed had threatened a collapse. These were factors which had prompted Witte to seek a settlement in the earlier stages of the war. Early in the summer of 1904, Witte had expressed a desire to meet Hayashi, the Japanese ambassador in London, to consult with him as to the best way to end the war. Hayashi consented to meet him somewhere on the continent but the matter was allowed to drop because of the opposition of the Tsar. (Dillon, *op. cit.*, 296.) Here again even the sanest of Russian official opinion was divided, for Baron Rosen, a diplomat of marked ability, affirmed that from the military standpoint Russia's case was by no means hopeless and inferred that success in the field might serve as an excellent means of quieting the internal political disturbances of the Empire which were becoming more and more threatening. (Rosen, *op. cit.*, vol. 1, 260.)

what it wanted, and ably counselled by the Elder Statesmen that maintained a calm attitude throughout the difficult negotiations, never allowing itself to be swayed in its decisions by the discordant demands of a war-excited populace or the military party always ready to demand an extreme and aggressive policy.

The appointment of the plenipotentiaries was of immense importance to both powers concerned. In Japan the selection caused less difficulty than in Russia. The position as head of the Portsmouth Mission was first offered to Prince Ito, who had negotiated the treaty of 1895, and whose appointment would have been pleasing to Russia.[14] But Ito declined and the task fell to the late Marquis (then Baron) Komura, who was at the time Minister of Foreign Affairs. The second Japanese plenipotentiary was Mr. (later Baron) Takahira, the Minister in Washington.[15]

Russia's choice at first fell upon her Ambassador to Paris, Mr. Nelidoff, who declined because of ill health,[16] and then upon her ambassador to Rome, Muravieff, a man ill-suited to the task, who fortunately refused the post, alleging poor health, and on August 11th Witte was named as first plenipotentiary.[17] The task was entrusted to him in a personal interview with the Tsar in which His Majesty expressed a desire that the conference should result in peace, but added that he would not pay a kopeck of indemnity or cede an inch of Russian territory. These conditions were in direct con-

---

[14] Howe, op. cit., 169. The British Ambassador in St. Petersburg reported to Meyer a conversation with Count Lamsdorff in which the latter said to him that if he knew whom Japan was going to appoint as plenipotentiaries it would aid him greatly in selecting Russia's representatives. He added that if Ito were to be sent Russia would send Witte as her first plenipotentiary.

[15] Lawton, Empires of the Far East, vol. 1, 246-247.

[16] Rosen, op. cit., vol. 1, 257.

[17] Witte, op. cit., 134.

flict with two of Japan's demands and were the out-standing points of controversy at the conference. With the controversy that centered on these points and which repeatedly threatened to bring to naught the work of the plenipotentiaries, we are not concerned.[18] Associated with Witte as Russia's second representative at Portsmouth was Baron Rosen, who had held the position of Russian Minister at Tokyo and was now his country's representative at Washington.[19]

The plenipotentiaries held their first meeting on August 9, 1905, in a building of the navy yard at Portsmouth. The credentials of the representatives of both nations were found to be satisfactory and at the second meeting on August 11th Baron Komura presented in writing the Japanese demands.[20] Following a procedure for which she could name innumerable precedents Japan asked for more than she expected to receive, with the intention of making necessary concessions during the negotiations. In the first article of these demands Russia was asked to acknowledge Japan's paramount position in Korea. By Article 2 Russia was to retire from Manchuria and relinquish all her concessions there which were an impairment

---

[18] *Ibid.*, 135.

[19] Realizing the magnitude of the task which confronted him Witte's first move after his appointment as plenipotentiary was an attempt, which proved unsuccessful, to change the personnel of the Japanese delegation through the substitution of Ito for Komura. (Dillon, *op. cit.*, 301.) Dr. Dillon, who was an intimate associate of Witte's, relates how the latter requested him to see Viscount Hayashi, the Japanese Ambassador in London, to propose that Ito be sent to Portsmouth in place of Komura and that he should be invested with full powers to arrange not merely a peaceful settlement but a cordial agreement for an alliance affecting all phases of the future development of the two nations. The Tokyo Cabinet was unable to agree to either of Witte's suggestions.

[20] A statement of these demands is to be found in several sources: *New York Times*, August 19, 1905; Lawton, *op. cit.*, vol. 1, 245-246; Dillon, "The Story of the Peace Negotiations," *Contemporary Review*, October, 1905, 460 *et seq.*

of Chinese sovereignty. Japan obligated herself by a similar engagement, excepting only the territory affected by the lease of the Liaotung Peninsula with Port Arthur and Dalny, which by Article 6 were to be transferred, with China's consent, to Japan. Japan also demanded cession to her of the southern branch of the Chinese Eastern Railway, which Russia had constructed from Harbin to Port Arthur. Sakhalin and adjacent islands were to be ceded to Japan and Russia was to reimburse her for the actual expenses of the war. Russian war vessels interned in neutral ports were to be surrendered to Japan; Russian naval strength in Far Eastern waters was to be limited and Japan was to be granted fishing rights along the coasts of Russia's Pacific possessions. Witte, as already stated, had received definite instructions on two points: namely, that there was to be no indemnity and no cession of territory. On the other hand it was these very points that the war party in Japan prized most highly. To meet this situation Witte resolved to base his tactics on principles which were calculated to appeal to public opinion in America.[21] This public opinion had been decidedly pro-Japanese during the war, but through Witte's wisely planned diplomacy the situation was in large measure reversed before the close of the negotiations, and there now remains no doubt that public opinion either in America or elsewhere would not have supported Japan had she decided to continue the war for a money indemnity. While, therefore, these questions of indemnity and the cession of territory, the latter having particular reference to the Island of Sakhalin, continually threatened to break the conference and prolong the war, the re-

---

[21] Witte, *op. cit.*, 139-140.

maining problems of discussion affecting Russia's position in Manchuria and Korea were easily adjusted.[22]

On September 5, 1905, the Treaty of Peace was signed,[23] bringing to a close one of the most bitter struggles of modern times.   Everywhere, save in Japan, the news of peace was received with rejoicing. The absence of any provision for an indemnity did cause considerable dissatisfaction in the Island Kingdom and some slight disturbances occurred in Tokyo.[24] In general, however, the impression has been created that Japan considered the treaty entirely inadequate. If such feelings existed in a marked degree at the moment they soon disappeared, and Japan found less cause for regret after she had made a careful appraisal of the gains she acquired at Portsmouth.   Let us turn, therefore, to a consideration of the Treaty of Portsmouth itself, and in particular to those clauses which concerned Manchuria directly.

Although Japan, in the course of her prewar negotiations with Russia, had stressed above all else the principle of the territorial integrity and the sovereign rights of China, her first interest so far as the treaty is concerned was her own paramount position in Korea. There is no evidence to indicate that Japan at this time had decided even as a purely theoretical matter, upon the annexation of Korea.   But her position at Seoul

---

[22] Dillon, "The Story of the Peace Negotiaions," *Contemporary Review,* October, 1905, 470.

[23] *Manchuria, Treaties and Agreements,* 70.   The fascinating story of President Roosevelt's efforts to bring Japan and Russia to a point of compromise on the subject of an indemnity and the cession of territory will be found in such works as Roosevelt, *An Autobiography;* Bishop, *op. cit.,* vol. 1; Dillon, *The Story of the Peace Negotiations;* Lawton, *op. cit.,* vol. 1; Howe, *op. cit.;* M. E. E., *His Book* (By Melville E. Stone, from the *Saturday Evening Post,* January 30, 1915), and Dennett, *Roosevelt and the Russo-Japanese War.*

[24] Gubbins, *op. cit.,* 264.

was no longer a matter of doubt, for Russia acknowledged not merely Japan's economic interests in Korea but her political and military interests as well. Article 3 of the treaty combined the second and third of Japan's original demands as presented by Komura. Both powers engaged to evacuate Manchuria, with the exception of the territory leased in Liaotung, and Russia specifically declared that she possessed in Manchuria no "territorial advantages or preferential or exclusive concessions" in impairment of Chinese sovereignty. This declaration was in fulfillment of what Japan had most urgently desired, for the position which Russia had persistently attempted to acquire in the "Three Eastern Provinces" since 1900 and her failure to limit her desires to the stipulations contained in the Convention of Evacuation of April 8, 1902, had been the cause of the greatest apprehension to the Japanese. Both powers engaged not to obstruct any general measures common to all countries, which China should take for the development of commerce and industry in Manchuria. As expressing the principle of the "Open Door" in a somewhat new form this clause became of great importance. By Article 5 Russia transferred to Japan, provisional upon the consent of the Chinese government, the lease of Port Arthur, Talienwan, and the adjacent territory, together with all privileges and concessions Russia had acquired in connection with the lease through her agreements made with China in 1898. Japan also received the southern branch of the Chinese Eastern Railway from Changchun to Port Arthur, a modification of her original demand in which she had asked for the entire line as far north as Harbin. It should be noted, too, that both powers were to exploit their Manchurian railways for purely commercial and industrial purposes with the exception of that section of the Japanese line in the leased territory.[25]

It will be recalled that during the construction by Russia of the Chinese Eastern Railway, guards had been employed for the protection of the line against bandits. Despite the fact that there was no treaty stipulation extending the privilege to Russia she greatly increased the number of such guards during the years of occupation after the Boxer uprising. Now by the peace settlement Russia and Japan reserved to themselves the right to maintain such guards to protect their respective railway lines in Manchuria. The number of guards was not to exceed fifteen per kilometer.[26]

With four exceptions the original Japanese demands were accepted with little change. The four which proved unacceptable to Russia were of varying importance to Japan. It was a difficult task for Japan to accept peace with no indemnity. In respect to Sakhalin there was compromise, and the clauses respecting interned Russian ships and the limiting of Russian naval strength in the Far East could not be considered major issues. And so, although it was said that the Japanese had been outwitted and outgeneraled in diplomacy and had been made to appear almost willing to wage a war for an indemnity, nevertheless, Japan received everything for which she had been fighting. She was assured a predominating position in Korea; Russia was to evacuate Manchuria; the principles of Chinese sovereignty and territorial integrity had been recognized; there was to be equal opportunity for the trade and

---

[25] Important so far as Japan was concerned, but not directly a phase of the Manchuria Question, was the fact that Japan received the southern part, about two-fifths, of the Island of Sakhalin. The fiftieth degree of north latitude was adopted as the northern boundary of the ceded territory. (Article 9.)

[26] See (1) of additional articles to the treaty.

commerce of all nations; and the Russian leasehold and railway as far north as Changchun were no longer Russian but Japanese. These in reality were the things which were of importance to Japan. She had rid Korea and South Manchuria of Russian influence and with the transfer of the Russian leasehold she might look confidently to a successful development of her own interests there. These considerations entirely outweighed the failure to receive an indemnity, desirable as that would have been to a nation burdened with a ponderous war debt.

The Treaty of Portsmouth had provided that the transfer of the Russian leasehold in Liaotung, together with all its rights and privileges, should be conditioned upon the consent of the Chinese Government. This provision was a necessary recognition of Chinese sovereignty in the territory which was to be transferred. By it China was permitted to save her face, but to Japan it was of great practical worth, for it enabled the Tokyo Government to adjust by negotiation a great variety of questions arising as a result of the transfer of the Russian concessions. The Portsmouth Treaty had been promptly ratified by both Japan and Russia during November [27] and this opened the way for the ensuing negotiations between Japan and China at Peking conducted by Baron Komura and Prince Ching. The discussions were carried on during December and on the 22nd, the Treaty of Peking was signed.[28] China went through the perfunctory performance of agreeing to all the transfers and assignments made by the Russian Government to Japan by Articles 5 and 6 of the Treaty of Peace. Japan agreed, in so far as circum-

---

[27] Ratifications were exchanged at Washington, November 25, 1905, *Manchuria, Treaties and Agreements*, 74.

[28] *Ibid.*, 78-83.

stances would permit, to conform to the original agreements concluded between China and Russia in respect to the leased territory,[29] and questions of controversy concerning Japan's rights in the leased territory and the concessions pertaining to it were to be decided by the Japanese Government in consultation with the Chinese Government. Having thus determined the status of their relationship in Manchuria the two powers concluded the treaty by an additional agreement of great interest. The importance of this agreement is such that a somewhat detailed discussion of it is merited.

The reader will recall that in October, 1903, China signed treaties of commerce and navigation with Japan and the United States, providing for the opening to trade of certain Manchurian towns. The opening of these towns had been vigorously opposed by Russia, while her Ambassador at Washington, Count Cassini, had attempted to create the impression that conditions in the provinces made the opening of trade centers impossible. Now by Article 1 of the additional agreement China agreed, following the evacuation of Manchuria by Russia and Japanese troops, to open a number ot cities in each of the three provinces to international residence and trade.[30]

---

[29] Ratifications were exchanged at Peking, January 23, 1906, *Manchuria, Treaties and Agreements*, 79.

[30] This engagement on the part of China applied to the following cities:

In the Province of Shengking or Mukden: Liaoyang, Hsinmintun, Tiehling, Tungkiangtzu, and Fakumen.

In the Province of Kirin: Changchun (Kuanchengtzu), Kirin, Harbin, Ninguta, Hunchun, and Sanhsing.

In the Province of Heilungkiang: Tsitsihar, Hailar, Aihun, and Manchuli.

On September 10, 1906, Tiehling, Tungkiangtzu, and Fakumen were declared open; on October 8, 1906, Hsinmintun was opened; on January 14, 1907, Changchun, Kirin, Harbin, and Tsitsihar were opened, and finally on June 28, 1907, Fenghwangcheng, Liaoyang Ninguta, Hunchun, Sanhsing, Hailar, and Aihun were opened. (*Manchuria, Treaties and Agreements*, 80.)

Japan agreed, when China became capable of affording full protection to the lives and property of foreigners in Manchuria, to withdraw her railway guards, provided Russia took similar measures. The presence of these guards had from the beginning been tolerated with disfavor by China and the agreement respecting their number contained in the Treaty of Portsmouth was perhaps no more welcome than the liberty Russia had assumed previous to the signing of the treaty, as her right. The acceptance of this article carried with it China's acceptance of the railway guards as a part of the Russian and Japanese railway concessions, while the wording of the article, "when tranquility shall have been re-established in Manchuria and China shall have become herself capable of affording full protection to the lives and property of foreigners" retained to Japan the right to maintain her guards even on the most flimsy pretext, especially so, since there was little prospect that Russia would withdraw her guards from the northern Province.[31]

During the war the Japanese armies advancing in Manchuria from the Korean border had been maintained in the field by a hastily constructed military railroad from Antung on the Yalu in a northwesterly direction toward Mukden.[32] Since she now controlled the southern section of the Chinese Eastern Railway, Japan realized the value of a connecting line with the Korean railways. She acquired, therefore, by Article 6 of the additional agreement the right to maintain and improve the line, creating thereby a commercial road. The right was to extend for fifteen years from the date when the conversion of the military line to a commer-

---

[31] Article 2 of additional agreement, *Manchuria, Treaties and Agreements*, 80.

[32] *The Japan Weekly Mail*, August 14, 1909, 183.

cial road was complete. It should also be noted that the opening of the Antung-Mukden Railway, as this road came to be known, completed the longest line of railway in the world, stretching from St. Petersburg in the west to Fusan in southern Korea.

Having in mind the development of trade and commerce between Manchuria and other sections of the Empire the agreement also provided for the linking of railway lines in south Manchuria with the imperial railways of north China.[33]   The two powers agreed that the forest wealth of the Yalu district should be exploited by a joint stock company composed of Japanese and Chinese.[34]   These stipulations in the treaty signed on December 22nd, which have been briefly outlined, were to form the basis on which Japan and China would attempt to harmonize their relationships in Manchuria.   To what degree the treaty proved an effective working agreement will be discussed in subsequent chapters.   It was, however, not the only document which bore directly on the Manchurian situation, for to the treaty and additional agreement were attached certain secret protocols which figured prominently in the controversies that arose concerning the rights of other powers in Manchuria.[35]   The most important clause of these protocols provided that the Chinese Government engage, for the purpose of protecting the interest of the South Manchuria Railway, not to construct prior to the recovery by them of the said railway any main line in the neighborhood of and parallel to that rail-

---

[33] Article 7 of additional agreement, *Manchuria, Treaties and Agreements*, 81-82.

[34] Article 10 of additional agreement, *Ibid.*, 82. See discussion of agreement of May 14, 1908, and regulations dated September 11, 1908, discussed in chapter 10.

[35] Summary of alleged secret protocols to the Sino-Japanese Treaty of December 22, 1905, in *Manchuria, Treaties and Agreements*, 83.

way, or any branch line which might be prejudicial to
the interest of the South Manchuria Railway.   Other
clauses provided for: engagement by China to borrow
from Japan one-half the capital required to construct
the Changchun-Kirin Railway; China was also to purchase from Japan the Hsinmintun-Mukden military
railway and to borrow from Japanese corporations one-
half the capital required for reconstruction of that portion of the line east of the Liao River.

Japan has long been the subject of bitter attacks by
those who considered that in the so-called secret protocols she definitely attempted to defeat the spirit if not
the letter of the "Open Door" doctrine in Manchuria.
This subject will be considered at some length in later
discussions of the "Open Door" as applied in south
Manchuria and of Japan's railway policies there.   But
occasion may be taken at this point to present evidence
which bears directly on the validity of the protocols
which has many times been called in question.   There
now seems to be no justification for the cloud of mystery which has enveloped these protocols.   They have
been considered first as "alleged" and secondly as "secret."   For neither of these qualifications does there
appear to be any justification.   Mr. Huntington Wilson,
Chargé d' Affaires of the United States at Tokyo, was
given a copy of the protocols which he transmitted to
the Department of State under date of February 16,
1906,[36] while clause three which stipulated that parallel
and competing lines to the South Manchuria Railway

---

[36] Millard, *Our Eastern Question*, 430.   As early as January 12, 1906,
Chargé Wilson informed the State Department that "certain protocols, con-
taining further arrangements of no small importance, were drawn up in
conjunction with the treaty and agreement; but, as I was informed at the
foreign office, these protocols are being kept secret for the present in accordance with an understanding with China."   United States *Foreign Relations*,
1906, Pt. 2, 996.

should not be constructed was communicated to the British Government during April, 1906.[37]   Two years later Sir Edward Grey, on March 24, 1908, stated that his government was informed the protocol bore the signatures of the Chinese representatives and that there could be no doubt as to its validity.[38]   Prior to this, on March 3rd, Sir Edward, in the course of discussion of railway interests in Manchuria, stated with reference to the same clause, that the existence of the agreement was not disputed by the Chinese Government.[39]   Although the Chinese did later deny the validity of the protocols, the case presented by them was far from convincing and until further evidence is forthcoming must lead inevitably to the conclusion that they were actually signed, and furthermore, that there was nothing secret about them.

During the course of the Russo-Japanese War, on August 12, 1905, the Anglo-Japanese Alliance was renewed for a period of ten years and its scope extended so as to include British India.   By the agreement either ally would at once come to the aid of the other, "If, by reason of unprovoked attack or aggressive action, wherever arising, on the part of any power or powers, either contracting party should be involved in war in defense of its territorial rights or special interests mentioned in the preamble."[40]   The renewal of this alliance, the signing of the Treaty of Portsmouth, and the successful negotiations resulting in the Treaty of Peking in December, 1905, all added to the prestige and the influence of Japan at large, but particularly with reference to her position in the Far East.[41]   Hav-

---

[37] *Parliamentary Debates*, March 24, 1908, vol. 186, 1191.

[38] *Ibid.*,

[39] *Parliamentary Debates*, March 3, 1908, vol. 185, 527.

[40] Treat, *op. cit.*, 202.

[41] After the renewal of the Anglo-Japanese Alliance in 1905 and the conclusion of the Russo-Japanese and the Franco-Japanese treaties in the summer

ing driven Russia from Korea and South Manchuria, and with the Peking Treaty as a basis for the development of her continental interests, Japan could anticipate a growth of trade in north China that might in some degree compensate her for the sacrifices of the war. For the first time in her history Japan experienced what it meant to be numbered among the Great Powers. Of these powers she was China's most intimate neighbor and in this capacity she entered upon a period in which her influence at Peking was comparable to that of her European rivals. These years were, outwardly at least, an era of reconciliation in which such accords as the Franco-Japanese entente of June, 1907; the Russo-Japanese agreement of July, 1907; the Anglo-Russian accord of August, 1907; the Gentlemen's Agreement between the United States and Japan of the same year, and finally the Root-Takahira notes of November, 1908, all appeared to find the happy mean of compromise by which conflicting interests were reconciled. In practically all of these agreements Japan played a leading part, while she was working out the course of her policy in Korea and Manchuria. Just what the purpose and spirit of that policy actually was it will be the task of following chapters to discuss.

---

of 1907, the Kaiser became alarmed lest these treaties might contain secret articles which might threaten the status quo and "Open Door" in China. He therefore urged a German-Chinese entente which he hoped the United States would join. The project came to nothing, since Roosevelt thought the time not ripe and he knew the opposition to be expected from the Senate. (Die Grosse Politik, XIX, ii, 533-642, and XXV, i, 73.)

CHAPTER VIII

THE OPEN DOOR IN MANCHURIA (1905-1907)

The signing of the Treaty of Portsmouth, and the subsequent settlement, in the Treaty of Peking, were the bases in which Japan sought a solution of the Manchurian question. The problem of harmonizing Chinese and Japanese aspirations in the "Three Eastern Provinces," where Japan now controlled the territory formerly leased by Russia, was of itself apt to lead to serious misunderstandings and disagreements. It was further complicated, as we shall see, by the interests of other powers, in particular Russia, Great Britain, and the United States, jealous of the markets which they already possessed or hoped to acquire in this rich section of the Chinese Empire. During the years, therefore, immediately following the Portsmouth settlement, or to be more precise, during the months in which the Russian and Japanese armies were evacuating Manchuria, the Tokyo Government was faced with a serious domestic problem, which soon acquired international aspects of the most grave and threatening character.

Any attempt to understand the international situation in the Far East during 1906 and 1907 must take full account of the national state of mind created in Japan by the Treaty of Portsmouth. The nation believed the war had been fought not merely to safeguard the sovereign rights of China in her northern provinces, but also for a more fundamental reason. This was the safeguarding of Japan herself as an independent and sovereign state. Both on land and sea the forces of Japan had been victorious, yet in the Portsmouth settlement Japan had been denied cession of territory, save in southern Sakhalin, and more important, a money indemnity, which she believed she might justly claim. The close of the war found her in possession of one tangible addition to her possessions —the Russian leasehold in southern Manchuria with the railway from Dairen to Changchun. The balance sheet of the war from the Japanese point of view presented an empty column of assets save for this one entry. Regardless of whether or not this view was a correct one; regardless of whether or not the nation as a whole was blind to certain other advantages she had acquired, the fact remains that this belief prevailed and must be kept in mind constantly if resulting controversies are to be seen in their true light.

The period allowed for the withdrawal of the Russian and Japanese armies from Manchuria had been fixed by a protocol signed on October 30, 1905, by staff representatives of the forces in the field.[1] In accordance with this arrangement the evacuation of Manchuria, with the exception of the leased territory and the railway zones, was completed by both Russia and Japan before April 15, 1907.[2] The railway guards, the existence of which was now recognized by the first of the additional articles to the Treaty of Portsmouth, were maintained apparently to the full extent of the stipulated number (15 men per kilometer of railway).[3]

---

[1] *Manchuria, Treaties and Agreements*, 77.

[2] Asakawa, "Japan in Manchuria," *Yale Review*, November, 1908, 268.

[3] *Ibid.*, 268-269. Asakawa here states that it was a matter of common knowledge that the total forces of Japan stationed along the railways and in the leased territory were limited to one division of her army, or 12,000 men more or less, under the command of the Governor-General of Kwantung. That the guards were not reduced further, he adds, was due to the inadequacy of the Chinese police and military forces in the face of great danger from mounted bandits. To repel the attacks of these the Japanese were compelled to detail guards to the passenger trains. There would seem to be no justification for or possibility of truth in the statement of one publicist who asserted that

While Japan was thus complying with the protocol of evacuation her domestic situation was far from enviable. As already stated, the Peace of Portsmouth was received by the nation with the utmost dissatisfaction. Outside of Japan her failure to secure the cession of Russian territory on the mainland or a money indemnity was regarded in circles hostile to her as a definite check to what was called Japan's long established and carefully planned policy of imperialism on the Asian continent. This was not the first occasion on which Japan had been accused of rattling the sabre in one form or another and it should therefore be profitable to examine carefully the course of this so-called aggressive policy.

One of the first questions confronting Japan, following her acquisition of Liaotung, was the disposition of the southern branch of the Chinese Eastern Railway from Changchun to Dairen and Port Arthur. To deal adequately with this topic we must retrace our steps to the spring of 1905 during the preliminaries of the Portsmouth meeting. It was at this time that Mr. E. H. Harriman, at the invitation of the American Minister in Tokyo, Mr. Lloyd C. Griscom, determined to visit the Far East with a view of extending American commerce there. With this general idea of the extension of American trade, he had conceived a plan for a round-the-world transportation line under unified American control, the route to go by way of Japan, Manchuria, Siberia, and European Russia, thus enabling the United States to take a commanding position

---

"Although the greater part of the Japanese army had returned to Japan, detachments were still stationed in the principal cities and towns. Unadulterated military rule prevailed." (Millard, *America and the Far Eastern Question*, 179.)   With most of the Japanese forces withdrawn it is inconceivable that "unadulterated military rule" could have prevailed.

in the Orient.[4] Mr. Harriman and his party reached
Yokohama on August 31, 1905, where he was received
cordially in both financial and official circles. On September 4th, the day before the Peace of Portsmouth
was signed, Mr. Harriman attended a dinner at the
American legation at which practically all the Ministers of State were present. On this occasion Harriman
hinted at the plan he had in mind. On September 12th,
after disorders occasioned by the signing of the Treaty
had subsided, Mr. Harriman was received in audience
by the Emperor. In the meantime he had interested a
number of financiers in his plan. He then visited Manchuria and Korea, returning to Tokyo on October 9th.
During his absence Mr. Griscom had worked inces-
santly to persuade the Japanese Ministers to consider
favorably Harriman's plan.[5]

The result of these negotiations was that on October
12th, 1905, a memorandum of preliminary understanding was drawn up by Count Katsura, representing the
Japanese Government on one hand, and Mr. Harriman
representing himself and associates on the other. This
understanding provided for the formation of a Japanese Corporation, under Japanese law, to provide capital for the purpose of purchasing the southern branch
of the Chinese Eastern Railway, acquired by the Japanese Government. The two parties were to have joint

---

[4] Kennan, *E. H. Harriman a Biography*, vol. 2, 1. Mr. Harriman planned
first to acquire control of the Japanese section of the Chinese Eastern Railway,
which was then in a very unsatisfactory physical condition, reconstruct it with
American capital and make it the eastern part of his proposed round-the-
world route. In the second place he proposed to buy the Chinese Eastern
Railway which he thought the Russians, having lost Port Arthur, would gladly
sell and then acquire transportation or trackage rights over the Transsiberian
to the Baltic Sea.

[5] *Ibid.*, 3-9. In his interviews with Premier Katsura, Count Inouye, and
the Minister of Finance he took the position that co-operation with the United
States would be in every way profitable to Japan, furnishing her with capital
and facilitating her trade.

and equal ownership in the properties acquired.[6]   Although a Japanese corporation in which he and his associates would have a fifty per cent interest was not all that Mr. Harriman had wished, he felt at least that it was a starting point, and the future might hold a wider and fuller development of his original plan.

Only three days after the departure of Mr. Harriman from Yokohama, Baron Komura arrived at Tokyo from the United States bearing with him the Treaty of Portsmouth, and in less than a week the Japanese Government determined on an entire change of policy.   In the first place, Baron Komura was opposed to the Katsura-Harriman understanding, claiming it to be inconsistent with Article 6 of the peace treaty which called for the consent of the Chinese Government before Japan could exercise any legal rights in the property of the railway line in south Manchuria.   Beyond this, however, Komura was convinced that the Japanese nation, disappointed with the peace settlement, would not tolerate the sale of the one thing it had acquired in the war, to a Japanese-American syndicate.   It is probable, too, Komura realized better than his fellow ministers the possibilities of Japanese development in south Manchuria and was satisfied the nation, of itself, could raise the capital necessary for that development without selling a portion of its interests to Americans.[7]   Nor is it beyond reason to suppose that Komura had already sensed a growing feeling on the part of the Japanese that the execution of President Roosevelt's

---

[6] *Ibid.*, vol., 2, 13.   It may be noted that Mr. Henry W. Denison, who had long been an adviser of the Japanese Government, was to be the arbitrator in cases of dispute between the new Corporation and the Japanese Government. In time of war the railroad was to be under the control of the Japanese Government.

[7] Kennan, *op. cit.*, vol. 2, 15.

scheme for bringing the belligerents together had defeated Japan in the pursuit of just aspirations on the continent. Japanese statesmen, of course, knew well that Mr. Roosevelt had rendered the nation invaluable service, but it is not surprising that a considerable section of the populace and the majority of the war party failed to share this view.

Commenting on this sudden change in the Japanese policy Mr. Kennan, a careful student of Far Eastern affairs, says: "In the thwarting of Mr. Harriman's plans there seems to have been no intentional breach of faith on the part of the Tokyo authorities. It was simply a case in which one branch of the government acted independently, and concluded a treaty that nullified action taken almost simultaneously by another branch."[8] This entire incident is of more than passing interest, for its significance has been entirely overlooked by writers whose object has been to place Japan in a difficult and unenviable position. One fact would seem to stand out pre-eminently. Had Japan possessed a deep-seated and sinister scheme of continental aggression, whose object was the elimination of all foreign competition in China save her own, and the purposeful violation of the "Open Door" doctrine, it is difficult to explain why the Katsura Government vacillated between one policy and another, or came near to disposing of half its interests in the Manchurian railway to American capitalists. Until such time as more evidence is brought forward less favorable to Japan, we

---

[8] *Ibid.*, 17. On January 15, 1906, Mr. J. Soyeda, president of the Industrial Bank of Japan, wired Mr. Harriman after the return of Baron Komura from Peking, that obtaining the consent of China entailed having the Manchurian Railway worked by a company composed exclusively of Japanese and Chinese shareholders, following in that the terms of the original concession to Russia. It was also stated that if outside capital was necessary another consultation would probably be held with Mr. Harriman.

are forced to conclude that Tokyo had no definite policy in the closing months of 1905, and that there was little, if any, substance to her co-called continental imperialism.

The uncertainty which surrounded the whole question of Japan's future policy in south Manchuria made of that question a convenient football in the turmoil of domestic politics. This fact was the more important because political life needed little to stimulate it in view of the already bitter feeling between the civil or peace party and the military. The situation led early in 1906 to the reorganization of the Ministry when Marquis Saionji became premier.[9] This selection was, in the view of Mr. Millard, a compromise between the extreme military and antimilitary wings of the government. The situation was at least clarified, for by May 24, 1906, when Marquis Saionji had returned from an unofficial visit to Manchuria an important council of statesmen was held at the Imperial Palace in which it was understood that a policy in keeping with the "Open Door" doctrine was vindicated.[10] Less than a month later on June 7, 1906, an Imperial Ordinance was issued sanctioning organization of the South Manchuria Railway Company.[11] On August 1st, the Government forwarded to Viscount Terauchi, chairman of the commission on organization, conditions pertaining

---

[9] Millard, *op. cit.*, 178.

[10] United States *Foreign Relations* (1906) 190-191, Chargé Wilson to the Secretary of State, Tokyo, May 24, 1906. At the same time the Nichi Nichi Shimbun, an organ of considerable authority, summarized the Government's intentions as follows: (1) To respect the sovereignty of China, and the principle of equal opportunity; (2) To avoid a display of military force and to take measures to acquaint the people of Manchuria with Japan's sincerity of purpose; (3) To take the utmost care not to give any cause of offense to southern China on account of Japan's Manchurian policy or any occasion for agitation for the purpose of recovering concessions.

[11] *Manchuria, Treaties and Agreements*, 85-86.

to the establishment of the company, and on August
18th the articles of incorporation were approved by the
government.[12]   Concerning its status and the nature of
its business, the company received certain orders from
the Japanese Government.   It was to operate seven
lines of railway, which, with the exception of one, had
been ceded to Japan by Russia;[13] these lines were to be
constructed to the standard gauge of four feet eight
and one-half inches; the principal stations were to be
equipped with all necessary accommodations for trav-
elers; for the convenience of the railways, mining, marine transportation, management of lands and buildings in the railway zone, and other activities sanctioned
by the government were to be undertaken by the company, and finally it was to make all arrangements for
public works, education, and sanitation in the railway
done.   The establishment of the company was sanctioned by the Ministry of Communications on November 1st, and the head office was located at Dairen.[14]

Both the president and the vice-president were to be
appointed by the Government.   The directors were
also to be chosen by the Government from among the
shareholders, while the auditors were to be selected at
the general meeting of shareholders.   Baron S. Goto
became the first president of the company in November,
and Mr. Z. Nakamura the first vice-president.   The
Government reserved the right to issue such orders as
might be necessary to superintend the business of the
company and in case the decisions of the company or
the conduct of its officers should be in violation of the

[12] *Ibid*, 87-94.

[13] The seven lines of railway included: (1) The Dairen-Changchun main
line; (2) The Nankuanling-Port Arthur line; (3) The Tafangshen-Liushutun
line; (4) the Tashihchiao-Yingkow line; (5) The Yentai-Yentai coal line;
(6) The Suchiatun-Fushun line; (7) The Antung-Mukden line.

[14] *Economic Development of Korea and Manchuria*, 250-251.

laws and regulations of the company, or detrimental to the public welfare, the Government retained the right to cancel the decisions and dismiss the officers.[15] The authorized capital was Yen 440,000,000 and the right to hold shares was limited to the Chinese and Japanese Governments and to Chinese and Japanese subjects. By virtue of the physical properties, appraised at Yen 100,000,000 ,which the Japanese Government invested in the Company, one million shares were allotted to the Government. To a great extent, therefore ,the South Manchuria Railway Company was modeled after the Chinese Eastern Railway Company to which it was successor in the Japanese zone. Unlike the railways of Japan, it was established as a joint-stock company in accordance with the commercial law of Japan. But as already noted, there was ample provision for government regulation of its activities. The seven railways mentioned in note 13 were acquired by the company from the Government in April, 1907, when the evacuation of Manchuria by the Japanese armies was completed.[16] The establishment of a company independent of the Government, although in reality under government control, indicated that sane counsels were to prevail in Tokyo. Had a system of government ownership of the South Manchuria Railway been adopted, following the existing system in Japan, the storm of abuse heaped upon Japanese activities in South Manchuria during 1906 and 1907 would probably have been trebled.

This brings our story to a consideration of the much discussed and misunderstood subject of the "Open Door" doctrine and its application in Manchuria dur-

---

[15] Articles 13 and 14 of Imperial Ordinance No. 142, June 7, 1906. *Manchuria, Treaties and Agreements*, 86.

[16] *Economic Development of Korea and Manchuria*, 261.

ing the years just mentioned. Through the more recent period of Japan's rise to the position of a world
power the Anglo-Saxon nations have gained most of
their impressions of Far Eastern affairs through the
works of untrained observers and paid publicists.
Many of these books have contained an astonishing
mixture of fact and fallacy, which is responsible in no
small measure for the distrust and lack of mutual appreciation so characteristic of the relations of Orient
and Occident. No treatment of a subject such as *International Rivalries in Manchuria* can hope to be adequate which fails to discuss some of the controversial
questions which have of themselves threatened the
peace of the Far East and with which international
rivalries are most intimately bound. Just such a question is presented in the case of Japan's application of
the "Open Door" doctrine in South Manchuria from the
close of the Russo-Japanese War until the complete
opening of Manchuria to foreign trade in 1907.[17]

The origin of the doctrine which has come to be
known as the "Open Door" is said to be found in instructions which Daniel Webster, American Secretary
of State, gave in 1843 to Caleb Cushing as Envoy Extraordinary and Minister Plenipotentiary to China.
These instructions made it apparent that the Government of the United States would find it impossible to
remain on terms of friendship with China if greater

---

[17] There is a great mass of secondary material dealing with this subject,
most of which, however, is of no value to the historian. The purpose of the
writer is to come to an accurate conclusion as to what was the attitude of the
Japanese Government with respect to the "Open Door" as applied to South
Manchuria. "Alleged" and "reported but unconfirmed" violations of the Doctrine by individual and private Japanese interests while of interest in the
general topic are not the primary concern of this discussion. The reader will
observe that the evidence here used is in practically all cases from the United
States *Foreign Relations* series, one of the final and most authoritative sources
to which the historian is able to turn on this question.

privileges or commercial facilities were granted to
the subjects of other governments than were granted to
the citizens of the United States. The American Government secured most-favored-nation treatment in the
treaty signed the following year and "thus was laid
the foundation of the policy of the 'Open Door' or
equality of opportunity."[18]

The years 1897 and 1898 have become historically
infamous as those in which contending European
powers secured strategic leaseholds on the coasts of
China, entrenched themselves in what were called
"spheres of influence," and threatened in fact a break-
up of the entire Empire. Such a situation as that presented by the "spheres of influence" foreshadowed the
defeat of all principles of equal opportunity for trade
and commerce and even endangered the territorial integrity of China. The power holding a "sphere of influence" became there economically dominant. The
system tended to produce in China rival economic
kingdoms which could lead only to international rivalries of the most bitter kind. Alarmed by this situation the British House of Commons passed resolutions
during 1898 in support of the principle of free and unrestricted commerce in the treaty ports of China.[19]

John Hay became Secretary of State for the United
States on September 30, 1898. He had been American
Ambassador in London and was well acquainted with
England's desire to maintain the principle of equal op-
portunity for trade. In his position as Secretary of
State he was confronted with the problem of formu-
lating a policy to meet American interests in China,

---

[18] *Origin of the Open Door Policy*, as outlined by Charles Evans Hughes,
Secretary of State, in an address delivered at Philadelphia, November 30, 1923,
in *Current History Magazine*, January, 1924, 577.

[19] *Parliamentary Debates*, Fourth Series, vol. 54, 309, 340.

now seriously threatened by the "spheres of influence."
The situation demanded prompt action. Hay therefore
dispatched his first circular note, on September 6, 1899,
to London, Berlin, and St. Petersburg, on November
13 to Tokyo, on November 17 to Rome, and November
21 to Paris.[20]   Although there was a slight difference in
the wording of some of the notes, essentially the following proposal was set forth, as contained in the note
to Mr. Buck, the American Minister in Tokyo:

Sir: This government, animated with a sincere desire to
insure to the commerce and industry of the United States and
of all other nations perfect equality of treatment within the
limits of the Chinese Empire for their trade and navigation,
especially within the so-called "spheres of influence or interest"
claimed by certain European Powers in China, has deemed the
present an opportune moment to make representations in this
direction to Germany, Great Britain, and Russia.

To obtain the object it has in view and to remove possible
causes of international irritation and re-establish confidence so
essential to commerce, it has seemed to this government highly
desirable that the various powers claiming "spheres of interest
or influence" in China should give formal assurances that—

First. They will in no way interfere with any treaty port or
any vested interest within any so-called "sphere of interest" or
leased territory they may have in China.

Second. The Chinese Treaty tariff of the time being shall
apply to all merchandise landed or shipped to all such ports
as are within said "spheres of interest" (unless they be "free
ports"), no matter to what nationality it may belong, and that
duties so leviable shall be collected by the Chinese Government.

Third. They will levy no higher harbor dues on vessels of
another nationality frequenting any port in such "sphere" than
shall be levied on vessels of their own nationality, and no higher
railroad charges over lines built, controlled, or operated within
such "sphere" on merchandise belonging to citizens or subjects
of other nationalities transported through such "sphere" than
shall be levied on similar merchandise belonging to their own
nationals transported over equal distances. . . .[21]

---

[20] United States *Foreign Relations,* (1899) 128-143.
[21] *Ibid.,* 138-139.

To this proposal of the American Secretary of State, Viscount Aoki, the Japanese Minister for Foreign Affairs, replied on December 26, 1899, as follows:

Mr. Minister: . . . . I have the happy duty of assuring your excellency that the Imperial Government will have no hesitation to give their assent to so just and fair a proposal of the United States, provided that all the other powers concerned shall accept the same.[22]

All the powers addressed by Secretary Hay replied favorably, with the reservation that the other powers should concur, except Russia, who was silent on the subject of uniformity of railroad charges and harbor dues.[23] When, on March 20, 1900, he had received all the replies Hay informed the Powers concerned that the United States Government considered the assent given by all as final and definitive.[24]

In the Boxer uprising of 1900 the representatives of the United States were guided in their attitude toward China by a telegram of Secretary Hay addressed to the Powers on July 3, 1900, declaring for the territorial integrity of the Empire.[25] This statement of American attitude came to be closely associated with the position taken by the United States the year previous, but further than this had nothing to do with the "Open Door" doctrine; rather was it a means through which the "Open Door" might be maintained. The note of July 3rd, therefore, constituted merely a statement of the attitude of the United States Government. It could not be considered a *modus vivendi*, since it was merely a one-sided declaration of policy, nor an integral part

---

[22] *Ibid.*, (1899) 139.

[23] *Ibid.*, 141-142.

[24] *Ibid.*, 142. Lord Salisbury excluded Kowloon from his assent.

[25] This telegram was dispatched to the United States Embassies in Berlin, Paris, London, Rome, and St. Petersburg, and to the United States Missions in Vienna, Brussels, Madrid, Tokyo, the Hague, and Lisbon. United States *Foreign Relations*, (1900), 299.

of the note of 1899.   Great Britain and Germany pledged themselves to maintain the territorial integrity of China in their agreement of October 16, 1900,[26] and to dispatches of the British and German Governments, John Hay replied on October 29th, reaffirming the position of the United States respecting impartial trade and the integrity of the Chinese Empire.[27]   As already stated, in a previous chapter, Germany had no intention of applying the principle of the integrity of China to Manchuria and after the Boxer Rising it was in Manchuria that the Russian aggression presented the greatest threat to the effective maintenance of the "Open Door."   In the Russian reply to Hay's note of September 6, 1899, it will be noted that Count Muravieff made specific mention and assurance respecting the Chinese tariff but avoided the subject of railway charges and harbor dues.   The story of Russian activities in Manchuria during the succeeding years which led eventually to the Russo-Japanese War has already been told.

On January 13, 1905, John Hay dispatched another circular letter to a number of the powers[28] dealing with the subjects of the "Open Door" and China's territorial integrity.   This note stressed the desire of the United States to "perpetuate the broad policy of maintaining *the integrity of China and the 'open door'* in the Orient."   It is important to note the two points stressed, as this has a distinct bearing on later interpretations of the doctrine.[29]

During the early months of 1906 the American State Department received urgent representations from

---

[26] United States *Foreign Relations*, (1900), 354.

[27] *Ibid.*, 355, 373.

[28] The circular letter was dispatched to the American representatives to Austria, Belgium, France, Germany, Great Britain, Italy, and Portugal.

[29] United States *Foreign Relations*, (1905), 1.

American traders in the Far East that they were prevented from entering Manchuria by way of Newchwang, the treaty port in the south, while Japanese agents were allowed free access to the country. The State Department therefore requested *Chargé* Wilson in Tokyo to request the Japanese Government to give the matter its close attention.[30] The Japanese Government promised to do so, although it had heard of no discrimination. At the same time the British Ambassador at Tokyo made representations to the Government on behalf of his nationals seeking a removal of restrictions to trade in Manchuria applied during the period of evacuation by the Japanese and Russian armies.[31]

The American State Department instructed Mr. Wilson, on March 24, 1906, that its agents in China reported that the action of Japanese authorities in Manchuria during military occupation tended to establish Japanese commercial interests in such a way as to leave little or no opening for other foreign trade by the time the territory was evacuated. The solicitude of the United States in regard to the "Open Door" in Manchuria was expressed.[32] In response the Japanese Foreign Office explained that the temporary restrictions placed upon foreigners were due to military necessity and that the "Open Door" would be observed in Manchuria.[33] The position of the Japanese Govern-

---

[30] *Ibid.,* (1906) pt. 1, 170.

[31] By the memorandum concluded between the Commanders of the Russian and Japanese forces no foreigners were permitted to pass between the zones in Manchuria still occupied by the two armies, except in very special cases. It was claimed by some of the foreign nationals that Japanese nationals were permitted absolutely free access to this zone thus giving them a distinct advantage in the establishment of their trade. (United States *Foreign Relations,* (1906), pt. 1, 171-172.)

[32] United States *Foreign Relations,* (1906), pt. 1, 174.

[33] Marquis Saionji to *Chargé* Wilson, April 11, 1906, encl. in *Chargé* Wilson's

ment was made clear in a memorandum presented in Washington on April 12th.   In this Japan stated that it was impossible to admit foreigners into the territories occupied by her troops immediately after the conclusion of peace.   The temporary nature of the measure was again stressed and the memorandum concluded with a solemn avowal of the intention of the Government to respect the "Open Door."[34]   The memorandum gave further expression to Japan's decision to open Manchuria before the complete withdrawal of troops.

A short time later the American State Department was informed that goods of the British-American Tobacco Company arriving at Dalny and Mukden were subject to duties and likin taxes, from which the shippers of Japanese tobacco were exempt.[35]   The collection of duties at Newchwang, while no customs houses were in operation on the Russo-Manchuria border or at Dairen in the Japanese leased territory, also caused the American State Department to urge upon China, Japan, and Russia the establishment of customs houses at centers where goods entered Manchuria, or to make Newchwang a free port.[36]

The final victory of the peace party in Japan as against the aggressive tendencies of the Militarists,

---

letter to the Secretary of State, April 12, 1906, *Ibid.*, 179.   See also *Ibid.*, 180, memorandum handed to the Secretary of State by the Japanese *Chargé*, April 12, 1906.

[34] In this connection it is interesting to note Mr. Roosevelt's comment with reference to the Japanese and Russians in the conference and negotiations which culminated in the Peace of Portsmouth.   "I am bound to say that the Japanese have impressed me most favorably. . . . .   They have always told me the truth.   They are a very secretive people and I speedily learned that I must never read into anything they said one word more than was actually down in black and white . . . . the Russians . . . . lied so to others that they finally got into the dangerous position of lying to themselves. . . . ."   (Bishop, *op. cit.*, vol. 1, 418.)

[35] United States *Foreign Relations*, (1906), 186

[36] *Ibid.*, (1906) 220-224.

which took place following the return of Marquis Saionji from Manchuria in May, 1906, was another avowal that Japan was seeking to clear Manchuria of her armies as rapidly as possible and to abide by her pledge respecting the "Open Door." An intimate appreciation of the uncomfortable position of the Japanese Government was given at the time by the American Ambassador, Mr. Wright. Nor was the press of Japan blind to the danger threatening the national reputation through "seeming" violations of the doctrine, it being pointed out that when a liberal policy, inevitable from the first, should be adopted, the Japanese would be said to have yielded to pressure rather than to the dictates of their own free judgment and volition.[37]

Agitation among American members of the business community in Shanghai had continued to increase during the early months of 1906 and this was not surprising. The Russo-Japanese War had not served the interests of trade in Manchuria during the course of the conflict, and the foreign business community was impatient to resume commercial activities in north China as soon as fighting had ceased. This was found to be impossible by reason of the military restrictions imposed by the Japanese commander, and a sort of feverish excitement resulted when reports openly accused the Japanese authorities with wilfully excluding American and British traders from Manchuria while their own nationals were permitted to gain a foothold, tending toward a monopoly, under the guise of serving the requirements of the retiring armies. With a view, therefore, of placing the exact situation prevailing in Manchuria before the American Minister, Mr. Rock-

---

[37] *Ibid.*, 194-195, Ambassador Wright to the Secretary of State, No. 8, incl., 3.

hill, at Peking, and through him to the State Department in Washington, three American merchants representing the Shanghai American commercial interests visited Manchuria in June, 1906. These visitors were afforded every facility by the Japanese authorities for pursuing their investigation and on July 2nd their report was submitted to the American Minister.[38] This document is of unusual interest not merely for what it contained, but because certain writers intent on proving a case against Japan have used phrases of the report, which, taken apart from the context, are entirely misleading.

At Newchwang, through which practically all the foreign trade of South Manchuria had hitherto passed, the investigators reported that orderly conditions prevailed under Japanese jurisdiction, and added:

It does not follow that any interference existed on the part of the Japanese authorities administering the foreign settlement with the ordinary customs administration under the Chinese system. . . . No interference on the part of the Japanese with the ordinary course of trade was discovered and adequate facilities which had previously been commanded for military purposes, now exist for the transport of goods by cart and boat on the Liao River. The import trade was, however, in a very depressed condition, as although the stocks were not large, no demand existed from the interior.[39]

[38] Complaints of Shanghai American Commercial Interests concerning conditions in Manchuria. Correspondence forwarded to Washington by Mr. Rockhill in dispatch No. 354, dated Peking, July 18, 1906. United States *Foreign Relations*, (1906), 209 *et seq.*

[39] United States *Foreign Relations*, (1906), 209-12. The investigators dwelt on some factors which they considered adverse to general import trade. These, however, it will be noted, were carefully characterized as "alleged" actions of Japanese in Manchuria. Principal among these was the charge that the Japanese were importing their own merchandise freely into Manchuria by way of Dalny and the South Manchuria Railway, paying neither duty nor likin thereon to the Chinese authorities, and that this privilege was granted only to Japanese subjects. It was alleged that a heavy impost was levied on all goods from Chinese ports entered at Port Arthur and that while other foreign traders had been stopped from doing business in the interior towns of Manchuria the

Referring to a charge made against the Japanese that a heavy likin was exacted on goods going to the interior from Newchwang, an impost which had not been made in the past and from which Japanese traders passing their goods through by rail were exempt, the investigators said they had no proof of the alleged violation despite the fact that the Japanese Government had made available every facility for pursuing the investigation.[40]

Feeling that they were possessed of the most reliable evidence which it would be possible to obtain concerning the Manchurian market the investigators felt constrained to write:

After a most comprehensive inquiry it is most difficult, if not impossible, to offer any satisfactory evidence to substantiate the theory that the Japanese Government, through the instrumentality of either its military or civil authorities, is at present purposely interfering with or placing any obstacles in the path of other nations for the industrial exploitation of this important part of the Chinese Empire.[41]

Bitterness, however, still characterized the attitude of most of the foreign commercial community toward the Japanese in Manchuria and their alleged violations of the principle of equal opportunity for trade and commerce. On August 9th, Viscount Hayashi, Minister of

---

Japanese had free access thereto with their goods upon which they were protected by their authorities from the payment of local levies to which (native) Chinese traders were subject. That this alleged condition of affairs might cease the United States Minister at Peking was urged to advocate: (1) That the Chinese Government be pressed to resume the effective administration of the Manchurian provinces at the earliest possible date; (2) that an efficient Chinese customs administration be established to regulate trade entering the country through the borders now under Japanese and Russian control, and (3) that a uniform system of currency be established.

[40] United States *Foreign Relations*, (1906), 211. From the tenor of the report it would appear that the chief explanation of the slack trade which was particularly harsh on American and British interests, lay in the unsettled condition in which large sections of the country, the scene of recent hostilities, still remained.

[41] United States *Foreign Relations*, (1906) 212.

Foreign Affairs, interviewed by one of Japan's most powerful newspapers, declared that his country would adhere strictly to the principle.   He intimated that parts of Manchuria would be opened as early as September, although by treaty Japan had the right to remain in military occupation until April, 1907.[42]   Ambassador Wright had numerous conversations with Viscount Hayashi during this period and was impressed with the "frankness and fairness" of the Japanese Minister.   There was no doubt in the mind of the American Ambassador as to Japan's policy.   In short he was convinced that equal opportunity for all nations in the trade and commerce of Manchuria was Japan's fixed policy and that this policy would be strictly maintained.[43]   This view was substantiated in dispatches from Minister Rockhill at Peking to the Secretary of State during October.   His intimate association with the progress of affairs in China afforded excellent opportunity for him to judge impartially the motives of the Powers and in particular those of the Japanese. Yet despite the flood of adverse criticism, Mr. Rockhill wrote on October 11th that although the competition of the Japanese for a large share in the markets of South Manchuria would be sharp, he had not the remotest doubt that the United States and other nations interested in the trade would be offered every opportunity to take a full share of it. [44]   With the completion

[42] *Ibid.*, (1906), 216-217.

[43] *Ibid.*, 217. On August 11, 1906, Ambassador Wright wrote to the Secretary of State from Tokyo: "I am persuaded that but comparatively small quantities of Japanese goods are going into Manchuria at this time."

[44] *Ibid.*, 226. Mr. Rockhill pointed out that the Japanese needed capital to develop both Manchuria and Korea. Foreign capital he believed essential to them to insure the success of enterprises such as the South Manchuria Railway. Regarding its own interests from the most selfish of standpoints the Japanese Government would hardly dare to repel foreign assistance or put foreign capital under any disadvantage.

of the evacuation of Manchuria by the armies in April, 1907, and the announcement shortly following that a customs house would be established immediately at Dairen, two of the most serious causes of irritation were removed and the question of Japan's maintenance of the "open Door" in Manchuria ceased to arouse such widespread alarm.[45]

It now seems apparent that the history of the "Open Door" doctrine has been complicated by a great many factors. The interpretation of the original Hay notes has given rise to controversy. The principle of the territorial integrity of China has been confused with the doctrine of the "Open Door" and by many considered an integral part of the doctrine. Failure on the part of critics to define the doctrine clearly has led to such confusion that careless writers have characterized actions which had nothing to do with the "Open Door," as violations of the doctrine. Finally, discussions at the Washington Conference in 1921 revealed that there was a fundamental difference in the interpretations

---

Indicative of American business methods at the time, which had far more to do with the lack of American trade in Manchuria than any alleged actions of the Japanese, is the following statement of Minister Rockhill:

"Unfortunately, our people have not conducted their business in China as other nations do, especially the Japanese and Germans, establishing direct relations with their customers. The greater part of all our merchandise, if we exclude petroleum and a few other articles of trade, is handled by foreign or Japanese firms, who either import them directly from the United States, or get them through commission houses, usually in Shanghai. Our interest in most of our products ceases the day they leave the factory or the port of shipment in the United States. . . . . The little brief excursion recently taken by the American Shanghai merchants to Newchwang and adjacent localities was, I think I am right in saying, the first they had made to a market only 800 miles away, and which they rightly consider one of the most important they have in China. This apparent lack of interest, for it can only be apparent, is recognized by American business men with whom I have spoken as deplorably short-sighted and discriminates more against us than any other cause, be it Japanese or Chinese."

[45] United States *Foreign Relations*, (1907), pt. 1, 130. Minister Rockhill to the Secretary of State, Peking, May 17, 1907, No. 621.

placed upon the original "Open Door" doctrine by the United States and Japan. A discussion, therefore, of the actual status of the doctrine in that period under view requires no further argument to justify it.

The occasion for the "Open Door" notes of John Hay in 1899 was the desire of the United States Government to insure to the commerce and industry of all nations perfect equality of treatment within the Chinese Empire and especially within the so-called "spheres of influence or interest."[46]   In order that this desirable condition of affairs might be brought about the Powers claiming "spheres of influence or interest" and certain other powers were asked to give formal assurances on three specific points. These, as already mentioned, concerned noninterference with a treaty port, equitable administration of the Chinese treaty tariff and avoidance of discrimination in the matter of railway charges and harbor dues.[47]   In his subsequent note of July 3, 1900, Secretary Hay adopted this method of acquainting the powers with the attitude of the United States Government concerning the territorial integrity of the Chinese Empire.[48]   From a technical point of view this communication had nothing to do with the note of 1899. It could not even be considered in the light of an international understanding or *modus vivendi,* for no reply was asked and none received from the Powers, as was the case in the "Open Door" notes. This view is reinforced by the American circular note of January 13, 1905,[49] which stressed the desirability of maintaining two distinct principles contained in America's policy toward China. The framer of this note evidently re-

---

[46] United States *Foreign Relations,* (1889), 138.

[47] *Ibid.,* 138-139.

[48] *Ibid.,* (1900), 299.

[49] *Ibid.,* (1905), 1

garded the situation in this light, and therefore made special reference not only to the "Open Door" but also to the territorial integrity of the Chinese Empire.

By reason of loose interpretation and the use of general terminology, the "Open Door," in a popular sense at least, has come to mean anything and everything involved in the policy of the United States toward China. Regardless of what the explanation of this may be the fact remains that there is no justification for such a view. Secretary Hay's original "Open Door" notes indicated clearly and beyond any shadow of reasonable doubt what were the questions on which the Powers gave formal assurance, and it was the observance of these which the United States considered as constituting an effective "Open Door." Let it be noted further that far from creating a blanket agreement against special interests in China, the "Open Door" notes took cognizance of the existing so-called "spheres of influence or interest" and were intended as a guarantee against certain types of action in the "sphere" where it was claimed special privileges were to be enjoyed. Although these privileges were not very clearly defined they had to do largely with railway and mining rights.[50] The "spheres of influence" continued to exist side by side with the "Open Door" doctrine, the only change being that the actions of the Powers within their respective "spheres" were limited by the three specific stipulations contained in Secretary Hay's notes of 1899.

---

[50] An examination of the note addressed by Secretary Hay to Great Britain (United States *Foreign Relations*, [1899,] 131-133) reveals that the United States Government was concerned primarily with a sincere desire that the interests of its citizens should not be prejudiced through *exclusive* treatment by any of the controlling Powers within their so-called "spheres of interest" in China. The same note states that the "Government of the United States will in no way commit itself to a recognition of *exclusive* rights of any power" in China.

Lack of evidence on the basis of which Japan could be convicted of violation of the letter of the "Open Door" has led some writers to find cases of violation in spirit. From the legal standpoint the only act which could constitute a violation of the doctrine in spirit would be one which wilfully prevented the realization of the purpose sought through the three stipulations of the original Hay notes.[51] There would seem to be no room for controversy on this point, since there is no doubt as to the actual meaning of the three stipulations, which again impresses one with the belief that had the doctrine been broader in scope than actually specified the existence of "spheres of influence" would have been entirely incompatible with it.[52]

During the period under review in this chapter, and in fact until 1921, Japan interpreted the "Open Door" doctrine in the light of the note which John Hay addressed to Mr. Buck in Tokyo on November 13, 1899, and from a technical point of view this note required nothing other than a fulfillment of the three definitely worded and specific provisions. It would seem, too, that in January, 1905, the American Government had no idea of confusing the principle of the territorial integrity of China with the "Open Door" for both were specifically mentioned as separate and distinct. The evidence does not indicate, however, whether the State Department had broadened its interpretation of the three stipulations of the original Hay notes. At the Washington Conference, however, Baron Shidehara, representing Japan, speaking on January 18, 1922, before the Committee on Pacific and Far Eastern Questions, noted that the principle of the "Open Door"

[51] Crandall, *Treaties, Their Making and Enforcement*, 371-372.
[52] As is the case under the Nine Power Treaty of 1922.

had undergone considerable changes in its application since it had originally been initiated by Secretary Hay. He added that it was then limited in scope both as concerning its subject matter and the area of Chinese territory to which it applied. On the other hand the principles formulated in the draft Resolution, which was at the time before the Committee, were of an entirely different scope from the policy of the "Open Door" as conceived in 1899.[53] To this statement Mr. Hughes, the chairman of the Committee, replied that while Secretary Hay presented certain definite points in the proposal he made, he made it clear what was the scope and purpose of the policy that he advocated.[54] The United States, therefore, did not regard the statement of principles recorded in the Resolution before the Committee as a new statement but rather as a more definite and precise wording of the principle that had long been admitted, and to which the Powers concerned had given their unqualified adherence for twenty years.[55] And so the question of the "Open Door" in any period of its application is complicated by varying interpretations which the Powers have placed upon it and in the case of the United States and Japan it is now evident that a definite conflict in interpretation existed. More will be said on this point in subsequent chapters in which there will be an attempt to examine Japanese action in Manchuria in the light of her declarations made during 1906 and 1907.[56]

---

[53] *Conference on the Limitation of Armament*, 1250.

[54] *Ibid.*, 1254.

[55] *Ibid.*, 1258-1260.

[56] In connection with the interpretation of the "Open Door" given in this chapter it is interesting to note that Tyler Dennett, (Americans in Eastern Asia, 647 and 648) makes the following statement, in answer to the question, what had the United States obtained by the "Open Door" negotiations of 1899-1900:

"Not so much as is popularly supposed. The United States had not secured more than already accrued to it under the 'most-favored-nation' clauses in the treaties. The preferential railway and mining privileges had in no way been disturbed. Although the United States expressly stipulated that it did not recognize the spheres of influence the replies to the notes had in each case afforded an opportunity of reaffirming that there were such spheres . . . . as a matter of fact only the partition of the Empire had been halted. The Hay notes, which are believed to have been drafted by Rockhill, were as significant in their omissions as in their contents. . . . . . These notes have been popularly mislabeled. They did not secure a complete open door. . . . . The United States was making no specific demand for the open door for investments. . . . . The United States merely demanded an open door for trade in that part of China in which American merchants were already interested. . . . ."

CHAPTER IX

RAILWAY POLITICS IN MANCHURIA, 1907-1910

It is not surprising that in the years immediately following the Russo-Japanese War the subject of railway politics played such an all-important part in the Manchurian question. From the period of 1905, international relationships in the "Three Eastern Provinces" have involved intimately a greater number of Powers than formerly, and as a result have become more complicated. The old Manchurian problem, that which pertained to the period when Russia alone claimed the country as her "sphere of influence," had now given place to the creation of a dual "sphere" with Russian influence pushed to the less important north, while Japan, now in possession of the former Russian leasehold and railway in the south, became dominant there.

The Russo-Japanese War had not been fought without centering the vision of sections of the business world on Manchuria. The Russian method of exploitation during the years in which she pushed southward to Dalny, and later when she had established a virtual protectorate over the country, had not been conducive to international trade. The great bulk of the export trade in the south had centered at Newchwang, but the political situation which had existed from 1900 to 1905 gave no encouragement to the stabilization or development of markets. The course of the war changed this situation. The victory of Japan was regarded as a triumph for free and unrestricted business competition in the former Russian "sphere." The war had temporarily destroyed the entire Manchurian market and this fact served to enhance the value of that market in the eyes of those who had traded there or who wished now to extend their commercial operations to this market. Thus when peace was made there were powerful commercial interests in the Far East prepared to resume and expand their trade in the "Three Eastern Provinces." When, therefore, these interests found that the market would not be open to them until the Japanese armies had been withdrawn, their impatience knew no bounds and unfortunately they spared no effort to accuse Japan of all kinds of willful discrimination. However, it was not surprising that both American and British interests, who with the Japanese were most closely involved in the Manchurian trade, should become alarmed at what to them appeared as a direct attempt to close the door to international trade. As already stated, repeated assurances by Japan that she would observe the "Open Door" did not dispel this impression, nor did the investigation of American business men from Shanghai put an end to the rumors. Even Japan's actual observance of the stipulations of the Portsmouth Treaty prior to April, 1907, failed to assure these interests that they would have free access to the market.

All this was indicative of a new spirit of competition in Manchuria, and Japan's position there was regarded with great jealousy. Of this there can be no doubt. Furthermore, every act of the Tokyo Government which seemed to increase its own influence in Manchuria called forth denunciation of Japan's continental imperialism. In the struggle for trade supremacy existing in China such a result was inevitable, as the course of events was soon to show.[1]

---

[1] In this connection it will be well for the reader to disassociate from his mind any preconceived ideas respecting the international position and motives

Having fought the war largely over the question of Russian influence in Manchuria, Japan, it must be assumed, attached considerable strategical importance to the region of the "Three Eastern Provinces." It was natural also that her political interests in Manchuria should increase with the transfer to her of the Russian leasehold and railway. Nevertheless, it must also be assumed that Japan's policy of developing Manchuria was largely promoted by economic motives. The South Manchuria Railway Company, which was to be the chief agency of Japanese progress there, was merely a joint-stock company, the primary, if not the sole business of which was to make money. This could only be accomplished by a natural and healthy development of the territory through which it ran, and to this end the Japanese administration directed all its efforts. This should be borne clearly in mind for it was on the basis of this policy that acts of the Japanese, which were later called in question, are to be understood. Even as early as October, 1906, it appeared to observers in a position to judge intelligently of Far Eastern events, that Japan would offer every opportunity to other nations to participate in the trade of South Manchuria. This policy was doubtless purely utilitarian, for above all else, Japan needed capital to develop her enterprises and an ever increasing business, to make profitable the venture of the South Manchuria line.[2]

Because of all these circumstances Japan probably argued that prior to the extension of railway lines in Manchuria a paying traffic should be created for the line she was already operating. With the natural out-

---

of the Powers during the period under review. A careful reading of this chapter should establish whether these ideas are tenable in the light of what we know concerning the diplomacy of the period.

[2] United States *Foreign Relations*, (1906), 226. Minister Rockhill to the Secretary of State, No. 427.

let of her leased territory at Dairen, Japan was also concerned lest Newchwang, the old treaty port and outlet of the Chinese railway in the west, should prevent the growth of export business by way of the South Manchuria line. A policy, which while observing the principle of the "Open Door," would tend to establish legitimately Japanese commercial supremacy in Manchuria, did not appear unnatural to the nation.[3] If the interests of any foreign power were to be recognized there, Japan felt justly that she had the prior right. This right she believed was reinforced by reason of the

---

[3] Another factor in Japan's special position in South Manchuria is also worthy of attention. On none of the foreign-loan-built railways of China was American material permitted to compete, except in rare and insignificant cases. The argument has been pressed by the enemies of Japanese-American friendship that Japan would pursue a similar policy in her sphere of influence in Manchuria as regards the development of her railway lines there. But the fact that such is not the case is demonstrated by the following official statement from the books of the South Manchuria Railway Company:

VALUE OF PURCHASES OF MATERIAL MADE BY SOUTH MANCHURIA RAILWAY, 1907-1908 UNTIL AUGUST 1, 1920

Administrative Year	Material imported direct from the U.S.	Total of material bought by the Company	Percentage of direct imports from the U. S.
	Yen	Yen	Per cent
1907-1908............	18,917,580.93	28,430,902.82	67
1908-1909............	959,321.17	6,350,381.10	15
1909-1910............	642,723.57	12,995,215.52	5
1910-1911............	582,815.38	11,749,425.44	5
1911-1912............	865,005.34	9,290,849.11	9
1912-1913............	548,711.40	5,255,170.91	10
1913-1914............	946,601.21	9,112,582.05	10
1914-1915............	781,836.69	5,694,479.55	14
1915-1916............	2,275,230.48	9,629,702.81	24
1916 1917............	3,099,585.54	18,036,199.53	17
1917-1918............	13,775,597.86	39,650,411.70	35
1918-1919............	26,460,773.36	70,166,326.10	38
1919-1920............	16,152,885.07	50,544,421.97	32
1920 (4 months only)..	1,805,440.19	7,798,782.73	23
Grand Total......	87,814,108.19	284,703,851.43	31

(Rea, "Daylight in Manchuria," in *The Far Eastern Review*, November, 1920.)

war she had just fought, and lastly there were natural economic grounds that under conditions of free competition among nations in the Manchurian market would tend to establish Japanese commercial supremacy.[4]

---

[4] No foreign nation save Japan had any considerable export trade in Manchuria; Japan's demands for the products of Manchuria had been instrumental in enabling the latter to import increasing quantities of merchandise of western nations; to the opening of the Japanese market had been due largely the remarkable development of Manchuria, and this mutual dependence and development between Japan and Manchuria was bound to increase. This may be assumed to be the case confronting Japan in her new field of action. (Asakawa, "Japan in Manchuria," *Yale Review*, November, 1908, 275-276.)

That Japanese trade supremacy in Manchuria was due to natural economic causes and not to her alleged policy of discrimination and violation of the "Open Door" is supported by the figures in the following tables:

TABLE SHOWING TOTAL VALUE OF ALL ARTICLES EXPORTED FROM AND IMPORTED TO NEWCHWANG (DIRECT) TO AND FROM FOREIGN COUNTRIES DURING THE YEARS NOTED.

Country	Exports	(lbs.)	Imports (pounds sterling)	
	1900	1901	1900	1901
United Kingdom....	531	149	491	37
United States.......	....	....	55,014	7,396
Japan..............	526,108	970,663	192,428	247,624
Hong Kong........	66,135	88,356	150,714	357,695
	1902		1903	
	Exports	Imports	Exports	Imports
United Kingdom....	252	5,901	1,670	6,172
Hong Kong........	78,573	385,302	91,584	372,565
United States.......	....	4,089	....	14,607
Japan..............	1,041,395	280,843	1,235,262	324,947
	1904		1905	
United Kingdom....	5,439	320	5,188	2,763
Hong Kong........	64,270	393,364	67,162	623,583
United States.......	....	....	....	67,668
Japan..............	155,051	205,034	937,227	*773,179
	1906		Average 5 years	1898-1903 excluding 1900
United Kingdom....	20,716	2,079	573	8,773
Hong Kong........	379,734	82,158	81,714	299,710
Japan..............	383,847	1,109,984	1,081,670	239,313
United States.......	178,612	1	....	33,356

* Including Formosa.

(Diplomatic and Consular Reports, China, 1901, 1904, 1905, and 1906 in *Accounts and Papers*, vols. CVI, XCVII, LXXXVIII, and CXXIII.)

In its final analysis, therefore, the policy of the Japanese Government in Manchuria centered about three points:

1. The best interests of Japan in South Manchuria would be served through the successful development of the South Manchuria Railway.

2. While claiming South Manchuria as a "sphere of interest" the "Open Door" would be observed toward the trade and commerce of all nations.

3. Japanese influence in South Manchuria must be strong enough to prevent the recurrence of such diplomatic chaos as had characterized Manchurian affairs between 1898 and 1905.

Bearing in mind these basic points, which the Tokyo Government considered essential to the preservation of peace in Manchuria, and the safeguarding of Japan's special interests on the continent, we are now in a position to turn to the international situation once more, this time as manifested in railway politics.

The reactions of Chinese diplomacy toward the Japanese advance in Manchuria during the years under review were of varied character. This subject will be dealt with at length in the following chapter. Suffice it to say here that Peking did not take kindly to the new masters of Liaotung, and in the main the efforts of Chinese officialdom were directed to making the position of Japan in Manchuria a most difficult one. An example of this type of Chinese diplomacy is found in the case of the Hsinmintun-Fakumen Railway controversy.

The idea of extending the Imperial Railways of north China from Hsinmintun (west of Mukden) to Fakumen had long been considered. Fakumen was originally one of the gates in the palisade constructed during the Ming dynasty from the Great Wall in a northeasterly direction across the Sungari and beyond, to keep back the Mongol hordes. It had now become a town of some importance and a favorable point from which to develop trade to the south or from which a line might be extended into the rich grain country of the north.[5] It was in the spring of 1907 that the subject of the Fakumen extension was again discussed in Peking. The whole affair was surrounded with secrecy; so much so that the Japanese Government received no intimation of what was in progress until August when negotiations between the Peking Government and the British construction firm of Pauling and Company, for the building of the line, were well under way.[6] Japan immediately warned Peking that on the basis of the protocol annexed to the Peking Treaty of December 22, 1905, the Hsinmintun-Fakumen scheme was unacceptable.[7] This warning had no effect on the Chinese Government for the negotiations with Pauling and Company continued. The Japanese warning was repeated in October, calling forth an evasive reply from Peking. Again in November Japan, for the third time, cautioned Peking that the extension to Fakumen would not be acceptable, but instead of heeding this China secretly concluded a contract with the construction firm almost simultaneously with the receipt of the third warning from Tokyo.[8] By November when this contract was signed China had sent T'ang Shao-yi to

---

[5] Kent, *Railway Enterprise in China*, 74.

[6] Kawakami, *American-Japanese Relations*, 80.

[7] The clause referred to by Japan follows: "The Chinese Government engage for the purpose of protecting the interests of the South Manchuria Railway, not to construct, prior to the recovery by them of the said railway, any main line in the neighborhood of and parallel to that railway, or any branch line which might be prejudicial to the interests of the above mentioned railway." *Manchuria, Treaties and Agreements*, 83.

[8] Bland, *Recent Events and Present Policies in China*, 219.

Manchuria as Governor of Mukden where he was to assist the Viceroy in resisting the advance of Japanese influence. Possessed of a masterful personality T'ang soon dominated Mukden, and it became a part of his policy (of which more will be said later) to hamper Japan by the establishment of British and American vested rights especially in the matter of railways and mines. Part of T'ang's policy consisted in promoting the Hsinmintun-Fakumen railway extension, which he eventually intended to continue northward to Tsitsihar. This would allow the development of a vast fertile region by the North China Railway system and Tientsin, instead of by the Japanese lines and Dairen.[9] There is no doubt but that China was fully aware she was violating a treaty stipulation and that Japan's opposition would most certainly be encountered. Not only did Peking know of Japan's attitude, but T'ang Shao-yi himself, at the time he signed the secret contract, had in his possession a copy of the official dispatch addressed to the Chinese Foreign Office by the Japanese Minister in Peking stating explicity the position of the Tokyo Government.[10]

In February, 1908, Japan proposed to indorse the extension if China would promise to extend the line to Tiehling or some other suitable point on the South Manchuria Railway. China refused and suggested that the question be referred to the tribunal at the Hague.[11] Japan declined to accept this solution and the matter came to a deadlock, until toward the summer of 1909 China abandoned the scheme. The controversy was finally settled by the Chino-Japanese agreement of September 4, 1909. By article 1 of this

---

[9] *Ibid.*, 218-219.
[10] *Ibid.*, 219.
[11] Kawakami, *op. cit.*, 86.

agreement China engaged, in the event of undertaking to construct a railway between Hsinmintun and Fakumen, to arrange previously concerning it with the Japanese Government.[12]

It seems proper at this point to discuss in detail some of the questions raised by this attempt of China to extend her northern railways, and the opposition furnished by Japan. It is reasonable to ask, in the first place, whether there was any justification for Japan's protest. Great Britain as the ally of Japan, and because it was a British firm to which China had granted the concession for the Hsinmintun-Fakumen extension, was deeply interested in the controversy. Questions were asked in the House of Commons as to the attitude of the Government, to which Sir Edward Grey replied on March 3, 1908, that Japan was not contesting the right in principle of China to extend her railway system west of the Liao River. Japan, he said, was opposing the application for the construction of a particular line on the ground that an agreement was arrived at in 1905 between China and Japan by which the former country engaged not to construct any main line of railway in the neighborhood of and parallel to the South Manchuria Railway or any branch line which might be prejudicial to that railway. The existence of that agreement (the secret protocol to the Treaty of Peking, December 22, 1905) he added, was not disputed by the Chinese Government. In conclusion Sir Edward said it was open to the contractors (Pauling and Company) to prove, if they could do so, to the satisfaction of Japan that the proposed line would not prejudice the South Manchuria Railway, and so would not violate the agreement.[13] The position of the British Government was

---

[12] *Manchuria, Treaties and Agreements*, 129.
[13] *Parliamentary Debates*, March 3, 1908, vol. 185, 527.

thus clear and unassailable. It will be recalled that the British Foreign Office had received a copy of the so-called "secret" protocols during April, 1906. They had been communicated by the Japanese Minister for Foreign Affairs to Mr. Wilson, *Charge d' Affaires* of the United States at Tokyo, and by him transmitted to the Department of State under date of February 16, 1906.[14] It is hardly reasonable, therefore, to regard them as "secret" nor could the American and British Governments have been unprepared for action which Japan would take, should China violate the agreement.

In the light of the international diplomacy in Manchuria from the latter part of 1907 to 1910, it is evident that political rather than economic motives prompted China to grant the Hsinmintun-Fakumen concession to a British firm. It has been claimed, and probably with some truth, that the extension had long been considered in Peking.[15] It is evident that the Fakumen line would have opened to agricultural development a fertile and promising country. Yet it is also true that China granted the concession at a time when the profitable operation of Manchuria railways was still a question of doubt. The concession was given in violation of an agreement, which present evidence indicates to have been a valid agreement. Finally it was given to a British firm, whose government was Japan's

---

[14] Millard, *Our Eastern Question*, App. F., 430-433. The defense of China, when she did call in question the validity of the protocols, was weak. On January 28, 1908, T'ang Shao-yi, "who signed the Peking agreement" is stated to have denied there was a clause debarring China from paralleling the South Manchurian road. He stated that the question had been discussed and references to it in the minutes of the conference were simply a record of the discussion. *(Ibid,* 433.) Attempting to build a case for China writers have become involved in a mass of statement and misstatement. In the above reference T'ang Shao-yi is spoken of as the negotiator of the Peking Agreement, in another case (see Millard, *America and the Far Eastern Question*, 250-251) he is referred to correctly as the secretary to the Chinese negotiators.

[15] Kent, *op. cit.,* 74.

first ally. Less outstanding facts than these would substantiate the theory that China was playing a political game. If she could interest British and American capital in seeking exclusive concessions in Manchuria, especially if these were in violation of agreements between China and Japan, there was reason to believe that the relations between Japan on the one hand and Great Britain and the United States, jealous of their trade in Manchuria, on the other, might be strained to a point of advantage if not actual rupture. At all events, Peking argued that it was a safe game to seek for British and American interests in Manchurian railways at the expense of Japanese. This, in fact, was the conclusion of contemporary writers.[16] Nor did the seed of political unrest thus scattered by China fall on stony ground. During the months of 1907 and 1908 in which the Hsinmintun-Fakumen controversy was at its height, Willard Straight, then consul-general of the United States at Mukden, kept himself intimately informed on these negotiations. To his mind they seemed to offer an opportunity for the realization of Mr. Harriman's plans and for the creation of Anglo-American-Russian cooperation in Manchuria. For some reason, which we will discuss later, Straight believed a combination of this kind to be necessary, for he did not consider the United States was politically strong enough to counterbalance Japanese influence.[17]

---

[16] Kawakami, *op. cit.*, 86, believed that China's object was to create friction among the Powers; Bland, *op. cit.*, 218, says that the Hsinmintun-Fakumen concession was part of T'ang Shao-yi's scheme for arresting Japan's policy of peaceful penetration into Manchuria. Harrison, *Peace or War East of Baikal*, 176, considered the later scheme of the Chinchow-Aigun Railway as more of a political than a business affair. This route was further removed from the Japanese line than the Fakumen extension. The inference concerning the Hsinmintun-Fakumen road as a political or economic scheme, is clear.

[17] Graves, "An American in Asia," in *Asia*, February, 1921, 160-161.

Taking the most charitable view possible of Chinese diplomacy at this period, makes it impossible to ignore the political motives which affected the Peking authorities in the entire course of this unfortunate affair. It is too much to suppose that China had forgotten the "secret" protocols which made the granting of the extension to Fakumen illegal and impossible. Mr. J. O. P. Bland, who signed the concession, is emphatic in his statement that China knew well what the results of her action would entail. There can be little doubt, therefore, that China was playing a political game. She hoped that Japan would not dare to oppose British interests. A notoriously corrupt government in Peking was testing the Anglo-Japanese Alliance on the basis of its own political standards.

It has been claimed that Japan's whole attitude toward the Hsinmintun-Fakumen road was in violation of the pledge given by the Tokyo and St. Petersburg Governments in the Portsmouth Treaty, namely, "not to obstruct any general measures common to all countries which China may take for the development of the commerce and industry of Manchuria.[18] Such a charge seems hardly justifiable for it is pertinent to ask the question,—was a secret concession awarded to a British construction company in violation of a treaty stipulation, a general measure common to all countries. The answer is obvious. The charge that the action of Japan was in violation of principles set forth in the Anglo-Japanese Alliance of 1905,[19] was certainly not recognized by the British Government, and as to there being an implication to disregard the "Open Door" in Manchuria[20] it is interesting to recall two facts. First,

---

[18] Hornbeck, *Contemporary Politics in the Far East*, 259.

[19] *Ibid.*, 259.

[20] *Ibid.*, 259.

the "Open Door" doctrine, as enunciated by John Hay, had nothing whatsoever to do with railway construction. Secondly, the original "Open Door" notes recognized the "spheres of interest or influence"[21] and limited the actions of the power claiming such "sphere" in three specific stipulations. These stipulations, however, did not touch upon the original "special interests" which gave rise to the "spheres," namely, priority in railway and mining rights.[22]

Apart from China and Japan, Great Britain was the only power interested to any considerable degree in the Hsinmintun-Fakumen affair. But the scope of railway politics in Manchuria soon broadened and from 1907 to 1910 the dollar diplomacy of American financial interests played the leading and most spectacular part. Willard Straight, who was intimately connected with Mr. Harriman and the New York financial group composed of J. P. Morgan and Company; Kuhn Loeb and Company, the First National Bank and the National City Bank of New York, while at the same time he was the consul-general of this country at Mukden, decided in August, 1907, to act upon plans he had conceived for the advance of American interests, commercial and political, in Manchuria.[23] He therefore drew up an outline of agreement, which would give to American interests the contract for a loan of some $20,000,000, carrying with it the right to establish a Manchurian Bank to cooperate with the Manchurian Government. The bank was to be the financial agent of the Man-

---

[21] Yen, *The Open Door Policy*, 53.

[22] Some authorities commenting on this period have entirely neglected the fact that in 1899 China had agreed with Russia that in the event of railways being constructed north of the Great Wall, Russian capital was to be employed. This right was transferred to Japan after the Russo-Japanese War. (*Manchuria, Treaties and Agreements*, 55.)

[23] Bland, *op. cit.*, 311.

churian administration in mining, timber, agricultural development, and the construction of certain railways.[24] This scheme was communicated to Mr. Harriman in September, 1907, but financial conditions prevented any action at the time. The next year Straight returned to the United States, at the request of Harriman, but before leaving Mukden he signed a memorandum of agreement for a $20,000,000 loan along the lines outlined the year previously. At the same time China sent T'ang Shao-yi to the United States as special ambassador to thank the American Government for the return of a portion of the Boxer indemnity. The real purpose of his visit was to complete the negotiations for the loan for which Straight had concluded the preliminary agreement.

A new factor entered the situation on Nevember 30, 1908. This was an exchange of notes between the United States and Japan known as the Root-Takahira Agreement stipulating for mutual respect of each other's interests in the Far East.[25] In November also both

[24] Graves, *op. cit.*, 161.

[25] United States *Foreign Relations*, (1908), 510-511.

"Willard Straight was an official in the employment of the State Department. He could not negotiate with financiers for the investment of American capital in China unless the Secretary of State authorized the negotiations. . . . . There was manifestly some hesitation on Mr. Root's part in lending official support to the project. . . . . The Secretary was disposed to back up an enterprise which looked towards American entrance into Manchuria by means of the "Open Door," but he was at the time negotiating an agreement with Japan, and he did not want to assume an attitude or to lend vigorous assistance to a project which would arouse Japanese opposition. While, consequently, he had no objection to the submission of Tang's plan to Mr. Harriman and he was willing to approve of it from the point of view of American national interest, he did not wish Mr. Harriman to venture in as a result of any positive encouragement from the government. The initiative and the responsibility were to be Mr. Harriman's. The State Department was to play the part of a complacent abettor. . . . . The attitude of the American Government changed later, but it was not the originator of the plan for seeking the extension of American influence in China by suggesting or by urging the investment of American capital. The initiative and the energy came from two individuals, Edward Harriman and Willard Straight." *(Croly, Willard Straight*, 270-271.)

the Empress Dowager and the Emperor Kuang Hsu
died suddenly. Yuan who had been supporting T'ang's
mission to the United States was unable to retain
power under the Regent, Prince Chung. He accordingly retired from office in January, 1909, and T'ang
left the United States shortly afterward.[26] But while
China had given up the idea of completing the loan negotiations, the American financiers were now thoroughly interested in the development of Mr. Harriman's plans. These were none other than the original
scheme of 1905, with an alternative scheme that conferences held early in 1909 had provided. A definite
contract was to be secured from the Chinese Government for the building of another railroad in Manchuria
which might be used as a threat to force the sale of the
Japanese and Russian lines. If this failed it might still
be built as an alternative line.[27] Straight had already

---

[26] Graves, op. cit., 161-162.

[27] Ibid., 162. Straight tells of these developments as follows: "In November, Mr. Schiff, who was in close touch with Mr. Gregory Wilenkin, formerly
the Russian financial agent in the United States and, then the Russian agent
in Japan, had been advised that there was still some possibility that Russia
would be willing to sell the Chinese Eastern Railway, if Japan would agree to
sell her Manchurian line. Mr. Schiff wrote to his friend Baron Shibusawa, to
ask whether the Japanese would be willing . . . . to sell the South Manchuria Railway to American interests provided the Russians would sell the
Chinese Eastern Railway. This proposition the Japanese turned down."

The fantastic not to say absurd proportions of the whole Harriman plan
were outlined after the latter's death in a letter from Straight to J. P. Morgan
and Company and to Kuhn, Loeb and Company.

"The proposition (Mr. Harriman's plan) was as follows: The Russian
Government and the French interest in the Russo-Chinese Bank are not satisfied with the present policy and position of that institution into which a large
German element has been introduced. It is proposed therefore either (a) to
inject new life and thus oust German control or (b) to extend the activities of
the semi-government Siberian Bank to Manchuria and China in order to check
the growth of Japanese influence. In either case English and American, together with French capital, would be used to bolster waning Russian prestige
in the Orient, besides insuring for themselves the political support of the Russian government in their enterprises in Manchuria and Mongolia.

"Leaving Siberia out of the discussion, the most promising field for the
Group's Eastern activities would be Manchuria and Mongolia. It should in

these regions be possible to act as partners, not as lenders alone, for the political situation, particularly in the former, forces China to grant terms more favorable than could be secured elsewhere, while in neither region is popular sentiment, a growing obstacle to foreign investment in the South, an important factor.

"These being the premises the following program is suggested:

"I. Co-operating Anglo-American interests should, as already proposed, secure the contract for financing, constructing and operating the Chinchow-Amur Railway, Russian political acquiescence, at least, if not support, being assured either by permitting the Russo-Chinese Bank to handle Pauling's construction accounts or by giving that institution a share in the flotation.

"II. The Manchurian Bank should be taken up as part of the general scheme, but would not necessarily be the next step which should be—

"III. The purchase of the Chinese Eastern Railway by the Chino-American British Company which shall operate the Chinchow-Amur Line. Prior to such purchase the American Government should interchange with Russia notes similar to those exchanged with Japan on November 30, 1908. Russia, in order to secure such a political entente, would be willing before selling the railway to withdraw the railway guards and recognize fully China's sovereignty and administrative right within the so-called 'Railway Settlements' over which the Chinese Eastern Railway now claims jurisdiction.

"IV. The withdrawal of the railway guards and the abandonment of the claim to administrative rights would force Japan in view of her obligations under the Treaty of Portsmouth and the Komura Agreement either to follow suit or to stand convicted of international bad faith.

"Considering her alliance with England the Russo-Japanese and Anglo-Russian ententes and the notes exchanged with us in November last, Japan's opposition to a Russo-American entente would hardly be a diplomatic probability. The possible extension of a participation which would satisfy Japanese 'amour propre' and not produce Chinese distrust, timely reference to the contract which Mr. Harriman signed for the joint operation of the South Manchurian Railway and which was ignored but never cancelled by Japan and the judicious manipulation of the American and European attitude toward the war loan conversion and treaty revision which Japan now contemplates, should render impossible any overt act of hostility or any very serious intrigue which could in any way be attributed to Japan."

The entire scheme, as may be seen at a glance, was to force the hand of the Japanese. There was no possibility of the Japanese giving a willing consent, and Straight must have had some conception of the limits of American action in such matters. His belief in the Harriman proposal was simply indicative of a brilliant imagination carried away by a grand American project. As Mr. Croly himself points out, "It was unreasonable to ask Japan to surrender valuable privileges without a 'quid pro quo' or without preparing for the use, if necessary, of some form of compulsion." (Croly, *Williard Straight*, 306 et seq.)

The influence which the visit of Count Ito to Harbin might have had upon the subsequent negotiations concerning Manchuria is commented upon by Mr. Croly in the following words: "Mr. Harriman had approached the Russian Government through its Department of Finance, and this Department was at that time favorable to the idea of selling the Chinese Eastern Railway. M. Kokovtsoff was as good as his word. He arranged and held a conference with

prepared a memorandum concerning the acquisition of the two lines (the South Manchuria and the Chinese Eastern Railway) and T'ang Shao-yi had informed him that China would co-operate with an international syndicate in purchasing the lines on behalf of the Peking Government. It was this memorandum which Straight believed (probably correctly) was the basis of the Knox neutralization proposal.[28]

To secure as strong representation as possible in their Far Eastern activities the American group, already referred to, was organized early in June, 1909. Mr. Harriman died during September, but despite this fact plans of the American Group went forward and on October 2, 1909, Straight, together with Pauling and Company, signed with the Viceroy of Manchuria an agreement for the construction of a railroad from Chinchow on the Gulf of Liaotung to Aigun on the Amur. The road was to be financed by the American Group while construction was in the hands of Pauling and Company, who had received the original concession from the Chinese Government for the Hsinmintun-Fakumen extension.[29]

With the death of Harriman, however, the genius of this dangerous and futile scheme was gone. An im-

---

Prince Ito at Harbin just previous to the assassination of that statesman. Prince Ito had been one of the Japanese political leaders who in 1905 had favored the sale of the South Manchuria Railway to Mr. Harriman. When the two men met they discussed among other subjects the possibility of an agreement between Russia and Japan for a less exclusive policy in Manchuria." (Croly, *Williard Straight*, 310-311.)

However, it is to be noted that it was Ito's visit to Harbin that paved the way for the later co-operation between Japan and Russia in July, 1910. In fact, it was alleged that Japan and Russia had exchanged notes late in 1909 wherein the two Powers discussed the question of opposition to the Chinchow-Aigun project. This, however, seems to have been one phase of a campaign carried on by the Jingo press in Japan. Harrison, *Peace or War East of Baikal*, 340-41.)

[28] Graves, *op. cit.*, 162-163.
[29] *Ibid.*, 163.

perial edict approving the preliminary agreement was issued on January 21, 1910,[30] but on the same day the Russian and Japanese Governments declined to enter the neutralization plan which had been proposed in the meantime by the American State Department.[31] Nevertheless negotiations were pursued for the drawing up of a final agreement for the Chinchow-Aigun railway but as Japan and Russia had formally protested against the scheme at Peking, the agreement was not signed.[32] Straight went to St. Petersburg in the summer of 1910 in the hope of reaching some understanding with the Russians. Nothing came of this move and with the British Government taking an attitude decidedly favorable to claims of Japan and Russia, there remained little hope for the success of the project. The British Government had been pressed to take an active part in promoting the Chinchow-Aigun railway but on March 23, 1910, Sir Edward Grey stated in Parliament that His Majesty's Government was unable to do so, as it was bound to pay some regard to provisions of the Anglo-Russian agreement of 1899.[33] Nor did the British Government find anything unreasonable in the attitude of either Russia or Japan.[34]

The British Government, in fact, took an entirely sympathetic attitude toward the views of both these powers. It was bound to the former by the Anglo-Japanese Alliance, and its action was governed in respect to the latter by the Scott-Muravieff notes of 1899. Sir Edward Grey's view of the whole Manchurian trouble was explained in the House of Commons on

---

[30] *Manchuria, Treaties and Agreements*, 140.

[31] United States *Foreign Relations*, ser. 5946, 248-251.

[32] Bland, *op. cit.*, 320, and United States *Foreign Relations*, ser. 5945, 255.

[33] *Parliamentary Debates*, (C) March 23, 1910, vol. 15, 1037.

[34] *Parliamentary Debates* (C) April 27, 1910, vol. 17, 426.

June 15, 1910, and this tended to clarify the situation, although questions continued to be asked the Government.[35]

During the course of the Chinchow-Aigun railway controversy, the American Government had advanced a suggestion to the Powers concerning Manchurian railways which has come to be known as the Knox's neutralization proposal, and it now remains to describe in some detail this vain attempt on the part of the United States to settle the Far Eastern question. On October 7, 1909, the American State Department was informed of the preliminary agreement for the Chinchow-Aigun railway, which had been signed at Mukden on October 2nd.[36] One month later, on November 6th, a note of Secretary Knox was presented to the British Government stating two comprehensive pro-

---

[35] *Parliamentary Debates* (C) June 15, 1910, vol. 17, 1389. Sir Edward explained at length that the Chinchow-Aigun railway was promoted by American financiers and a British firm of contractors, who had applied and had been promised a concession from the Chinese Government. To this Sir Edward had no objection to offer, but he did object when asked to bring diplomatic pressure to bear on the Chinese Government to put this agreement into effect. The obstacle to such action lay in the understanding between Great Britain and Russia respecting railway construction in North China. Sir Edward made it clear, however, that the agreement did not obligate the British Government to discourage British firms from applying for or promoting railways in Manchuria.

He pointed out that the Chinchow-Aigun railway as proposed was to cross the Russian line in North Manchuria and extend to the Russian frontier. The British Government, therefore, in the face of the Anglo-Russian agreement could not take an active part in supporting the proposed line until the Chinese Government had come to terms with Russia concerning it.

As to Japan, Sir Edward said that nation had not opposed the line in principle, but had asked for participation, which he considered a reasonable demand on the part of Japan. Had Japan stated that she wished a railway monopoly in Manchuria there would have been a distinct breach of the Open Door, he believed. If she made use of her position there to give preferential rates to her own people as against others, that again would have been a breach of the Open Door. But when Japan states that she has an interest in Manchuria, which justifies her in wishing for participation in railways which to some extent may compete with the Japanese line, it could hardly be considered an unreasonable demand.

[36] United States *Foreign Relations*, (1910) ser. 5945, 231.

posals.[37] The first of these proposed that the Manchurian railways be placed under an impartial administration by some plan investing in China the ownership of the railroads through funds loaned for the purpose by interested powers. The plan provided that an international syndicate of the participating powers should supervise the railroad systems during the term of the loan to China. The second proposal provided that in case the first suggestion was not entirely feasible, then the British and United States Governments might support diplomatically the Chinchow-Aigun arrangement and invite interested powers to participate in financing and constructing the line. The first of a number of serious blunders that characterized American diplomacy in the neutralization scheme was to be found in this, the first note. Secretary Knox referred to the completed agreement concerning the Chinchow-Aigun Railway, which as a matter of fact had not been ratified by the Chinese Government at this time. A bitter dispute was to arise over this for certain foreign governments later believed that the United States, to use the language of the street, was attempting to "put one over." The fact that the note was addressed to Great Britain rather than to Japan and Russia, who were most closely interested in Manchurian railways, was, to say the least, far from tactful. It is evident, too, that in the alternative scheme for co-operation in the Chinchow-Aigun Railway the powers referred to by Secretary Knox were probably Germany and France, certainly not Japan and Russia.

Sir Edward Grey replied on November 25th. The British Government expressed approval of the principle

---

[37] *Ibid.*, 234. The Secretary of State to Ambassador Reid, Washington, November 6, 1909.

contained in the first proposal, but suggested postponement of its consideration as already negotiations were
under way for a large loan to China. As regards the
second proposition Sir Edward suggested that Japan
should be invited as an interested party to participate
in the Chinchow-Aigun road.[38] Notes were dispatched
from Washington to Tokyo, Peking, Paris, Berlin, and
St. Petersburg on December 14th. But Ambassador
O'Brien at Tokyo was instructed to communicate only
the substance of the memorandum which had been sent
to the British Foreign Office. He was also to say that
the British Government had signified its approval of
the general principle involved.[39] This could not be considered a frank statement of Great Britain's position,
and when this later became known, it created further
suspicion of the motives of the United States Government. On the same day Knox replied to Sir Edward
Grey giving reasons why the American plan should be
adopted immediately.[40] The purpose of the note in
reality was to inform the British Government that
Washington intended to proceed with its Manchurian
proposals despite Grey's advice for postponement. On
the following day Ambassador O'Brien was instructed
to assure Japan that the United States would welcome
her co-operation,[41] while *Chargé* Fletcher at Peking
was instructed to urge the Chinese Government to
consent to the participation of Japan and other interested powers in the Chinchow-Aigun railway.[42] A

---

[38] United States *Foreign Relations* (1910), ser. 5945, 235. The Minister of
Foreign Affairs to Ambassador Reid, London, November 25, 1909.

[39] *Ibid.*, 236, Secretary Knox to Ambassador O'Brien, Washington, December
14, 1909.

[40] *Ibid.*, 236, Secretary Knox to Ambassador Reid, Washington, December 14,
1909.

[41] *Ibid.*, 237, The Acting Secretary of State to Ambassador O'Brien, Washington, December 15, 1909.

[42] United States *Foreign Relations*, (1910), ser. 5945, 237, The Acting Secretary of State to *Chargé* Fletcher, Washington, December 15, 1909.

subsequent note of December 18th from the American Ambassador to Baron Komura reiterated the assurance of the previous note and outlined all phases of the American proposals.[43] At about the same time *Chargé* Schuyler at St. Petersburg presented to the Russian Minister for Foreign Affairs an important *aide-memoire* which differed, however, from the note to Komura in that no mention was made of the Chinchow-Aigun railway proposal.[44] This led the Russians to suppose that they were not to be considered as participants in the building of the road should the alternative suggestion of the American Government be adopted, and Iswolsky replying informally said he was disappointed the plan had not been worked out in detail. By this time it had become evident that the State Department at Washington had not considered minutely the enormous financial undertaking its plan involved, and thus was not in a position to know whether the plan was practical.

The German response was given most informally on December 24th. The method of procedure of the Berlin Foreign Office was interesting. Ambassador Hill merely received a telephone message stating the Government agreed with the general principles laid down in the ambassador's memorandum.[45] Efforts of the United States Government to advance the neutralization proposal, including a further statement of its position to Japan, and a declaration of the Government's purpose in the American press, took place during January. This latter was an unusual procedure and was

---

[43] *Ibid.*, 237, Ambassador O'Brien to Baron Komura, Tokyo, December 18, 1909.

[44] *Ibid.*, 239, *Chargé* Schuyler to the Russian Minister of Foreign Affairs, December, 1909.

[45] *Ibid.*, 240, Ambassador Hill to the Secretary of State, Berlin, December 24, 1909.

largely for the purpose of quieting rumors in the foreign press, but far from accomplishing its purpose, it created more rumor.[46]   The replies of the Japanese and Russian Governments declining to accept the neutralization proposal came at practically the same time and employed almost identical arguments to justify their actions.[47]   It was obvious that the two powers had been brought together by what they considered a threat to their special position in Manchuria and that their action, although taken independently, was nevertheless the result of a common policy to protect that position to the utmost of their ability.   Both powers were explicit as to the reasons for their action.   Russia declared that the sovereignty of China and the "Open Door" in Manchuria were not threatened, and added that an international administration would seriously injure Russian interests, both public and private, an argument which applied largely to the Chinese Eastern Railway and auxiliary works.   Russia stated further that this line was an integral part of the transsiberian route, and finally that there seemed to be no assurance that the practical application of the American scheme would meet with success.   As to the Chinchow-Aigun railway Russia considered it of the greatest strategic and political importance and as regards any project for financial participation in railway construction in Manchuria, St. Petersburg declared it reserved the privilege to examine such project from the standpoint of its political and strategic interests and of the interests of the Chinese Eastern Railway.

Japan considered that the most serious obstacle to the acceptance of the neutralization proposal lay in the

---

[46] *Ibid.*, 243-245.

[47] *Ibid.*, 248-251.   Ambassador Rockhill to the Secretary of State, St. Petersburg, January 22, 1910, and Ambassador O'Brien to the Secretary of State, Tokyo, January 24, 1910.

fact that it contemplated a serious departure from the terms of the Treaty of Portsmouth. That peace settlement, in the view of Tokyo, had not been too generous. Such as it was, it was permanent, and had been strengthened by the Peking Convention of December 22, 1905, and the Government did not feel disposed to depart from the terms of that settlement. Nor did Japan see in the condition of affairs in Manchuria a just reason of adopting a system of railway administration different from that existing in other parts of China. The principle of the "Open Door" was declared to have a great significance there because by the Portsmouth Treaty the Japanese and Russian railways were operated for purely commercial and industrial purposes. Finally the replacing of a national by an international regime of railway administration, in the view of Tokyo, was merely the substitution of political expedients for economy and efficiency. Japan, however, agreed in principle to the Chinchow-Aigun proposal, reserving final judgment until necessary details were known. On February 4th the French Government rejected the neutralization proposal,[48] and on the 23rd the German Government gave assent to the general principles involved.[49]

Russia's emphatic pronouncement that the Chinchow-Aigun railway project would be exceedingly injurious both to the strategic and economic interests of the Empire was presented to the State Department by the Russian embassy in Washington on February 24th,[50] and with it, all hope of the adoption of the alter-

[48] United States *Foreign Relations*, (1910), ser. 5945, 256, Ambassador Bacon to the Secretary of State, Paris, February 4, 1910.

[49] *Ibid.*, 260.

[50] United States *Foreign Affairs*, (1910), ser. 5945, 261, Memorandum from the Russian Embassy, Washington, February 24, 1910.

native proposition of the American Government vanished. There was the implication in the Russian note that the American Government was merely interested in providing a new field for the investment of American capital. If such were the case the Russian Government was not averse to the construction of a railroad from Kalgan to Urga.[51]

And so the attempt of the American Secretary of State, attractive in theory, but impossible in practice, came to naught. It now appears that the Knox neutralization proposal will be relegated to the category of diplomatic blunders. Not that the plan itself was unworthy of a nation such as America. On the contrary, it had many points which recommend it. The fact that it may have appeared as a clever political move to give the United States a firmer grip on Far Eastern trade, to promote the interests of Americans in Far Eastern finance, does not in any way alter the situation. Behind the ulterior motive which always prompts those selfishly interested in international diplomacy, was the working of a laudable and high principle, which sought to help China to help herself. This fact should be stressed, for it will not soon be forgotten that the neutralization proposal was conceived without intimate knowledge of a highly involved situation; the first proposals to European governments threw wisdom and

---

[51] As Secretary Knox was the exponent of Dollar Diplomacy, the Russian reply probably held more than a veiled hint of biting sarcasm. On March 9th, Knox requested Baron Rosen for more information concerning the Kalgan-Urga Railway and stated that he was unaware of the agreement of 1899 to which Russia had referred in her memorandum of February 24, 1910. By this agreement China had engaged not to build railroads to the north of Peking with foreign capital other than Russian, and Russia was willing not to insist on the execution of this obligation by China only on condition that railroads build with capital provided by international syndicates should not be an evident menace to the security of the Russian frontier and should not injure the interests of Russia's railroad enterprise in Manchuria. (United States *Foreign Relations*, (1910), ser. 5945, 261.)

tact to the winds, and the course of the negotiations created intense suspicion that the motive of the American Government was not a disinterested one. Far from hastening the time when China might assume complete control of her Manchurian provinces, the Knox proposal encouraged the powers holding concessions there to entrench themselves to the full extent of treaty stipulations. On July 4, 1910, Japan and Russia signed a convention engaging to maintain and respect the *status quo* in Manchuria and to co-operate in the development of their respective railway lines there.[52] The understanding was a perfectly legitimate one, but its announcement at this particular time signified that Japan and Russia were entirely unsympathetic toward the diplomacy of the Knox proposal.

Perhaps it may be said with justice that no time in the period under review could have been less suitable for the presentation of the Knox plan. The reader will recall the months of uncertainty following the close of the Russo-Japanese War when Tokyo's policy in Manchuria was the political plaything of the military as opposed to the peace party. A bitter domestic struggle had resulted in a victory for the latter party. Japan had determined to develop her special interests in Manchuria in keeping with the policy of the "Open Door." In the development of that policy she had become the subject of repeated and unjustifiable attacks. She was accused of violating the "Open Door;" her treaty rights respecting the building of parallel and competing lines to the South Manchurian had been called in question; and foreign capitalists had attempted to use this as a club to force the sale of the Japanese road. When the

---

[52] *Manchuria, Treaties and Agreements,* 141-142. See also Dennis, *Foreign Policies of Soviet Russia.*

importance which Japan attached to the South Manchuria Railway is recalled, it is not surprising that mutual interests found their greatest protection in a closer relationship between Japan and Russia. This is not to infer that the best interests of Manchurian development were served thereby. It is merely a statement of the inevitable result of the diplomatic blundering which sought to internationalize Manchurian railways at a time when even the most tactful approach to the subject would probably have met with a similar failure.

CHAPTER X

CHINO-JAPANESE RELATIONS, 1906-1913

It is now necessary to recall that on December 22, 1905, China and Japan concluded the Treaty, or Convention of Peking as it is sometimes called, by which China consented to the transfer to Japan of the former Russian leasehold and concessions in South Manchuria. The treaty, and certain "secret" protocols attached to it, also provided the basis of settlement of a large number of questions which concerned Chino-Japanese relationships in Manchuria. With the establishment of Japan's position in Liaotung it became evident that interpretations of the two powers relative to these problems were by no means synonymous. It thus developed that during the years in which Japan was protecting what she considered her legitimate interests against the onslaught of railway politics, described in the previous chapter, she was also confronted by a series of more or less grave controversies with the Government at Peking. If these Chino-Japanese debates concerning the Manchurian settlement are to be viewed in their true light; if one is to understand both the attitude and action of the Japanese Government during the period, the international background presented by railway politics must be borne constantly in mind. It is inconceivable that the position of Japan can be understood or correctly interpreted during these Chino-Japanese negotiations unless the broader aspects of Far Eastern diplomacy, involving the great European powers and the United States, are considered as a vital part of the same story.

It was this broader conception of the whole international problem of the Far East which led Willard Straight in his later life to a change of heart, and to the realization that the only practical receipt for a Far Eastern settlement or an "Open Door" in North China lay in a frank and cordial joint policy between the United States and Japan.[1] As Straight looked back on those active years, when he was carried forward in the whirl of Far Eastern politics by his own brilliancy and youth, he changed his views and sympathies on things Chinese and things Japanese. "Chinese incompetency, dilatoriness, utilitarianism and down-right dishonesty slowly alienated the warm sympathy of his earlier dreams. Correspondingly he came, in his own exasperation, to realize more clearly some of the conditions with which successive but unsuccessful Japanese ministries had been contending."[2]

An interpretation of these conditions which Japanese negotiators faced in Peking and Manchuria from 1906 to 1913 is the subject of this chapter. It is not the purpose of the writer to justify the at times aggressive policy of Japan, nor to excuse the hopelessly corrupt and incompetent game played by China. Rather is it his purpose to explain as accurately as possible and sympathetically the motives which prompted this chapter in the history of diplomacy. It will not be found that the responsibility for these misunderstandings rested solely upon one nation. It is less important therefore to assess the blame, than to understand the fundamental cause of these international troubles.

In September, 1905, Japan had acquired the former Russian leasehold at the tip of the Liaotung Peninsula

---

[1] Marvin, "Willard Straight" in *Japan*, December, 1924, 36.
[2] *Ibid.*, 45.

with the railway stretching north to Changchun. This
territory usually referred to as the Province of Kwantung comprised something more than 1,000 square
miles.[3]   And by 1907, at the time when active negotiations commenced for the settlement of Chino-Japanese
problems in Manchuria, it contained a population of
405,685, only five per cent of whom were Japanese.[4] In
this province Japan established a new governor-gen-
eralship which assumed the administration of the province and in addition supervised the military, diplomatic,
consular, judicial, and railway affairs of the entire
Japanese zone south of Changchun.[5]   It was here that
Japanese activities in Manchuria were to center. The
governor-general who has always been a military man
was assisted by a civil governor.[6]   The system savored
somewhat of a military administration, but was a very
effective one, and its character is not surprising when
the conditions prevailing in the surrounding territories
of Manchuria are considered. But the establishment
of an administration in Kwantung was a matter rest-
ing entirely with the Government of Tokyo. It was
not complicated by the broader and more intricate
aspects of international diplomacy. Far different were
the problems confronting Japanese statesmen in evolv-
ing a practical solution of other Manchurian enterprises in which Tokyo demanded that rights which she
claimed should have ample protection. It was said
during the years now under review, and it has been
asserted since that time, that the years 1906-1913

---

[3] *Economic Development of Korea and Manchuria*, 167. The province consists of a tract of the mainland, with the Gulf of Liaotung to the west, covering
an area of 1203 square miles and also of the adjacent islands, about 40 in
number, with a total area of 95 square miles.

[4] Asakawa, "Japan in Manchuria," in *Yale Review*, November, 1908, 269.

[5] *Ibid.*, 270.

[6] Recently a change has been effected in the system and the governor general is no longer required to be a soldier.

provided excellent examples of Japan's unprincipled and aggressive policy toward China and that the agreements reached between the two governments in this period were not settlements between equals, based upon friendly compromise, but rather the result of a vigorous shaking of the mailed first by Japan. Particular attention is called to this general conception for it is a wide-spread one. But so far as history is concerned it can only be maintained if founded upon irrefutable facts. One of the purposes of this chapter therefore will be to examine the negotiations of these years in an attempt to find a reasonable interpretation of diplomacy which has led to much controversy.

Among the first problems of settlement in postwar Manchuria was that of the Hsinmintun-Mukden Railway. An important line of railroad now connects Peking with Mukden, the capital of Manchuria. This railway belongs to the Chinese Government, but was built with British capital and is under British management, though operated by Chinese. When the line was under construction it was the intention of the railway authorities to construct a bridge over the Liao River with the object of extending the line to Mukden, but Russia, who looked upon Manchuria at that time as her "sphere of influence," prevented the extension of the line east of Hsinmintun, and the proposed construction of a bridge over the Liao was objected to on strategic grounds. When the Boxer disturbances broke out in Manchuria, the Russians advanced west of the Liao and occupied this railway east of Shanhaikwan as far north as Hsinmintun with the branch line between Yingkow (Newchwang) and Kaopantzu (the junction station on the line). It will be recalled that on April 8, 1902, Russia signed the Manchurian

Convention of Evacuation. By article 4 Russia agreed to return that portion of the railway occupied by her troops to its owners. China agreed not to permit a third power to undertake or share the defense, construction, or working of the line, or to occupy the territory so restored.[7] During the Russo-Japanese War when the general headquarters of the Japanese Army advanced to Mukden the field railway department laid a light rail line for temporary use between Mukden and Hsinmintun.[8]

Article 2 of the "secret" protocols of the Peking Treaty of December 22, 1905, provided for the sale by Japan to China of the Hsinmintun-Mukden line. China had engaged to reconstruct the line and to borrow from a Japanese corporation one-half the capital required for that portion east of the Liao River.[9] When in April, 1907, the South Manchuria Railway Company assumed the management of the lines held by the Japanese Government in South Manchuria, China approached Japan through the Foreign Ministry in Tokyo asking cession of the Hsinmintun-Mukden line and at the same time a like overture was made to the South Manchuria Railway Company through the Ministry of Communications at Peking.[10] In response to these advances an agreement was signed at Peking on April 15, 1907, for the cession of the line,[11] and

---

[7] *Manchuria, Treaties and Agreements,* 66-67.

[8] Private correspondence (information from the files of the South Manchuria Railway Company).

[9] *Manchuria, Treaties and Agreements,* 83.

[10] Private correspondence with the South Manchuria Railway Company (information from the files of the Company).

[11] *Manchuria, Treaties and Agreements,* 98-100. The purchase price of the railway was fixed at Japanese gold yen 1,660,000. The period of the loan for the Hsinmintun-Mukden line was 18 years. The security for the loan from the South Manchuria Railway Company, which provided the capital was the real property of the section of the railway east of the River Liao. The agreement for the handing over by Japan of the Hsinmintun-Mukden Railway together with the rolling stock and equipment was signed on May 27, 1907 (*Ibid.,* 101.)

final arrangements for the loan and sale of the railway were completed on August 18, 1909.[12] Following the transfer, the Hsinmintun-Mukden line was converted to standard gauge and since that time has developed a fair business, yielding moderate returns annually. The loan advanced for construction by the South Manchuria Railway Company is being paid as installments fall due and the loan agreement terminated in 1927.[13]

Interesting in the course of its development is the story of the Kirin-Changchun railway which connects the northern terminus of the South Manchuria Railway with the capital of Kirin Province. The line is seventy-nine miles in length and is of standard gauge. In concluding the "secret" protocols of December, 1905, China had agreed to borrow from Japan one-half of the capital required for the construction of this road.[14] Accordingly on April 15, 1907, at the time Japan ceded to China the Hsinmintun-Mukden Railway, China agreed to borrow from the South Manchurian Railway Company one-half the capital required for the construction of the Kirin-Changchun line.[15] A supplementary agreement concerning particulars of the loan was concluded in November, 1908,[16] and construction work was commenced in May, 1910, the line being opened to traffic in October, 1912. Chiefly owing to mismanagement the Kirin-Changchun railway lost money rapidly, but in 1917 Japan agreed with the Peking Government to assume management of the

---

[12] *Ibid.*, 122-124.

[13] Private correspondence (information from the files of the South Manchuria Railway Company).

[14] *Manchuria, Treaties and Agreements,* 83, Art. 1.

[15] *Ibid.*, 98-100. The period of the loan was fixed at 25 years and the security for the loan was the real property of the railway and its earnings.

[16] *Manchuria, Treaties and Agreements,* 120-122.

line. Since that date the railway has grown in prosperity and is now considered the most profitable in Manchuria for its running mileage.[17] The South Manchuria Railway Company has invested 6,500,000 yen in the line, but although this company has undertaken to manage the railway, it is, in fact, one of the Chinese Government roads. The director is a Chinese official appointed by the Peking Government, and practically the entire staff is Chinese.

A question concerning which there was much controversy at the time, and much idle debate since, was that of the Antung-Mukden Railway, stretching in a southeasterly direction from the capital of Fengtien Province to Antung on the Korean border. This line had its beginning in the light military railway constructed between Antung and Mukden by the Japanese Army during the Russo-Japanese War. The length of the line is 188 miles; the gauge was two feet, six inches, and in order to hasten construction to keep pace with the advancing Japanese Army by avoiding tunnels and bridges the line followed wide detours and steep grades with the result that the hauling capacity of engines was necessarily very small. This was one of the lines acquired by the South Manchuria Railway Company from the Japanese Government in April, 1907.[18] The future development of the line had been provided for by article 6 of the additional agreement to the Peking Treaty of December 22, 1905. This provided that:

The Imperial Chinese Government agree that Japan has right to maintain and work the military railway line constructed between Antung and Mukden and to improve the said line so

---

[17] Private correspondence with the South Manchuria Railway Company (information from the files of the Company).

[18] *Economic Development of Korea and Manchuria*, 261.

as to make it fit for the conveyance of commercial and industrial goods of all nations. The term for which such right is conceded is fifteen years from the date of the completion of the improvements above provided for. The work of such improvements is to be completed within two years, exclusive of a period of twelve months during which it will have to be delayed owing to the necessity of using the existing line for the withdrawal of troops. The term of the concession above mentioned is therefore to expire in the forty-ninth year of Kuang Hsu. At the expiration of that term the said railway shall be sold to China at a price to be determined by appraisement of all its properties by a foreign expert who will be selected by both parties. The conveyance by the railway of the troops and munitions of war of the Chinese Government prior to such sale shall be dealt with in accordance with the regulations of the Eastern Chinese Railway. Regarding the manner in which the improvements of the railway are to be effected, it is agreed that the person undertaking the work on behalf of Japan shall consult with the commissioner dispatched for the purpose by China. The Chinese Government will also appoint a commissioner to look after the business relating to the railway as is provided in the agreement relating to the Eastern Chinese Railway. It is further agreed that detailed regulations shall be concluded regarding the tariffs for the carriage by the railway of the public and private goods of China."[19]

It is now evident that Japan did not appreciate the enormity of the task confronting her in converting the light military line into one suitable for commercial purposes. Had she done so Japan would not have conceded that "the work of such improvements is to be completed within two years, exclusive of a period of twelve months during which it will have to be delayed owing to the necessity of using the existing line for the withdrawal of troops." According to the customary interpretation of this clause the work of reconstruction was to be completed by December, 1908, and as is now well known Japan had by no means com-

---

[19] *Manchuria, Treaties and Agreements*, 81.

pleted the task by that time. Apart from the fact, however, that Japan was undoubtedly attempting to strengthen her position in Manchuria and that China was using all means in her power to obstruct such advance, it is quite clear that the wording of the article in question was unfortunate. Technically the limits of the period of reconstruction work were not fixed and on this basis Japan might claim that her actions were within the meaning of the treaty. However this may be, the sudden activity of Russia, in deciding to reconstruct the Amur Railway and to double-track the transsiberian line, apparently stirred the Japanese Government into a sudden realization of the danger of further delay in the reconstruction of the Antung-Mukden Line.[20]

During the years immediately following the close of hostilities private negotiations were carried on between Japan and China with a view to making the Antung-Mukden Railway available as speedily as possible as a connecting link between the Korean and South Manchurian systems. Through this method of procedure nothing was accomplished and in January, 1909, the Japanese Government proposed officially to China that commissioners be appointed to survey the line.[21] This was agreed upon and a joint survey of the proposed route with the exception of a small section, some twenty miles in length between Mukden and Chenhsiang-tun, was completed early in April. As the route of this small section of the road was to be determined by the two Governments, Japan, in order to avoid further delay, proposed to commence work on that portion of the line east of Chenhsiang-tun which had

---

[20] *Far Eastern Review*, June, 1911, 15.

[21] Japan's Official Statement re the Antung-Mukden Railway, in *The Japan Weekly Mail*, August 14, 1909, 183.

already been surveyed, and announced her desire to begin purchase of the land required for railway purposes.[22]   But in reply to this China raised questions of controversy concerning police authority in the railway zones and the withdrawal of railway guards. Japan urged China to accede to her request.   In response to these appeals China, on June 24th, forwarded to Tokyo a reply which in the opinion of the Japanese Government "if concurred in would nullify the provisions of the arrangement of 1905 on the subject of the Antung-Mukden Line, and utterly destroy the value of the railway."[23]   China now disregarded the survey made by the joint commissioners and revived the question of police authority and railway guards, and raised other issues which Tokyo believed should be the subject of separate and independent negotiations.   Finally China declared that the work of improvement must be confined to the existing track and that no broadening of the gauge could be permitted.

It appears that China had no just ground upon which to raise these issues for these matters were explicitly cared for in treaty stipulations.   Her only ground for protesting further action on the Antung-Mukden Line by the Japanese lay in establishing her interpretation of the time limit clause as the correct one.   This she did not do, but chose rather to cloud the issue with questions which had no legal justification in the controversy.   By the end of July, Japan was still unable to secure a modification of the Chinese attitude, and determined, therefore, to take action independent of the Chinese authorities to carry out the work of reconstruction according to what the Government con-

[22] *Ibid.*, 183.
[23] *Ibid.*, 183.

ceived as its treaty rights and in harmony with the survey of the commissioners of the two Powers.[24]

In accordance with this decision Mr. Ijuin presented Japan's ultimatum to the Waiwupu on the afternoon of August 6, 1909. At six o'clock that evening the Tokyo Government was informed that the note had been presented and at eleven o'clock the Japanese Prime Minister issued formal sanction for the commencement of construction on the Antung-Mukden Line.[25] It would seem that the Peking Government never entertained a serious intention to obstruct, save by prolonging the negotiations, Japan's plan for reconstructing the railway. On the day following the presentation of the Japanese ultimatum the Chinese Government replied it would not insist on its objections to changing the existing gauge or to the introduction of such rectifications of the line as were technically necessary, and it was suggested that these rectifications might be determined by commissioners appointed by the two countries. Japan replied that this had already been accomplished by a joint commission. To this response China gave her assent and the Japanese Government instructed Consul-General Koike at Mukden to sign a memorandum with the Viceroy of the "Three Eastern Provinces," Hsi Liang, and the Chinese Governor of Mukden, Cheng. By this it was agreed that the standard gauge would be adopted, the survey of the line was approved, while certain other details were left for future negotiations.[26]

Although the South Manchuria Railway Company had actually commenced some of the work of recon-

---

[24] *Ibid.*, 183.

[25] *Japan Weekly Mail*, August 14, 1909, 182.

[26] *Manchuria, Treaties and Agreements*, 128. The agreement was signed on August 19, 1909.

struction on August 7, 1907, the delay occasioned by the protracted negotiations between Tokyo and Peking prolonged the work until October, 1913, at a total cost of 22,000,000 yen. The first standard gauge express was dispatched over the line on November 3rd of the same year.[27] With this outlay the line has brought only meager returns. Yet at the outbreak of the World War in 1914 it formed one of the links in the world's international highway connecting Europe with the Far East.

The story of the Antung-Mukden Railway has been capitalized by the enemies of Japan. It has been characterized as typical of her China policy, but this position cannot be maintained in the light of the other agreements reached with China during the period. This is not to say that the action of Japan in the Antung-Mukden case was free from objectionably aggressive features. These were certainly present, and although they are not to be justified on ethical, they are easily explained on strategic grounds. The reader is already conversant with the Japanese attitude toward the whole Korean and South Manchurian question. These two territories had now become for practical purposes a Japanese sphere, or what might be called a necessary buffer zone against the reappearance of the Russian menace. One of the most important factors in the maintenance of such a zone was the Antung-Mukden Railway. By treaty stipulation both Japan and Russia had agreed that their railroads would be developed in Manchuria for purely commercial purposes, yet it would be absurd to deny that political considerations played no part in directing the course

---

[27] Private correspondence with the South Manchuria Railway Company (information from the files of the Company).

of such development. The strategic value of the Antung-Mukden Line had been demonstrated in the war with Russia, and for commercial purposes it was the connecting link between the Korean roads and the South Manchuria Railway. It is not surprising, therefore, that the force of these arguments prevailed in Tokyo. The case might have been different if the Government of Peking had enjoyed the respect of the Mikado's ministers. But as the progress of the negotiation soon disclosed, neither the purposes nor the methods of Peking's officialdom were calculated to inspire the Japanese with either respect or restraint.

Further matters concerning railways and mines in Manchuria which had become the subject of controversy between China and Japan were adjusted by a convention signed on September 4, 1909.[28] The first clause of this agreement as already stated brought to a close the long and bitter diplomatic wranglings that followed China's proposal to extend the Imperial Government Railways from Hsinmintun to Fakumen. China now recognized the railway between Tashichao and Yingkow as a branch line of the South Manchuria Railway, to be surrendered to China at the expiration of the lease of the main line.[29]

One of the most important questions which confronted Mr. Ijuin, the Japanese Minister at Peking, in the negotiations attending the conventions signed in September was that of the Fushun and Yentai collieries. The rich Fushun mines had been considered

---

[28] *Manchuria, Treaties and Agreements,* 129-130.

[29] In 1908 China requested Japan, on the strength of the Russo-Chinese agreement of 1898, to destroy the branch railway connecting Yingkow with the South Manchuria Railway. But Japan desired to operate this line and to extend it from the terminus at Niuchiatun to a point nearer the port of Newchwang.

by Russia as appertaining to her railway concession,[30] and when Japan took over the railway she continued operation of the colliery. A distinction was made in the original agreement of 1896 between rights acquired on state land and those on private property. China now contended that if Russia had been entitled to half of the coal area, the other half had been forcibly taken by her from its Chinese owner and hence was beyond Russia's power to transfer to Japan.[31] In the convention of September, 1909, China recognized in regard to the mines both at Fushun and Yentai the right of the Japanese Government to exploit these properties, and Japan agreed to pay a tax upon the coal so produced. All other mines along the South Manchuria Railway and the Antung-Mukden Railway, it was agreed, should be exploited as joint enterprises of Japanese and Chinese subjects.[32]

China had also desired to extend eastward to the inner city of Mukden the Hsinmintun-Mukden Railway from its inconvenient location west of the tracks of the South Manchuria Railway. Japan, holding the intervening land, had refused to consent to this extension unless she also was allowed to make a similar extension

---

[30] *Manchuria, Treaties and Agreements*, see article 6 of contract for the construction of the Chinese Eastern Railway, September 8, 1896, 15, and article 4 of agreement concerning the southern branch of the Chinese Eastern Railway, July 6, 1898, 48-49.

[31] Asakawa, "The Manchurian Conventions," in *Yale Review*, November, 1909, 261.

[32] According to the settlement of the Fushun colliery affair, the original Chinese owner from whom Russia is said to have forcibly taken a half of the Fushun colliery, was to receive compensation. It may be remarked that the right of working mines appertaining to a railway is a usual part of a railway concession in China. For example, the Kiaochow-Tsinan Railways (German), Chinese Eastern Railway (originally Russian, now part Japanese), Shankaikwan Railway (British), mines and railways in Chekiang (British), in Shansi (British), in Honan (British), in Szechwang (part British, part French), in Anhui (British). Such rights terminate with the expiration of the railway concession. (*Ibid.*, 265-266.)

of her railway to the inner city. By article 5 of the September agreement Japan withdrew her objection and two years later, on September 2, 1911, an agreement for the extension of the Peking-Mukden Line was signed.[33] Both of these agreements marked a conciliatory attitude on the part of Tokyo.

Another problem which had been the occasion of constant friction between Japan and China concerned a district known as Chientao. The territory between Mount Paik-tu (Pe-tow) and a tributary of the Sungari known as the Tumen (not the larger river of the same name which forms a part of the accepted boundary line between Manchuria and Korea), a district of indefinite area called Chientao, had for many years been settled by Koreans and at times had been considered by the Korean Government as a part of its domain, or at least as neutral territory between Korea and China. China, however, had always regarded it as her own and administered it as part of Manchuria. Upon reports that the Korean settlers were subject to harsh treatment at the hands of the local Chinese authorities, the Japanese Resident-General in Korea, without raising the question of territorial sovereignty, insisted upon the right of protecting the Korean settlers. China contended that the Koreans had become Chinese subjects by their act of voluntary settlement and were no longer subject to the Japanese protectorate.[34]

By the Chientao agreement of September 4, 1909, Japan recognized China's territorial sovereignty in the region. China promised to open four towns in Chientao to world commerce. It was agreed that Koreans already residing in a defined area of the territory should

[33] *Manchuria, Treaties and Agreements*, 130.

[34] Asakawa, "The Manchurian Convention," in the *Yale Review*, November, 1909, 262-263.

be allowed to enjoy special rights of domicile but other Koreans and foreigners were to be confined to the open marts. Korean residents were to be under Chinese jurisdiction and were to receive the same treatment and protection as Chinese residents. The Japanese consular officers were to be given the right to attend court but not to sit as judges, and in important cases involving the lives of persons reserved the right to apply to the Chinese authorities for a new trial.[35]

There is no question as to the power of Japan to have forced a settlement in the Chientao affair, which would have given her, through the Korean administration, complete control over the district. But she did not attempt this. She recognized Chinese sovereignty in the region and waived any claim to the exercise of extraterritorial jurisdiction. True it is that Japanese consular officers were given the right to attend court and, in cases involving the lives of Koreans, to apply to the Chinese for a new trial, but such rights were in no way comparable to those exercised under full extraterritorial jurisdiction. Had there been more substance and less shadow to Japan's so-called aggressive policy she would beyond doubt have demanded and secured from China such jurisdiction in Chientao. The

---

[35] *Manchuria, Treaties and Agreements*, 135-136. Note that by article 6 the Government of China undertook to extend the Kirin-Changchun Railway to the southern boundary of Yenchi, and to connect it at Hoiryong (Hueining) with a Korean railway, and such extensions were to be effected upon the same terms as the Kirin-Changchun Railway. The date of commencing the work of the proposed extension was to be determined by the Government of China, considering the actual requirements of the situation, and upon consultation with the Government of Japan. The settlements of September 4, 1909, concerning Chientao and mines and railways in Manchuria were regarded as indicating more favorable relations between Japan and China. The terms of the agreements were looked upon as indicating friendly mutual compromise in which the rights and interests of both parties were upheld. (United States *Foreign Relations*, (1909), 117.)

incident is simply another example of the conciliatory nature of the settlements reached at the time.

Another problem which required diplomatic settlement by the Governments of Tokyo and Peking concerned forest lands on the right bank of the River Yalu, which forms the southern part of the border between Manchuria and Korea. It will be remembered that a Russian lumber concession on the left bank of the Yalu was one of the principal difficulties in the diplomatic tangle leading to the Russo-Japanese War. The timber lands which now formed a subject of negotiations between Japan and China had nothing to do with the former Russian claims.

The forest area on the upper Yalu was not exploited until the late years of the Manchu Dynasty. Extensive forest areas stretching south of the Long White Mountains had remained untouched for centuries. The territory had afforded a refuge to brigands and a field for exploitation by adventurers. It was at the end of the Kuang Hsu Era that a group of Shantung immigrants organized a timber company and professed that they had secured the right to exploit the forests of the upper Yalu. In reality all the company did was to collect a stated commission on the timber rafts floated down the river, taking no part itself in the cutting of timber. While this state of affairs existed the Chinese authorities at Antung also levied a tax on timber rafts coming down the river. This tax amounted annually to a considerable sum, but it found its way largely into the pockets of corrupt Chinese officials and resulted in no contribution to the general administration or to the district from which it arose in particular.[36]

---

[36] Private correspondence with the South Manchuria Railway Company (information from the files of the Company).

At the outbreak of the Russo-Japanese War, Antung was one of the first towns in Manchuria occupied by the Japanese Army, and military necessity required the opening of a military administration office, which temporarily assumed charge of the local government. During this period the receipts derived from the tax on timber rafts were employed in the local administration. At the close of the war the administration of Antung was handed over to the Chinese Government and by article 10 of the additional agreement to the Peking Treaty of December 22, 1905, the Chinese Government agreed to the formation of a joint stock forestry company composed of Japanese and Chinese capitalists, for the exploitation of the upper Yalu forest lands. The Japanese and Chinese shareholders were to share equally the profits of the undertaking, and a detailed agreement concerning particulars of the concession was to be concluded at a later date.[37]   In consequence of this understandinig an agreement between the two Governments was concluded on May 14, 1908.[38]   By this agreement the capital of the Company was fixed at $3,000,000; the term of the Company's rights was to extend for twenty-five years (a period which might be extended if agreeable to the Chinese Government) and the district in which timber might be cut was defined. The Company was formed on September 25th of the same year and commenced its operations immediately.[39]

China, however, has not participated in the operations of the Company to the limit of her rights according to the agreement of May 14th. Practically all the investments in the Company are Japanese, China hav-

---

[37] *Manchuria, Treaties and Agreements*, 82.

[38] *Ibid.*, 118-120.

[39] Private correspondence with the South Manchuria Railway Company (information from the files of the Company).

ing been content to confine her contributions to securing title to the forests and rights of exploitation. The chief officials of the Company are Chinese appointed by the Mukden Government, which it would seem looks upon the timber company as a sort of Government concern. A net profit has been returned each year since active operations were commenced and the company is making a considerable contribution to the development of the district.[40]

A further problem requiring settlement in this period was the customs administration in South Manchuria. Under the Russian regime in the Liaotung Peninsula Dalny had been created a "free" commercial port. For this reason no Chinese customs existed at Dalny during the Russian occupation and the Chinese customs did not function in the Leased Territory while it was under Russian control. The reader will recall that during 1906 and the early months of 1907, while the Japanese armies were being withdrawn from Manchuria, foreign commercial interests desiring to re-establish their markets in Manchuria complained repeatedly that Japanese goods were permitted to enter Manchuria free of duty at Dairen, while the merchandise of other nations admitted at the port of Newchwang was required to pay the regular tariff duties. It was therefore realized at an early date that the establishment of Chinese custom houses at Dairen was greatly to be desired.[41]

A commercial treaty which China had concluded with the United States in January, 1904, had provided for the opening to foreign trade of certain Manchurian towns, but owing to outbreak of hostilities between

---

[40] *Ibid.*

[41] United States *Foreign Relations*, (1906), 198, Minister Rockhill to the Secretary of State, Peking, June 26, 1906.

Russia and Japan and the occupation of Manchuria by the belligerents China had been unable to establish her customs houses and to complete arrangements for the formal opening of the cities in question.[42]   On April 27, 1906, the Japanese Government notified the Chinese Government that Antung must be opened to foreign residence and trade by May 1st, and Mukden on June 1st of the same year, in compliance with the Sino-Japanese commercial treaty.   On these dates China should have opened customs houses at these two places.   On July 13th, therefore, Mr. Rockhill presented a memorandum to the Chinese Foreign Office setting forth that the United States Government would insist upon the fulfillment of treaty obligations.[43]   The American Minister informed the Peking Government that China must establish at once a custom house at Antung and another as near as was practicable to Dalny (Dairen). A third custom house was to be established in North Manchuria to impose duties on Russian goods entering the provinces.   These demands were made with the view that duties might be levied on all goods from abroad without discrimination.   China promised to open the customs at Antung immediately and discussions concerning the customs at Dalny would be undertaken at once with Mr. Hayashi, the newly appointed Japanese Minister to Peking, who arrived from Japan on July 14th.

More than a month later, however, on August 30th, Mr. Rockhill reported to the Secretary of State that notwithstanding constant pressure, he was unable to get the Chinese Government to fix the date for opening

---

[42] *Ibid.*, 204, Minister Rockhill to the Secretary of State, Peking, July 16, 1906, No. 352, (inclosure).

[43] *Ibid.*, 204, Minister Rockhill to the Secretary of State, Peking, July 16, 1906, No. 352, (inclosure).

customs at Antung or to take any action whatsoever for the establishment of customs anywhere in Manchuria. Japan by this time had stated that she would not permit the establishment of customs at Dalny, unless they were established simultaneously in the north on the Russian frontier. Mr. Rockhill was informed that the Chinese Government had not even broached the matter to the Russian legation in Peking, an attitude which was characteristic of the Government.[44] Despite the careless attitude of China, Viscount Hayashi commenced negotiations with the Waiwupu soon after his arrival in Peking. But China insisted that the whole customs question concerned herself alone and that there was no need for hurrying a settlement.[45] The Japanese Government had already notified the Powers that Dairen would be established as a free port on September 1st.[46] The situation did not change materially until the early months of 1907, when T'ang Shao-yi, who in many respects was considered one of the ablest ministers of the Chinese Foreign Office, was appointed Governor of Fengtien or Mukden Province, and finally on May 30th an agreement was signed by Viscount Hayashi, Minister of Japan, and Sir Robert Hart, Inspector General of the Imperial Chinese Customs, for the establishment of a maritime customs house at Dairen.[47] The customs house was opened on July 4th.[48]

This agreement contained several clauses of interest, exemplifying in particular that Japan was in large measure following precedent established by other foreign powers in their relationships with China. The

[44] United States *Foreign Relations*, (1906), 220, Minister Rockhill to the Secretary of State, August 30.

[45] *The London Times*, Weekly Edition, August 24, 1906, 533.

[46] *Ibid.*, 537 and August 31, 549.

[47] *Manchuria, Treaties and Agreements*, 103-106.

[48] *The London Times*, Weekly Edition, July 5, 1907, 421.

chief of the custom house at Dairen was a Japanese
(Germany had made a similar ruling at Kiaochow),
who at that time was a member of the Chinese customs
service.   The following of German precedent was a
satisfactory arrangement for Japanese trade predomi-
nated in South Manchuria.   And article 6 went so far
as to mention that its provision was based on the regulations governing Germany at Kiaochow.[49]

It is very probable that Japan was influenced to
some extent by foreign opinion in encouraging China
to establish her customs at Dairen.   The position and
attitude of the Japanese was constantly watched by the
other foreign Powers in the Far East.   Japan knew
that it would be comparatively simple to suppress
smuggling at a customs port, while the problem would
present far greater difficulties on the borders of the
leased territory adjoining the interior of China.

On June 29th Mr. Rockhill was informed by Prince
Ching that other cities in the three provinces of Manchuria had been opened to international trade,[50] and in
July experimental regulations for the establishment of
customs houses in North Manchuria were concluded by
representatives of China and Russia.[51]

The settlement of the customs question cleared the
way for a more equitable development of trade in Manchuria.   With Dairen opened as a free port, and the
imposition of the stipulated customs tariff on goods imported into the interior beyond the boundary of the
leased territory, and the export tariff on all goods
shipped from the port of Dairen that had come from
the interior of Manchuria (thus retaining the leased

[49] *Manchuria, Treaties and Agreements*, 104-105.

[50] United States *Foreign Relations*, (1907), pt. 1, 130.

[51] *Ibid.*, 138, fixes the date of the agreement as July 28th, while *Manchuria, Treaties and Agreements*, gives July 8th, (see 113).

territory as a free zone), there remained no grounds for the allegation that Japan was attempting to close the Manchurian market to all international trade save her own.[52]

Other negotiations between Tokyo and Peking concerned the telegraph connecting Kwantung and Chefoo and the Japanese telegraph lines in Manchuria. The first agreement adjusting this question was signed on October 12, 1908.[53] Prior to the Russo-Japanese War

[52] It is interesting in the cause of an accurate narrative to note the report of Consul-General W. D. Straight of Mukden in March, 1907, just prior to the opening of the Dairen customs (Consular and Trade Reports, March, 1907, 102-103). ". . . . It has been frequently stated that the Manchurian markets would be reserved for special exploitation and would not afford an equal opportunity to all those desirous of sharing in their profitable development. It is not unnatural that such should have been the case; that during the military occupation advantages not free to all were enjoyed by the privileged few. It would be a mistake, however, to consider that within such a limited period and during such a troublous time it would have been possible to establish relations sufficiently close to constitute a serious menace to the interests of the general commercial community. . . . ." As is well known, the sympathies of Consul-General Straight leaned decidedly toward the Chinese. His remarks for this reason are the more significant.

[53] MacMurray, op. cit., 760-762. The first thing which Russia had undertaken, when she had secured the leasehold of Kwantung Territory in Manchuria was, through interests of the Great Northern Cable Company, a Danish institution, to lay a submarine cable across the Bay of Pechili in order to communicate between the Russian Consulate in Chefoo and the Russian Headquarters established then in Port Arthur. The cable was solely for military purposes.

In undertaking this work, which might have called forth some international complications, the Russian authorities acted in a free-handed manner, neither negotiating for the sanction of the Chinese Government nor consulting the wishes of any other Powers. On the other hand the Chinese Government, assuming an nonchalant attitude, permitted the work to go forward unmolested. Russia on the 21st of August, 1900, officially announced the completion of this cable line and telegraphic service was opened to the public with rates as follows:

To and from Port Arthur..........6 cents in large silver.
To and from Japan.................$1.02.
    etc.   etc.   etc.

At the time the war broke between Russian and Japan, the cable in question was cut on the Chefoo side. By whom or by which party of belligerents has not been disclosed.

Then followed a long period of negotiation between the Governments of

there had been a cable connecting Chefoo on the Shantung Peninsula with Port Arthur in Kwantung. During hostilities the cable was cut and it was now decided that the cable would be restored by joint action of both Powers. Article 2 dealt with the Japanese telegraph lines in Manchuria outside of the leased territory and the railway zone. These were military cables laid by the Japanese army during the war and China maintained Japan no longer had a right to operate them. Therefore, the Tokyo Government which had continued to operate the lines until 1908 now agreed to sell them to China. There were also certain telephone lines operated by the Japanese in Manchuria, but these were not turned over to China since it was not practical to do so, China having no telephone system which could assume their management. China also agreed (article 3) to construct between the Japanese Railway and certain large towns in Manchuria telegraph lines which were to be placed for a period of fifteen years at the exclusive disposal of the Japanese Government tele-

---

Japan and China as to whether the cable should be restored and, if so, by whom.

Finally, on October 12, 1908, the Sino-Japanese Cable Agreement was concluded, as the result of negotiations carried on between Count Ishii, the then Vice-Minister of Foreign Affairs for Japan and the Chinese Government delegates, Messrs. Wang Pang and Dresing who visited Japan en route from the International Telegraph Convention at Lisbon in 1908, where they represented their Governments.

The essential points of the clause regarding Chefoo-Kwantung cable given in Art. I of the Sino-Japanese Cable Agreement are:

I. That a new cable be laid between Chefoo and a certain point in Kwantung Leased Territory; the cable from this Territory to a point 7½ miles off Chefoo shall be owned by Japan and the remaining 7½ miles by China.

II. That China shall erect a telegraph from the shore where the said cable terminates to the Japanese Post Office at Chefoo, making arrangements to appropriate certain hours to meet the particular need of Japan, and that during these hours the Japanese Post Office at Chefoo may have a direct communication with the said cable service, and further the said Office may use the Japanese syllabary "Kana" for telegraphic messages to facilitate the communication of Japanese people residing there.

graph service. Two subsequent agreements defining details of this arrangement were signed on November 7th.[54]

The final agreement between China and Japan, negotiated during the period under review, took the form of an exchange of notes on October 5, 1913.[55] On this date the Chinese Minister for Foreign Affairs addressed the Japanese Minister in Peking regarding the construction of railway lines in Manchuria, a subject which repeatedly had been discussed by these ministers. The note of the Chinese Minister stated that his Government had decided on a plan of co-operation with Japan with particular reference to railway loans. The first loan which China agreed to make from Japanese capitalists was to be for the construction of the following railways: (a) from Ssupingkai via Chengchiatun to Taonanfu; (b) from Kaiyuan to Hailungcheng, and (c) from the Changchun station of the Kirin-Changchun Railway to Taonanfu. These lines were to connect with the South Manchuria and the Peking-Mukden Railways. China further agreed that if in the building of railways from Taonanfu to Jehol and from Hailungfu to the city of Kirin it should be proposed to borrow foreign capital, negotiations would first be entered into with Japanese capitalists. The signing of this agreement was a very distinct victory for Japanese finance in the development of Manchuria, and the question arises why did China concede these rights to Japan. It has been affirmed that in 1913 at the time of the counter revolution of the republicans against Yuan Shih-kai some Japanese were killed by Chinese at Nanking and it is alleged that the Japanese Govern-

[54] MacMurray, op. cit., 762 and 765.
[55] Manchuria, Treaties and Agreements, 148-150.

ment was appeased by the note of the Chinese Minister on October 5th.[56]

As suggested earlier in this chapter, it is essential to recall two factors in Manchurian history if one is to evaluate properly the course of Chino-Japanese negotiations between 1906 and 1913. The first is the question of the "Open Door" in Manchuria. The patience of the Japanese Government and of the Japanese people had been strained to a point of extreme danger by the attitude of foreign commercial interests in China. The columns of the foreign press were filled with the "violations" of the Japanese. From this continual assault Tokyo found relief only in the correct attitude of the British and American Governments. While ready to support their nationals should the "Open Door" be denied them in China, the attitude of these Governments was entirely sympathetic toward Japan and expressed confidence that the Mikado's Empire would not depart from its announced policy in the Far East. Nevertheless, the injustice of repeated attacks on Japanese policy could only serve to bestir the Tokyo Government to the end that everything which it could claim as a legitimate right in Manchuria, might be safeguarded.

The second factor to recall is that of railway politics. In the attempts of foreign capitalists to buy the South Manchuria Railway; in their later attempts to use the threat of a competing line to force the sale of the Japanese road, and in the bluff that competition would be forced upon Japan whether or not she permitted the sale of her Manchurian railway lines; in all of these schemes Japan saw the plans of those interests whose

---

[56] Gerard, *Ma Mission en Chine*, 312-313, and "Japanese Concessions in Manchuria," in *Far Eastern Review*, October, 1913, 181.

purpose was to force her out of the Manchurian market and to deprive her of what she considered her meagre fruits of victory. It was a period of the most trying diplomacy. Having driven Russia from South Manchuria at tremendous cost, it was not to be supposed that Japan would surrender the rights she had won at an exorbitant figure. Each attempt to thwart her advance was looked upon not merely as a violation of Japan's treaty rights but as a threat against the necessary consolidation of her position. Between 1906 and 1909 such threats appeared repeatedly, and each in turn reinforced her now well established policy. This policy was carefully conceived and for the most part applied with judgment and reserve. Having concluded peace with Russia and secured the consent of China to the transfer of the former Russian rights and leasehold by the Treaty of Portsmouth and the Peking Convention, respectively, Japan had determined to adhere to the settlement provided by these documents. Therefore, in the subsequqent Chino-Japanese negotiations, which have been related in this chapter, Japan required of China recognition of her position in Manchuria to the full extent permitted by the treaties of 1905. In view of the obstacles which China placed in the way of that policy, it is a tribute to Japan that her ministers were governed by reserve and dignity; that her policy was in keeping with treaty obligations, and acceptable to those powers which had commercial interests in Manchuria.

In passing judgment on Japanese diplomacy it must be recognized that the Antung-Mukden Railway agreement, of all those concluded by China and Japan between 1906 and 1913, was the only one in which the attitude of Tokyo may be described as arbitrary. In

all others there was a generous consideration of the
Chinese view, at a time when actions of the Peking
Government were by no means conducive to such an
attitude.   The China of those days was, with minor
differences, the China of the past.   The old policy of
playing one foreign power against another was still
the main feature in her futile attempt to repel the advance of invading interests and protect what little remained of the nation's sovereignty.   Both on the surface and behind the closed doors of Peking's political
life the wisdom and vitality of the Manchu dynasty
were things of the past.   Those inseparable attributes
of a vigorous government—integrity and service to the
nation— were conspicuously absent, a condition which
in Japan aroused the contempt of the growing power
of the military class, fresh from its victory in the Russian War.   And thus the surprising fact of the years
1906-1913 is not to be found in such an incident as the
settlement of the Antung-Mukden dispute, but in the
conciliatory features which marked Japan's whole
policy during these years.

CHAPTER XI

THE MANCHURIAN TREATY AND NOTES OF 1915

It has long been the philosophy of her statesmen that the whole world is China's enemy. Yet, if pent-up fears and hatreds, kindled in the breasts of her rulers during the past three-quarters of a century, were to break forth, the object of their revenge would not be a European Power or the United States, but Japan. This bitter relationship, which has developed during the present century, finds an explanation in the whole course of Chino-Japanese intercourse, as related in previous chapters. But it would seem appropriate to add a word in approaching the complexities of the subject now to be treated. It has been assumed by some students that the Japanese demands presented to China in January, 1915, require no explanation, and that there is little use in hunting for the motives which prompted their presentation. These critics accept the view that in 1915 Japanese statesmen, being human, and thus far from infallible, committed a grave blunder. What could be simpler? How else can the events of 1915 be explained? Perhaps this is the correct view, yet of this the writer is by no means convinced. Such an explanation takes no account of the traditions of Japan's code of diplomacy and disregards entirely her orderly and sagacious growth from a feudal state to a great world power.[1]

The writer is not unaware that too great a zeal to find for each and every action a motive well founded in national tradition may create motives which at the

---

[1] Dillon, *The Inside Story of the Peace Conference*, Chapter IX, Japan.

time never existed. Against such a tendency one must be constantly on guard. Nevertheless, it is inconceivable that the whole trend of national and international development may be discarded, and that the events which form history may be isolated and labeled as "Approved" or "Not Approved" on the simple standard of whether statesmen were sagacious or blundering. Japanese history provides an example, and the events of 1915 and those which followed must be regarded as a part of the longer period of Japan's relationship with China. But even this approach does not simplify the problem presented by the Manchurian Treaty and notes of 1915, which formed a part of the famous or infamous Twenty-One Demands.

Back through the centuries, so long as history retains any record, the civilization of China had persisted. Slowly, ponderously, irresistibly this civilization had grown. Her peoples were ruled, now by one, now by another dynasty, some of which were alien, yet even when conquered, China rose victorious and absorbed the conquerer into her life and made of him a Chinese.

Across the seas to the east lay the islands of Nippon, insignificant, harboring a young and uncultured race; so ran the Chinese view. Then came the westerner. In 1854 Japan turned her back on the policy of exclusion and seclusion. In the course of half a century her entire life was transformed.[2] She adopted the civilization of the west. Some of what she acquired was good but as might reasonably have been expected she also accepted the bad when it seemed profitable to do so.

During these years the life of China remained practically unchanged. While she witnessed first her own

---

[2] Gubbins, *op. cit.*, Chapter VIII *et. seq.*

defeat, and later that of Russia at the hands of Japan, her government failed to understand the foreigner, and she looked with contempt, perhaps with some jealousy, upon this upstart of the Pacific who had deserted the ancient culture of the East for the materialistic civilization of the barbarian.[3] The feeling of bitterness was increased by a multitude of forces in Far Eastern intercourse, but principally by the struggle, which we have seen, centered in Manchuria. China had rejoiced in 1895 when Japan was forced to return the leasehold in the Liaotung Peninsula. But in 1904 and 1905 China did nothing to protect her own sovereignty in Manchuria. She allowed Japan to fight her battle for the "Three Eastern Provinces" and reluctantly consented to the transfer of the Russian concessions to Japan at the close of the war. The years which followed provided Tokyo with a lesson which unfortunately was inevitably to be learned. The Far Eastern diplomacy which surrounded the Harriman scheme, the Hsinmintun-Fakumen Railway, the Chinchow-Aigun Railway, the schemes of the proposed Manchurian Bank, and the Knox Neutralization proposal, convinced Japan that her Manchurian interests were in jeopardy. She began to question whether the settlements, generally speaking moderate in character, which had been based on the Peking Convention of December, 1905, did provide a sufficiently strong guarantee of her special position in China.[4] This situation prevailed in the Far East in 1914 when Japan was called to the assistance of her ally, Great Britain, in the World War.

With Japan's declaration of war against Germany and the capture of Kiaochow we are not concerned. It

---

[3] Morse, *The International Relations of the Chinese Empire*, Vol. III, 153.
[4] Note the Root-Takahira Agreement of November 30, 1908, United States *Foreign Relations*, (1908), 510-511.

is sufficient to note that since hostilities took place on Chinese soil, China declared a war zone. The success of the Japanese troops is well known. After the military operations about Tsingtao friction between Japan and China increased. China demanded that the Japanese withdraw from the German railway between Tsingtao and Tsinan, the capital of Shantung. Japan refused to withdraw until the war was finished and the disposition of German rights settled by treaty. Tension increased in the capitals of the two powers and when on January 7, 1915, China proclaimed the revocation of the war zone, Tokyo replied sharply that such action would not be recognized. Popular ill-will was aroused in Japan and on January 18th the famous Twenty-One Demands were handed by Mr. Hioki, the Japanese Minister, to Yuan Shih-kai.[5] Relative to the demands, instructions had been given to Mr. Hioki by Baron Kato, the Japanese Foreign Minister, in Tokyo on December 3, 1914, and these instructions summarized the purpose of Japan's China-Policy. In order to provide for the readjustment of affairs consequent to the Japan-German war and for the purpose of ensuring a lasting peace in the Far East, Japan had determined to approach China with a view of concluding treaties on specific subjects. The demands were divided into five groups.[6] Group one dealt with the Shantung settlement; group two concerned the defining of Japan's position in South Manchuria and Eastern

---

[5] Treat, *op. cit.*, 209, and Hornbeck, *op. cit.*, 301-2.

[6] *The Sino-Japanese Negotiations of 1915, Japanese and Chinese Documents and Chinese Official Statement*, published by the Carnegie Endowment for International Peace, division of international law, No. 45, Washington, 1921.

A similar document to which reference is invited is: *The Chino-Japanese Negotiations: Official statement by the Chinese Government respecting the Chino-Japanese Negotiations brought to a conclusion by China's compliance with the terms of Japan's ultimatum delivered on May 7, 1915.* (With documents and treaties.) Peking, 1915.

Inner Mongolia; group three was to safeguard the best interest of the Han-Yeh-Ping Company; group four was intended to emphasize the principle of China's territorial integrity; group five represented certain "wishes" of the Japanese Government respecting foreign advisers employed by China. Mr. Hioki's instructions included the statement, "The Imperial (Japanese) Government are determined to attain this end (the acceptance of the demands by China) by all means within their power."

Group two, which concerned South Manchuria and Eastern Inner Mongolia, included the following demands:[7]

The Japanese Government and the Chinese Government in view of the fact that the Chinese Government has always recognized the predominant position of Japan in South Manchuria and Eastern Mongolia, agree to the following articles:

Article 1. The two contracting parties mutually agree that the term of the lease of Port Arthur and Dairen and the term respecting the South Manchuria Railway and the Antung-Mukden Railway shall be extended to a further period of ninety-nine years respectively.

Article 2. The Japanese subjects shall be permitted in South Manchuria and Eastern Inner Mongolia to lease or own land required either for erecting buildings for various commercial and industrial uses or for farming.

Article 3. The Japanese subjects shall have liberty to enter, reside, and travel in South Manchuria and Eastern Inner Mongolia, and to carry on business of various kinds—commercial, industrial, and otherwise.

Article 4. The Chinese Government grant to the Japanese Subjects the right of mining in South Manchuria and Eastern Inner Mongolia. As regards the mines to be worked, they shall be decided upon in a separate agreement.

Article 5. The Chinese Government agree that the consent of the Japanese Government shall be obtained in advance, (1)

---

[7] *The Sino-Japanese Negotiations of 1915*, 3-5. The text given is the official Japanese translation.

whenever it is proposed to grant to other nationals the right of constructing a railway or to obtain from other nationals the supply of funds for constructing a railway in South Manchuria and Eastern Inner Mongolia, and (2) whenever a loan is to be made with any other power, under security of the taxes of South Manchuria and Eastern Inner Mongolia.

Article 6. The Chinese Government engage that whenever the Chinese Government need the service of political, financial, or military advisers or instructors in South Manchuria or in Eastern Inner Mongolia, Japan shall first be consulted.

Article 7. The Chinese Government agree that the control and management of the Kirin-Changchun Railway shall be handed over to Japan for a term of ninety-nine years dating from the signing of this treaty.

Before proceeding to a discussion of these demands, the negotiations which continued until May, 1915, and the Manchurian Treaty which resulted, a brief account of the political situation in Japan will be given. This situation was an important factor influencing Japan's action, and the reader must view impartially each element in the unfortunate diplomacy of 1915 if he is to approach a truthful interpretation of the subject. At this time Count Okuma was at the head of the Japanese Ministry, while Baron Kato, head of the Doshikai Party, was Minister of Foreign Affairs. The domestic political situation was far from tranquil. Party strife was keen, while the more progressive elements in political life were waging their struggle for party government and a more responsible administration. Prior to the outbreak of the World War, the calling to power of the Okuma Ministry was regarded as epoch-making in the cause of responsible government.[8] In August all parties had united in support of the war. When, however, the Kiaochow campaign was completed the program of the government gave rise to differences of

---

[8] Hornbeck, op. cit., 167-168.

opinion. On December 25, 1914, Count Okuma approached the Diet on the question of increased army and navy appropriations and this the Diet refused by a substantial vote of 213 to 148. Okuma immediately dissolved the Diet, and a new election was called for March 25, 1915.[9]

During the interval before the election, the Government pushed its China policy with great effect. In the face of domestic political turmoil, Okuma and his followers were able to point to a strong and definite policy of advancing Japanese interests, both economic and political, in China. As an election cry it was most successful, and in the March elections Okuma and his Ministry were returned to power. It should be noted that after the election the Japanese demands were greatly moderated and the treaties which resulted were much less objectionable than the original demands. There is now no doubt that domestic politics entered very largely into the international situation and that there was by no means a unanimous opinion in Japan as to the wisdom of the nation's policy toward China.[10]

Conditions were very favorable to Japan's policy. The European Powers were fully occupied with the war, and Japan was thus protected from interference in two ways. The powers were in no position to come to the defense of their interests in China if threatened and that country found that her old game of setting one power against another was for the time being impossible. There is every reason to suppose that Japan was well aware of this. She had observed the play of this kind of Chinese diplomacy between 1906 and 1910, and the lesson was not lost upon her.[11] Nevertheless,

[9] *Ibid.*, 175 and 303.

[10] Treat, *op. cit.*, 210.

[11] Commenting on the outcome of the 1915 negotiations the *Manchester Guardian* stated on May 10, 1915, that even the program which China had

it must not be assumed that Japan's decision was made hastily or that it encountered no opposition.   Certain factors played strongly into the hands of the Imperialists who were ready on any pretext to increase their hold on China.   To these aggressive, but hardly wise councillors, it appeared that such a favorable moment should not escape.   The war had showed more clearly than anything else the value of Chinese mineral resources to Japan.   Particularly was this true as regards sources of iron.   The conciliatory treaties concluded regarding Japan's rights in Manchuria no longer afforded her interests ample protection.   And thus, argued the Imperialist, why should Japan not act when the other powers could not interfere.   It was an argument which could be used with great effect for in the whole of the Twenty-One Demands Japan asked very little that other nations had not, at one time or another, received from China.[12]   This was in no sense a justification of Japan's action, but knowledge of it is essential if her motives are to be appreciated.

The five groups of demands, as already noted, were presented to China, without warning, on January 18, 1915, with the stipulation that absolute secrecy be maintained by the Chinese Government.   Negotiations concerning the demands commenced at a conference held on February 2nd, but it will be necessary here to limit the discussion to Group II concerning Manchuria and Eastern Inner Mongolia.   Although by no means the most objectionable of the demands, those in Group II were sufficiently strong to raise grave question as to

---

then accepted, not to mention that which she rejected, could never have been put forward had not the hands of the Powers been tied by the war.   That it should have been put forward at such a time was in the opinion of this paper its most astonishing feature.   (6.)

   [12] In this connection the reader may note certain striking parallels in the actions of the allied squadrons at the time of the Tientsin Treaties.   The parallel extends even to the matter of rebellion within the Empire.

Japan's motives.[13]   The preamble attempted to secure
China's acceptance of a situation not in keeping with
the facts of history, for it would be absurd to suppose
that "China has always recognized the predominant
position of Japan in South Manchuria and Eastern
Inner Mongolia."   There was little of a surprising nature in the first article of the group asking for an extension of the Manchurian leaseholds to ninety-nine
years.   This was the term granted by China in most
of the foreign concessions and Japan had been unfortunate in falling heir to the Russian contracts of twenty-five years.   Articles 2, 3, and 4 of the Manchurian
group were particularly significant.   These, it will be
remembered, concerned the right to own or lease land,
to reside and travel and to carry on mining.   Consent
to these demands would have been a grave departure
from China's policy respecting treaty ports, concessions, and the so-called "spheres of influence."   Article
5, respecting railway loans in South Manchuria, was
natural enough and came as a direct result of the international railway schemes which had been used as a
club over the South Manchuria Railway during the
years 1906 to 1910.   Granted that Japan possessed special interests in these regions, Article 6, insuring that
her advice would be accepted in preference to that of
other foreign powers was not very surprising.   Nor
was the demand that the control and management of
the Kirin-Changchun Railway be given to Japan for
ninety-nine years a serious one from the Chinese point
of view.   Although a Chinese Government line, it had

---

[13] Of all the demands, those in Group V presented the most objectionable
features. Although these were presented as merely the "wishes" of the Japanese Government, their mere formulation was unwarranted and out of keeping
with Japan's expressed policy in China. *(The Sino-Japanese Negotiations of
1915, 2.)*

no connection with the Imperial Railways of north China. It was in reality merely a branch of the South Manchuria Railway, which line had furnished China with half the capital for the construction of the road. As pointed out in a previous chapter, this line, under Chinese management, was a financial failure, but since it has been taken over by the South Manchuria Railway Company in 1917, it has become the most profitable in Manchuria for its running mileage.[14]

While not so alarming as it has sometimes been represented, Group II of the Twenty-One Demands was nevertheless highly objectionable. It appeared as the demands of a victor to the vanquished, rather than as proposals of a friendly power to a weak neighbor. It would never have been made had not Japan realized her own power and China's weakness. Aware of the jealousy of the European nations, Japan would scarcely have dared to present the demands had those powers been free to resist her. All of which indicates more clearly the real issue raised by Japan's diplomacy. Her demands were objectionable, but their general nature was by no means new or unprecedented in the relations of the Powers with China. What remains as astonishing, and as yet unexplained, was the nature and time of Japan's presentation. Preliminary, therefore, to a discussion of the method pursued by the Tokyo Government is a brief statement of the course of the negotiations themselves.

---

[14] Article 7, however, was the subject of a bitter attack on the part of the *Far Eastern Review* which regarded the situation as follows: "The claim that the Kirin-Chang-chun Railway, a Chinese Government line, should be handed over to Japan for ninety-nine years marks the zenith of Japanese audacity. There has been no war with China in the immediate past. Japan is not imposing terms of peace upon China. Her only concern, so she has assured the world, is to preserve peace in the Far East and to fulfill her engagement with Great Britain. But does robbing China of one of her railways conduce to either of these ends?" (*Far Eastern Review*, February, 1915, 11,339.)

China presented a counterproject to Japan's original demands on February 12, 1915.[15]   China disclosed a full realization of the nature of the Japanese preamble and substituted for it a statement that Japan would always respect the sovereignty of China in the "Three Eastern Provinces."   All mention of predominant position and special interest enjoyed by Japan was omitted and Eastern Inner Mongolia was not mentioned. China agreed to the Japanese demands of Article I in respect to the South Manchuria Railway and the leased territory but to this was added "that in all other matters the provisions of the respective original treaties shall be adhered to."[16]   So far as the Antung-Mukden Railway was concerned China agreed to negotiate with Japan relative to an extension of the term of lease.[17] Peking also agreed to open new marts to trade in South Manchuria, and to permit merchants of Japan and all other countries to reside, trade, and carry on all kinds of commercial and industrial business, and to rent land after fair negotiations with the owners.[18]   Nothing was said in the counterproject regarding the right to own land or to travel freely.   China's opposition to the opening of Manchuria and Eastern Inner Mongolia to Japanese travel and residence, with the right to own land and carry on business was natural and proper, for, so long as extraterritoriality prevailed, intolerable conditions would result.   The Japanese scattered throughout the territory, would be subject only to their own consuls and their own laws.   This condition is one that Japan should have appreciated.   She had suffered from extraterritoriality, though not so severely as

---

[15] *Sino-Japanese Negotiations of 1915*, 8-10.

[16] *Ibid.*, Group II, clause 1.

[17] *Ibid.*, Group II, clause 2.

[18] *Ibid.*, Group II, article 3.

China, and her territory was not opened to travel and residence until the foreigners had consented to place themselves under Japanese jurisdiction. For this reason alone Japan should have been the last power to extend the application of extraterritoriality in China.[19] The right of prospecting new mines in South Manchuria was granted to Japanese syndicates desiring to do so for one year, and to work one-half of the mines discovered by this means, China retaining control of the other half.[20] China also agreed to give Japan the preference in all railway loans in South Manchuria.[21] Article 6 was accepted by China with only a minor change in the wording. Article 7 regarding the Kirin-Changchun railway was not mentioned. In its place China proposed the following article in the counter-project: "The existing treaties between China and Japan in regard to the 'Three Eastern Provinces' shall remain in force as heretofore, except as otherwise provided for in the present agreement."[22]

On the basis of the original demands and the counterproject, negotiations between the two powers were continued between Lou Tseng-tsing, the Chinese Minister for Foreign Affairs, and Mr. Hioki. For the sake of clearness and brevity the results of the negotiations will be given in the order in which the demands were originally presented, rather than as a chronological account of the various conferences which is needlessly confusing. There was considerable discussion on the subject of the preamble of Group II[23] but by the time of the Chinese reply of May 1, to Japan's revised de-

---

[19] Treat, *op. cit.*, 213.

[20] *Sino-Japanese Negotiations of 1915*, Group II, article 4.

[21] *Ibid.*, Group II, article 5.

[22] *Sino-Japanese Negotiations of 1915*, Group II, 10.

[23] *Far Eastern Review*, March, 1915, 11,399.

mands of April 26, Tokyo had dropped its claim to a special position in South Manchuria and the preamble to Group II declared that the object of the demands was the development of economic relations in South Manchuria.[24]

Concerning Article 1 of Group II Japan and China were in substantial agreement before the negotiations commenced. By March 9th, at the eighth conference, China had agreed to accept Japan's demand for the extension of the lease of Dairen, Port Arthur, the South Manchuria and the Antung-Mukden Railways.[25] Articles 2 and 3 were discussed in the conference of March 13th. By that time agreement had been reached on all points save the right to own land, the right to engage in farming, and the question of restricting Japanese in South Manchuria to treaty ports. China yielded on the question of farming, but Japan continued to insist on complete extraterritoriality for her subjects and thus questions involved in these clauses were not settled until after the last conference on April 17th.[26] Concerning mining rights, demanded in Article 4, Japan presented thirteen mining areas in which she desired concessions. China agreed, at the conference of March 23rd, to grant concessions in nine of these, but refused in the case of the remaining four which were located in Eastern Inner Mongolia.[27] China readily agreed to

[24] See final amended project of Chinese Government of May 1, 1915, and Preamble to the Treaty respecting South Manchuria and Eastern Inner Mongolia. (Sino-Japanese Negotiations of 1915, 26 and 44.)

[25] This left only one outstanding question—the provision in the original treaty with Russia which gave China the right to repurchase the southern branch of the Chinese Eastern Railway after a period of thirty-six years, that is in 1938. Consideration of this clause was postponed until a later date. (Far Eastern Review, March, 1915, 11,399.) See also The Sino-Japanese Negotiations of 1915, 67.

[26] Far Eastern Review, March, 1915, 11,400.

[27] Far Eastern Review, April, 1915, 11,440.

the section of Article 5 respecting loans for railways
to be constructed in South Manchuria, but Japan increased her demand at the conference of March 13th,
asking not only to be consulted before such loans were
made but that Japan be the sole power to make such
loans.[28]   This China refused and later the demand was
withdrawn.   The second part of Article 5 was agreed
to by China on March 23rd.[29]   Article 6 had been accepted by China in the counterproject but she formally
assented to it on March 23rd.[30]

The Kirin-Changchun Railway was not mentioned in
the counterproject, but on March 23rd China agreed to
an amendment of the loan agreement.[31]   When the conferences ended on April 17th, agreement had been
reached with respect to Articles 1 (with the exception
of the repurchase clause of the South Manchuria Railway Treaty) 4, 5, 6, and 7.   The questions which remained for settlement included: the language of the
preamble, the inclusion of Eastern Inner Mongolia
(with which we are not concerned), the repurchase
clause of the South Manchuria Railway Treaty, restric-
tion of Japanese in South Manchuria to Treaty ports,
Japenese ownership of land in South Manchuria, and
extraterritoriality as applied to Japanese holding leases
in South Manchuria.   Then Japan presented her revised demands of April 26th, in which she yielded on
the question of the preamble,[32] and made provision for
a modified extraterritoriality.   China's reply to these
revised demands was issued on May 1st at a conference
in which the Minister for Foreign Affairs read a mem-

---

[28] *Ibid, March,* 1915, 11,400.
[29] *Ibid.,* April, 1915, 11,440, and *The Sino-Japanese Negotiations of 1915,* 69.
[30] *The Sino-Japanese Negotiations of 1915,* 69.
[31] *Ibid.,* 69.
[32] *Ibid.,* 10-19.

orandum to the Japanese Minister. In this statement China yielded on all points save the ownership of land by Japanese.[33]

From the Japanese point of view it now appeared that nothing further could be gained through negotiation and on May 7th, Mr. Hioki presented to the Chinese Minister for Foreign Affairs the ultimatum of the Tokyo Government.[34] It demanded acceptance of Japan's amended project before 6 p. m. of May 9th and was accompanied by an explanatory note which, among other things, stated that the words "lease or purchase" in Article 2 of Group II might be replaced by the words "temporary lease" or "perpetual lease" or simply by "lease" on the clear understanding that it should mean a long-term lease with the privilege of its unconditional renewal.[35] China complied with the terms of the ultimatum on May 8th.[36]

On May 25th the Manchurian as well as the Shantung Treaty was signed by Mr. Hioki and the Chinese Minister of Foreign Affairs.[37] On the same day a series of notes was exchanged by the plenipotentiaries. These settled details arising out of the clauses of the treaty, such as that the lease of Port Arthur and Dairen should expire in 1997. The date for reversion to China of the South Manchuria Railway was fixed as 2002, and the clause in Article 12 of the original Chinese Eastern Railway Agreement providing that the Chinese Government might take over the railway after thirty-six years from the day on which it was opened to traffic, was declared null and void. The term of

---

[33] *Ibid.*, 19-23 and 26-29.
[34] *Ibid.*, 31-36.
[35] *Ibid.*, 36-38.
[36] *Ibid.*, 38-39.
[37] *Ibid.*, 39-63.

lease of the Antung-Mukden Railway was fixed to expire in 2007. The mining properties which might be prospected by Japanese subjects were specified in detail. China agreed to negotiate first with Japanese capitalists in case funds were sought abroad for the construction of railways in South Manchuria and Eastern Inner Mongolia.[38] The notes further provided that if China desired to employ foreign advisers in South Manchuria preference would be given to Japanese. The Japanese interpretation of the term "lease" was also included. It is to be noted that China agreed in the treaty to a fundamental revision of agreements and contracts relating to the Kirin-Changchun railway on the basis of terms embodied in railway loan agreements which China had entered into with foreign capitalists, and if in the future the Chinese Government granted to foreign capitalists in matters relating to railway loans, more advantageous terms than those in the various existing railway loan agreements, the Kirin-Changchun Railway Loan Agreement, should, if so desired by Japan, be further revised.[39]

To sum up the entire situation resulting from the Manchurian Treaty and Notes it may be said that Japan had gained the following: the extension of the term of her leaseholds in South Manchuria; permission for Japanese subjects to lease land[40] and to enter, travel, and reside in South Manchuria; the application

---

[38] It was also agreed that when the Chinese Government proposed to raise a loan abroad on the security of the taxes of South Manchuria and Eastern Inner Mongolia, (excluding, however, the salt gabelle and customs duties which are already made securities for the loans of the Chinese Central Government), they would first consult Japanese capitalists.

[39] Article 7 of the treaty respecting South Manchuria and Eastern Inner Mongolia. *(The Sino-Japanese Negotiations of 1915, 46-47.)*

[40] Japanese subjects have not as yet (1924) leased any land in Manchuria because the preliminary regulations which were to be drawn up before such lease could be made have not been drafted.

of a modified extraterritoriality with special provision for a joint tribunal in the case of civil suits arising out of land disputes between Japanese subjects and Chinese citizens; the opening of more Manchurian towns to international trade; and the revision of the Kirin-Changchun Railway Loan Agreement.

News of the settlement reached by China and Japan was received favorably in the foreign capitals and especially in London. The reason for this was evident. Great Britain, France, and Russia were involved in the European War and were unable to concern themselves with the settlement of Far Eastern problems. Nevertheless, there was frequent and heated debate in the House of Commons concerning the negotiations, and questions asked from the floor of the House occasioned the British Ministry no little embarrassment. Sir Edward Grey was questioned in Parliament as early as February 18th,[41] replying that he was not in a position to communicate information on the subject of the Twenty-One Demands which had been given to him confidentially by the Japanese Government. Similar questions were asked in Parliament on March 2,[42] when the Government was in possession of the full text of the Demands, to which Sir Edward replied in like manner. As late as March 4 the British Government had received no representations from the Chinese Government.[43] and it soon became evident that such interest as was manifested by the House was concerned with British vested interests in the Yangtze Valley.[44] Finally on March 11th, Mr. Primrose, Under Secretary of State for Foreign Affairs, voiced the position of the

---

[41] *Parliamentary Debates* (C) February 18, 1915, vol. 69, 1286.
[42] *Ibid.*, March 2, 1915, vol. 70, 639, (C).
[43] *Ibid.*, March 4, 1915, vol. 70, 977, (C).
[44] *Ibid.*, March 9, 1915, vol. 70, 1237.

British Government as the ally of Japan, stating that His Majesty's Government had no objection to the expansion of Japanese interests in China, provided that such expansion inflicted no injury on British interests.[45] Finally on April 20th, six days before the presentation of the amended Japanese proposals, Sir Edward Grey informed the House that the Government was not in a position to make a statement, but speaking generally he might say that His Majesty's Government, in its China policy, continued to be governed by the terms of the existing agreement (the Anglo-Japanese Alliance) between the United Kingdom and Japan. The purpose of this Agreement, he said, was the preservation of the common interests of all powers in China by insuring the independence and integrity of the Chinese Republic, and the principle of equal opportunity for the commerce and industry of all nations in China.[46] After the presentation of Japan's ultimatum it became known that the British Government had been in communication with Tokyo in regard to any possible bearing of the Twenty-One Demands on the Anglo-Japanese Alliance, but in the view of Downing Street, no occasion for a protest had arisen in that connection.[47] The Government believed that the Japanese ultimatum did not indicate that Tokyo's action was in violation of the Anglo-Japanese Alliance and in fact Sir Edward Grey's reply stated without reserve that no breach of the Anglo-Japanese Alliance had occurred.[48] It may be assumed that the British Government in this case regarded the technical aspects of the treaty with the exactitude which had marked its attitude in 1907 and

[45] *Parliamentary Debates* (C) March 11, 1915, vol. 70, 1721.

[46] *Ibid.*, April 20, 1915, vol. 71, 157-159.

[47] *Ibid.*, May 12, 1915, vol. 71, 1657.

[48] *Ibid.*, May 13, 1915, vol. 71, 1825-1826.

1908 when a British construction firm, backed by American capital, was attempting to promote railway schemes, contrary to Japanese interests in Manchuria.

The policy of the American Government during the course of the 1915 negotiations was cautious and correct in all aspects. Mr. Paul S. Reinsch, Minister to Peking, became aware of a feeling of tension between Tokyo and Peking as early as September, 1914. On October 2nd, Yuan Shih-kai asked the American Minister to request President Wilson to use his good offices in conferring with the British Government in order to prevail upon Japan to restrict her action in Shantung to the military necessities involved in the capture of Tsingtao.[49]   Despite the absolute secrecy demanded by the Japanese Government, the American Minister was informed of the nature of the demands on January 22nd.[50]   Later Mr. Reinsch was consulted by the Chinese Foreign Office respecting the demands and expressed the opinion that detailed negotiations of individual demands, with a view of granting only the least objectionable, would be likely to give more force to considerations of equity.   On February 19th the American State Department informed Mr. Reinsch that the demands under Group V were not being urged, and the full text of the original demands had been communicated to the various foreign offices.[51]   At this juncture the American Minister dispatched a telegram to President Wilson inviting the chief executive's per-

---

[49] Reinsch, *An American Diplomat in China*, 125, see also Reinsch, "Secret Diplomacy and the Twenty-one Demands," in *Asia*, November, 1921, 937. Quoting a remark of President Yuan during their visit: "From the information in my possession," he (Yuan) said, "I am convinced that the Japanese have a definite and far-reaching plan to use the European crisis in an attempt to lay the foundations of control over China."

[50] Reinsch, *An American Diplomat in China*, 131.

[51] *Ibid.*, 136.

sonal attention to the proposals which affected the rights and legitimate prospects of Americans in China, but a personal letter to Mr. Reinsch from the President had been mailed on February 8th. In this the President said: "I have had the feeling that any direct advice in China, or direct intervention on her behalf in the present negotiations, would really do her more harm than good, inasmuch as it would very likely provoke the jealousy and excite the hostility of Japan which would first be manifested against China herself . . . . For the present I am watching the situation very carefully indeed, ready to step in at any point where it is wise to do so.[52]

Certain possible solutions of the deadlock between China and Japan were suggested by the Department of State. These aimed to bestow desired benefits upon Japan, but at the same time to protect China and American interests in China.[53] But the lending of a sympathetic hearing to all matters which the Chinese wished to discuss was as far as the American Minister was permitted to go. On May 6th the American State Department had cabled counseling both governments to patience and mutual forbearance, but the advice came too late as the ultimatum was presented on May 7th.[54] Then on May 11th Washington cabled an identical note to Tokyo and Peking reasserting the principle of equal opportunity and reserving all American rights that might be affected by the Demands. This note was delivered by Mr. Reinsch to the Chinese Minister of Foreign Affairs on May 13th.[55]

---

[52] *Ibid.*, 137.

[53] *Ibid.*, 139.

[54] *Ibid.*, 148.

[55] Reinsch, *op. cit.*, 148.

When assessing the blame of the European Powers that secured leaseholds on the coasts of China during 1897-1898 it is well for the American

Some rather startling revelations with respect to American policy in the Far East in 1915 have been made as a result of the belated publication of the United States Foreign Relations volume for the year just mentioned. The particular portion of this correspondence that is of interest for our purposes has been excellently summarized by Dr. Payson J. Treat in an article, "Our Asiatic Neighbors," (Washington Historical Quarterly, Vol. XVII, No. 2, April, 1926.) We have learned, writes Dr. Treat, "that the American Department of State, after a careful scrutiny of the Japanese demands and in the light of information received from our representatives in Peking and Tokyo, informed Japan that in respect to sixteen of the demands it was not disposed to raise any question. These included the demands regarding Shantung Province, for which Japan was so roundly denounced in the United States four years later, and regarding South Manchuria and Eastern Inner Mongolia. Only five of the demands seemed objectionable to our State Department, two of these on the ground that they would be a violation of the principle of the 'Open Door' and three because they were 'clearly derogatory to the political independence and administrative entity of that country.' Japan acceded

student in particular to bear in mind the new light shed on the policy of our own government as a result of the publication of the volume of Foreign Relations for 1915. "We here learned for the first time that in 1900 our Navy Department desired to secure a coaling station at Samsah Inlet, north of Foochow, and Mr. John Hay sounded Japan to see if she would object to our securing such a lease in Fukien Province, which was a recognized Japanese sphere of interest. It doubtless will come as a surprise to many students of Far Eastern History to learn that so soon after Germany, Russia, Great Britain, and France had secured naval bases in China, the United States should have made such a proposal. Japan replied that she did not wish any power to secure a lease in that Province, and the matter was dropped. But this American proposal was the basis of Japan's demand that she should be consulted first if China needed foreign capital to work mines, build railways, and construct harborworks in the Province of Fukien." (Treat, "Our Asiatic Neighbors," in Washington Historical Quarterly, Vol. XVII, No. 2, April, 1926.)

to our suggestions in every case. Four of the demands
were dropped, and the fifth was changed to an exchange
of notes which, following our suggestion, stated that
China would not permit any Power 'to construct a dock-
yard, a coaling station for military use, or a naval base
or to set up any other military establishment on the
coast of Fukien Province, nor shall they allow any like
establishment to be set up with any foreign capital on
the said coast.'   In other words, there was absolutely
nothing in the Sino-Japanese treaties of 1915 to which
the American Government had taken the slightest offense.   Yet I am afraid it will be many years before
American opinion recognizes these simple facts."

Something still remains to be said, not primarily
concerning what Japan demanded in 1915, but concerning the manner of the demand, and also upon the subject of China's counterdiplomacy.   As indicated earlier
in this chapter, the world had less occasion for surprise
at the content of the Twenty-one Demands than at the
circumstances in which they were pressed.   It is only
from an examination, with this fact constantly in view,
that a more intimate conception of the international
forces at work in the Far East in 1915, may be attained.   It is now a generally accepted fact that since
her entry into the community of progressive nations,
Japan's main aspiration had been to play a leading and
civilizing part in the Far East.[56]   She had hoped to
play a directing part in leading China from the old into
a new world.   To Japan this seemed a legitimate and
profitable policy; and, it must be conceded, there was
nothing surprising in this desire to contribute to the
intellectual and moral advance of the Chinese.   But,
that Japan should assume such a role, met by no means

---

[56] Dillon, *The Inside Story of the Peace Conference*, 328 *et seq.*

the unqualified support of the European Powers. Russia, France, and Germany foiled Japanese plans in 1895; Russia displaced Japanese influence in Korea and Manchuria until 1904, and nationals of the United States and Great Britain (though for the most part unsupported by their governments) kept the question alive in the years following the Russo-Japanese War. To these obstacles was added China's constant disapproval of any advance in Japanese interests. In this respect China's attitude was not exceptional. Since the beginning of European intercourse with the Middle Kingdom, she had sought to defend herself by playing one power against another. She now conceived that her best policy lay in combining all the European nations against Japan. She had attempted to create friction between the signatories of the Anglo-Japanese Alliance in 1907 and 1908, but her diplomacy met with no success. Its aim, however, did not escape astute Japanese statesmen, and it presented a case diametrically opposed to the now firm and deeply rooted policy of Tokyo.

This policy as already stated sought to establish Japan as the dominant power in the Far East. The lesson her European rivals in China had taught her was plain enough, and it developed a materialistic philosophy which accepted the real facts of the situation and acted upon them. It is a matter of common knowledge that the positions held by European Powers in China were the result of the force of great national fleets which opened the gates to trade, wrung from China concessions and leaseholds, and deprived her of all save the name of sovereignty and territorial integrity. Japan had first observed, and then participated in these events. It appeared to her national interest to do so. Yet it must not be forgotten that in her diplomatic dealings with China until 1915, Japan had pursued a policy which could neither be termed aggressive nor lacking in sympathy and understanding for the problems of her great but seemingly helpless neighbor. She had not merely complied scrupulously with her treaty obligations, but had accepted the policy of the "Open Door" and had made that policy her own in the Japanese sphere in South Manchuria. The credit for this record which was Japan's until 1915, must go in large part, if not in its entirety, to the sagacious counsels of the Genro, the Elder Statesmen, who, having actively participated in the making of modern Japan, now in the days of their retirement, advised the younger councils of administrators in the shaping of their country's program.[57]

The events and tendencies here set forth simply indicate in what direction Japan was headed. Sometime between 1910 and 1914 what seemed the inevitable goal of Japan's Far Eastern policy became clear and, relatively speaking, simple. Experience had provided its own lesson. Japan's temperate policy had produced very definite but very unsatisfactory results. Her own interests in China had advanced but slowly and were accompanied by inadequate guarantees. The precariousness of her position had encouraged American capitalists to threaten such rights as she did possess. No moderation on Japan's part seemed capable of winning the sympathy of the Chinese Government, and the goal of Japanese ambition, which cannot be dismissed in a word as immoral, pernicious, and illegitimate, seemed further removed than before. The time had come for a change in policy. In an article con-

---

[57] Gubbins, op. cit., 302-303.

tributed to the *Shin Nippon* or "New Japan," a magazine published in Tokyo, in the November number of 1914, Count Okuma, then prime minister, said the tendency of the day justified the assumption that in the not distant future a few strong nations would govern the remainder of the world, and that Japan must prepare herself to become one of these governing nations.[58] How aggressive elements in Japanese public life subscribed to this view, the whole history of the Twenty-One Demands can best tell. In a word it meant that Japan would adhere to her ideals of dominance in the Far East.

Bearing this situation in mind and giving full weight to the force of this national philosophy, the procedure of the Japanese Government becomes more explicable. Greater significance attaches itself to the instructions given by Baron Kato to Mr. Hioki on December 3rd. The unusual procedure in presenting the demands to the President of the Chinese Republic, and not to the Minister of Foreign Affairs, loses some of its mystery, and the caution that the demands be kept secret becomes not unnatural.[59] During March, Japan moved additional troops to Manchuria, explaining that these contingents were being sent to relieve the garrisons. This was certainly a reprehensible act but not unnatural if Japan's policy was to be carried into effect.[60] It was simply indicative of the coercive measures which the Tokyo Government was prepared to take.

---

[58] Gubbins, *op. cit.*, 277-278.

[59] The fact that Japan published on February 14th a list of eleven demands as constituting the entire subject of the negotiations with China while actually omitting Group V and other strong demands appeared, however, as a distinct departure from Japan's ethical code. (Hornbeck, *op cit.*, 305.)

[60] The movement of these troops to Manchuria was in advance of the regular time for changing garrisons and as the new troops arrived the old were not withdrawn. (Hornbeck, *op. cit.*, 320-321.)

But the presentation of the ultimatum of May 7th remains as an unexplained and inexcusable blunder of Japan's diplomacy. China had already yielded to the great majority of Japan's demands, in some cases on the basis of compromise, and there seemed little reason to suppose that a settlement on all points could not be reached on a basis of negotiation. Nevertheless, in her anxiety to bring the negotiations to a close, a desire which was caused in no small measure by foreign disfavor toward the whole proceeding, Japan brought upon herself almost universal condemnation. Yet the tone of this document was greatly softened through the efforts of the Elder Statesmen, and, it is interesting to note, Baron Kato later declared that the ultimatum was sent at the request of Yuan Shih-kai as an eleventh hour expedient to save China's face. If such were the case Japan played the part, not of the knave, but of the fool.[61]   But regardless of whether the ultimatum was framed with the purpose of easing the situation for China, it stood as an astonishing political blunder and it is impossible to believe that Japan's statesmen could have been ignorant of and indifferent to the consequences it would involve.

The only optimistic and satisfying influence that remained after the negotiations were completed and the treaties signed was the outspoken criticism voiced in Japan at the government's drastic policy. This criticism grew steadily in strength, and the fall of the Okuma Ministry in the following year has been ascribed generally to dissatisfaction with its Chinese policy. It is clear that subsequent ministries have

---

[61] *Far Eastern Review*, 18, December, 1922, 728-729. See also Hornbeck, *op. cit.*, 326-328, concerning a discussion of Japan's ultimatum and the modification of her demands as compared with those put forth as last and final on April 26.

attempted to make amends for the sacrifice of Chinese friendship in 1915.[62] The character of these efforts will be considered in the following chapter.

China's position following the Revolution of 1911 and the establishment of the Republic in 1912 can only be described as most unfortunate. At no time could the Peking Government be considered as representative of China as a whole, and negotiations with it were sure to arouse bitter antagonism among the anti-Peking parties. Wisdom, patience, and sympathy were needed in dealing with China in those days of disorganization, and it may hardly be said that Japan's attitude in 1915 bespoke any of these. Torn by the force of a national upheaval, with an administration that could scarcely claim the name government, and unable to invoke the aid of the great European Powers, China presented a most unhappy and ineffective front to the militant diplomacy of Japan. According to a statement of President Yuan Shih-kai, to which reference has already been made, China was apprehensive of what Japan might do should the European Powers become involved in a western war. Peking, therefore, could not maintain that Japan's demands were a complete surprise, yet China was utterly unprepared to meet the emergency when it arose in the conferences of February and March, even after the Chinese counterproject of February 12th made substantial, far-reaching concessions to Japan. This fact in itself was indicative of the extent to which China was prepared to defend her interests and sovereign rights. It recalled the flabby attitude of the Peking Government in the years of the Russo-Japanese War and those which immediately preceded it. China's helplessness in this as in other situations aroused the pity rather

---

[62] Treat, *op. cit.,* 218-219.

than the sympathy of the outside world. For her unenviable position she had largely herself to blame, and in the playing of one power against another she merely sought once more to save what little she retained of sovereignty.

To conclude, the events of the early months of 1915 provided the Tokyo Government an expensive but an invaluable lesson. Japan soon recognized that she occupied an isolated position. She became the object of bitter hatred on the part of thoughtful Chinese, and in Europe and America her ambitions in the Far East were looked upon with suspicion not to say distrust. If the extent of Japan's misdemeanor was capable of absolute measurement it would probably be true that she has reaped unmerited abuse, the sincerity of which was open to question in the case of practically every power that condemned her. For, it may be added, if every foreign right in China which had been founded on force, as were the Japanese Demands in 1915, were abolished, China would find herself free from most of her embarrassing treaty obligations.

Having full regard for the facts and interpretations here set forth, it does not appear that the diplomacy of the Twenty-One Demands was the mere chance mistake of human and blundering statesmen. As striking but isolated events of a few months these demands are neither significant in themselves nor indicative of anything fundamental or otherwise in the Japanese national character. If, however, they are viewed in the wider, more comprehensive light of Chino-Japanese relations during twenty-five years, they are pertinent to an understanding of Far Eastern affairs. Events since 1915 have shown that the lesson of those dramatic days has not been lost upon Japan.

And, if it be true, that the world has entered upon a new era in the matter of international relations there is ample evidence to support the view that Japan will not be found wanting as a sympathetic and persistent supporter of the new order.

At precisely the same time that Japan was being so soundly rated in the United States and elsewhere because of the "notorious" Twenty-One Demands, she was being criticized by the State Department in Washington because of the establishment of alleged discriminatory freight rates. The complete detailed correspondence on this subject between the State Department and the Japanese Government is to be found in U. S. Foreign Relations, 1915, 594-625, and U. S. Foreign Relations, 1916, 446-450. From this correspondence it appears that the Japanese authorities in June, 1914, proposed to sanction reduced rates on through goods shipped to the interior of Manchuria from Japan only. The question from the American point of view was twofold: the arrangement of the rates so as to favor the ports of Dairen and Antung, as against the port of Newchwang; and a special reduction of thirty per cent which it was proposed to grant in the case of goods imported in Japanese bottoms.

Interest and a certain degree of apprehension on the part of American shippers was natural for most American goods were transported not by way of Japan but through Shanghai. Added to this was the fact that these goods were usually re-shipped only to the port towns of Manchuria and not to the interior in through shipments.

The negotiations continued on through 1915 and on January 25, 1916, the American Secretary of State wrote to Ambassador Guthrie in Tokyo: "The Rail-

way Administration (South Manchuria Railway) has
several times altered the conditions under which the
reduced rates will be granted.

"At first they were made applicable to specific goods
shipped from Japan. To obtain these special rates
American goods would have had to be shipped via
Japan. Subsequently, after objection made by various
interests, the special rates were made applicable to
goods in vessels of certain Japanese lines. This being
equally objectionable and not in harmony with the
agreements into which Japan has entered for the
preservation of equality of opportunity, it is now
sought to make the enjoyment of reduced rates a
matter of special contract, the approval of which by
this Government would apparently make it a party
to the discrimination.

"You are instructed to bring the matter once more
to the attention of the Foreign Office and point out
that, in view of this Government, the right of American goods to receive the reduced rates can not be made
to depend upon the route of shipment, the nationality
of the importing vessel nor upon the signature by
shipping companies of a contract with the railway,
granting preferential rates." (The Secretary of State
to Ambassador Guthrie, January 25, 1916, U. S. Foreign Relations, 1916, 447.)

While the establishment of the special rates proposed by the Japanese afforded ground upon which the
American Government was justified in making a formal
protest that the principle of equality of commercial
opportunity was being again threatened, there was
nothing particularly new or surprising in the entire
matter. The popular American slogan, "equality of
commercial opportunity," used to signify the "Open

Door" had been threatened and violated repeatedly by every power claiming special interests and influence in China. It would be mere pretense to assume that such violations were the exception rather than the rule. But to assume that the Japanese Government in its proposed rate changes in 1914-1916 was violating the "Open Door" doctrine of John Hay, the only interpretation of the doctrine having any status whatever as an international agreement, is incorrect. An examination of the American correspondence on this episode in American-Japanese relations does not support the view that the principles enunciated by John Hay were in any way violated.

CHAPTER XII

MANCHURIA SINCE 1915 AND THE WASH-INGTON CONFERENCE

Probably never before in the world's history did the idea of peace hold such a position in the minds of men of every continent, as at the close of the World War. There seemed a genuine belief that the old was to give place to a new and better order. But the hopes of the idealists were rudely crushed by the diplomats who wrote the Treaty of Versailles. Nevertheless, the cause of peace still lived, and, when a Conference on the Limitation of Armament was called on August 11, 1921, by the Government of the United States, to meet in Washington on November 11th, the third anniversary of the signing of the Armistice between the victorious Allied and Associated Powers and Germany, the announcement was greeted with international applause. The day had arrived when the Great Powers were to come together, and, with mutual consent, at least, limit the national extravagance in battalions and battleships.[1]

The exact and fundamental origins of the Washington Conference have yet to be discovered. The idea itself was by no means original with the American Government, or with the American people, for the theory of limitation of armament is very old. Certainly the Borah amendment to the naval bill of 1920 was not the real beginning.[2]

---

[1] The reader will not find in this chapter a detailed narrative of political developments in Manchuria since 1915. The chapter deals only with the more striking episodes in the international situation such as the new "Open Door" Policy, the Four-Power Consortium, and the aftermath of the Twenty-one Demands.

[2] Ichihashi, Y., lecturing on the Washington Conference at Stanford University, Monday, December 8, 1924.

In reality there were two conferences: the first, the Five-Power Conference on armament; the second, the Nine-Power Conference on Pacific and Far Eastern questions. It is with the second of these conferences that we are concerned here. The preliminaries to calling the conference were carried out in the usual diplomatic manner. On July 8th the American Government informally inquired of Great Britain, France, Italy, and Japan their attitude toward such a conference. The formal invitations were dispatched by Washington on August 11th,[3] the delay having been caused largely by Japan, a power that first desired to be satisfied concerning the nature of the Far Eastern questions which were to be considered. China was also asked to join the conference on August 11th, and three other Powers, Belgium, the Netherlands, and Portugal, were asked to participate on October 4th.[4]

It is not the purpose of this chapter to discuss the motives of the American Government in calling the Washington Conference. This subject has been discussed in numerous monographs, among the most interesting of which is that of Reboul, *Le Conflict du Pacifique.* But in order that the reader may be prepared for some of the conclusions reached, relative to the work of the Powers at Washington, it should be noted that with the exception of a very few, the delegates were all seasoned diplomats, long trained in the school of international affairs. In this respect, at least, the conference was not different from many which had preceded it. As to open diplomacy, openly arrived at, such a thing was not considered for a moment. The informal conferences were secret and no

[3] *Conference on the Limitation of Armaments,* 4.
[4] *Ibid.,* 6 and 8.

records were kept. Even the plenary sessions were restricted. Finally, the conference was in no way informal. Diplomatic usage and precedent were followed with a nice exactness.

The Pacific and Far Eastern Problem, with which the Second Conference was concerned, centered about China, and in so far as it was disposed of resulted in two treaties, the one on the "Open Door" policy, the other on the Chinese Customs Tariff, and a number of resolutions on such subjects as extraterritoriality, post offices, radio, the Chinese Eastern Railway, and other matters. In an attempt to present concisely the significant phases of these questions which concerned Manchuria it will perhaps be advantageous to depart slightly from the chronological development of the subject and consider first the new "Open Door" doctrine. This will be followed by a brief statement of what was accomplished by the Conference with respect to the Chinese Eastern Railway, the Anglo-Japanese Alliance and finally the Twenty-One Demands.

Such definition as it possessed was first given to the "Open Door" doctrine by the American Secretary of State, John Hay, in 1899. That definition setting forth the policy of the United States Government at that time was a check on the actions of a power within its so-called sphere of influence in China. The "Open Door" notes asked assurance from the Powers that within the said spheres of influence they would not practice unfair discrimination in the matter of tariff rates, railway charges, and harbor dues. An impartial application of these, the American Government believed, would insure equality of commercial treatment for its nationals in China. These requirements and these only constituted the "Open Door" doctrine in 1899 and the scope of the policy remained unchanged until it was redefined at the Washington Conference.

Approaching the subject of the "Open Door" doctrine at the Washington Conference a close student of the question has said: "It is no secret that the United States has been vitally interested in the Orient, not so much out of sympathy for China as on account of investments and trade.[5] And it may be assumed that such matters as post offices and wireless which figured in the Conference agenda were only preliminary to a discussion of the "Open Door." On November 21, Mr. Root, of the American delegation, introduced a resolution to the Committee on Pacific and Far Eastern Questions in which the Powers recognized the sovereignty and territorial integrity of China, and the principle of equal opportunity for the commerce and industry of all nations.[6] But in view of the fact that the terms of these principles had come to mean practically nothing so far as the attitude of the Powers toward China was concerned, further action was necessary if mere words were to be translated into reality. Accordingly on December 12th Dr. Wang, of the Chinese Delegation, asked the Powers represented at the Conference to disavow all claims to the so-called spheres of influence or any special interests which they claimed within Chinese territory.[7] Mr. Root then asked the Chinese Delegation for specifications of the restrictions from which they wished to be released.[8] On December 14th, therefore, Dr. Wang asked the cancellation of twenty treaties and agreements, among which were included such important documents as the Anglo-Japanese Alli-

[5] Buell, *The Washington Conference,* 280.
[6] *Conference on the Limitation of Armaments,* 890.
[7] *Ibid.,* 1146.
[8] *Ibid.,* 1146.

ance, the Root-Takahira Agreement of 1908, the Lansing-Ishii Agreement of 1917, a number of nonalienation agreements, and the Sino-Japanese Treaties, and exchange of notes of May 25, 1915.[9]   The Japanese delgation took exception immediately.   Mr. Hanihara stated that if there was a question of making the Treaty or Agreements of 1915 or the change or abrogation thereof, the subject of discussion at the Conference, "he desired to announce that the Japanese delegation could not agree to such a course."[10]   Thereupon the committee adjourned and for a month there was silence on the subject of the "Open Door" and the spheres of influence.   By that time the Committee was prepared to tackle the problem of the "Open Door" once again.   On January 16th, Mr. Hughes stated that

---

[9] *Ibid.*, 1152-1160.   The complete list of these agreements, the cancellation of which was asked by Dr. Wang, follows.   In compliance with the request of the Committee to furnish a list of restrictive stipulations from which China desired to be relieved the following was submitted:
"Sino-Japanese Treaties and Exchange of Notes of May 25, 1915."
"Inter-Power Agreements with Reference to China."
(1) Franco-Japanese Agreement, June 10, 1907.
(2) Anglo-Japanese Treaty, July 13, 1911.
(3) Russo-Japanese Convention, July 30, 1907.
(4) Russo-Japanese Secret Convention, July 30, 1907.
(5) Russo-Japanese Convention of July 4, 1910.
(6) Russo-Japanese Secret Convention, July 4, 1910.
(7) Russo-Japanese Secret Convention of July 8, 1912.
(8) Russo-Japanese Convention of July 3, 1916.
(9) Russo-Japanese Secret Treaty of Alliance of July 3, 1916.
(10) American-Japanese Exchange of Notes of November 30, 1908.
(11) American-Japanese Echange of Notes of November 2, 1917.
(12) Anglo-French Agreement of January 15, 1896.
(13) Anglo-Russian Agreement of April 28, 1899.
(14) Anglo-German Agreement, September 2, 1898.
"Commitments and Agreements which appear or have been alleged to create or recognize the existence of spheres of interest."
"Nonalienation Agreements."
(1) Hainan.
(2) Yangtze.
(3) Tongking Border.
(4) Fukien.
(5) Coast of China.
[10] *Conference on the Limitation of Armament,* 1160.

"it was idle to deal generally with the matter of equal opportunity and the so-called "Open Door" unless it was recognized that there was inherent in that principle the agreement that the committee was not attempting to obtain, either for the Governmnts represented on it or for their respective nationals, a general superiority of rights or preferential monopolistic advantages which operated to the exclusion of other Powers and their nationals."[11]   Mr. Hughes therefore wished to have a definite statement before the committee and to this end read his draft resolution on the "Open Door."

With a view to applying more effectually the principle of the Open door or equality of opportunity for the trade and industry of all nations, the Powers represented in this Conference agree not to seek or to support their nationals in asserting any arrangement which might purport to establish in favor of their interests any general superiority of rights with respect to commercial or economic development in any designated region of the territories of China, or which might seek to create any such monopoly or preference as would exclude other nationals from undertaking any legitimate trade or industry or from participating with the Chinese Government in any category of public enterprise, it being understood that this Agreement is not to be so construed as to prohibit the acquisition of such properties or rights as may be necessary to the conduct of a particular commercial or industrial undertaking.[12]

If the American Government hoped to dispose of the "Open Door" in a resolution of this kind, its purpose was defeated, for questions raised by the British Delegation now forced a more searching consideration of the doctrine.   These questions concerned the nature of monopolistic enterprises referred to toward the close of the Resolution.[13]   The following day, January

[11] *Ibid.*, 1214.
[12] *Ibid.*, 1214.
[13] Buell, *op. cit.*, 291-292.

17th, Mr. Hughes placed before the Far Eastern Committee a detailed resolution as follows:

The Open Door in China.

1. With a view to applying more effectually the principle of the Open Door or equality of opportunity in China for the trade and industry of all nations, the Powers other than China represented at this Conference agree:

(a) Not to seek or to support their nationals in seeking any arrangement which might purport to establish in favor of their interests any general superiority of rights with respect to commercial or economic development in any designated region of China;

(b) Not to seek or to support their nationals in seeking any such monopoly or preference as would deprive other nationals of the right of undertaking any legitimate trade or industry in China or of participating with the Chinese Government or with any Provincial Government in any category of public enterprise, or which by reason of its scope, duration, or geographical extent is calculated to frustrate the practical application of the principle of equal opportunity.

It is understood that this Agreement is not to be so construed as to prohibit the acquisition of such properties or rights as may be necessary to the conduct of a particular commercial, industrial, or financial undertaking, or to the encouragement of invention and research.

2. The Chinese Government takes note of the above Agreement and declares its intention of being guided by the same principles in dealing with applications for economic rights and privileges from Governments and nationals of all foreign countries whether parties to that Agreement or not.

3. The Powers, including China, represented at this Conference agree in principle to the establishment in China of a Board of Reference to which any question arising on the above Agreement and Declaration may be referred for investigation and report.

(A detailed scheme for the constitution of the Board shall be framed by the Special Conference referred to in Article I of the Convention on Chinese Customs Duties.)

4. The Powers, including China, represented at this Conference agree that any provisions of an existing concession which

appear inconsistent with those of another concession or with the
principles of the above Agreement or Declaration may be submitted by the parties concerned to the Board of Reference when
established for the purpose of endeavoring to arrive at a satisfactory adjustment on equitable terms.[14]

Mr. Hughes stated that the declaration in the first
article was intended to state "with such precision as
the subject admitted, what the "Open Door" principle
was understood to be."[15]

On January 18th, while the Hughes Resolution was
still before the Pacific and Far Eastern Committee,
there occurred one of the most significant events in the
entire history of the "Open Door" doctrine. Address-
ing the Committee on the subject of article 4, Baron
Shidehara stated in no uncertain language that the
"Open Door" as defined in the Hughes Resolution was
a far different doctrine from that initiated by John
Hay in 1899, adding that while it was true that the
"Open Door" was not a new invention, nevertheless:

it must be noted that the principle had undergone considerable
changes in its application since it had originally been initiated
by Secretary Hay in 1899. It was then limited in scope, both as
concerning its subject matter and the area of Chinese territory
to which it applied; it simply provided, in substance, that none
of the Powers having spheres of influence or leased territories
in China should interfere with treaty ports or with vested rights
or exercise any discrimination in the collection of customs duties
or railroad or harbor charges. The principles formulated in the
draft Resolution were of an entirely different scope from the
policy of the Open Door as conceived in 1898-1899; the draft
Resolution gave, in a certain sense, a new definition to that
policy.[16]

The issue raised by the statement of Baron Shidehara was a decidedly embarrassing one for the Ameri-

---

[14] *Conference on the Limitation of Armament,* 1224-1226.
[15] *Ibid.,* 1226.
[16] *Ibid.,* 1250.

can delegates for they were immediately forced to take an entirely illogical position. Mr. Hughes admitted that in the original statement of the policy by Secretary Hay there were specific points mentioned and added that the bearing of those points and the intent of the policy were clearly presented.[17] Then having presented to the Committee much of the early correspondence on the doctrine Mr. Hughes added that while it was true Secretary Hay had stipulated certain definite points, he made clear what was the scope and purpose of the policy he advocated.[18] Mr. Hughes therefore regarded the principles in the Resolution not as a new statement but rather as a more definite and precise statement of the principle that had long been admitted, and to which the Powers concerned had given their unqualified adherence for twenty years.[19]

Baron Shidehara objected to the application of a Board of Reference to concessions already existing,[20] and Sir Robert Borden of Canada suggested that Article 4 be dropped altogether.[21] As a result, the Hughes resolution was adopted without Article 4, for it appeared that the United States was prepared to agree with the view that the Conference could not interfere with interests that had already been acquired.

Finally on February 6th the treaty defining the new "Open Door" was signed.[22] Article 1 reasserted the principles of sovereignty and territorial integrity which had been guaranteed to China on so many occasions with questionable results, and the Root principles adopted at the beginning of the Conference. Article 2,

---

[17] *Ibid.*, 1250.
[18] *Ibid.*, 1256.
[19] *Ibid.*, 1258-1260.
[20] *Ibid.*, 1250.
[21] *Ibid.*, 1260.
[22] *Ibid.*, 1621-1629. Full text of the Open Door Treaty.

it appeared, was an obstacle to the formation of such agreements as the Anglo-Japanese Alliance and the Lansing-Ishii Agreement. The "Open Door" Resolution was embodied in Articles 3 and 4 but omitted mention of the Board of Reference which was made the subject of a resolution. In Article 5 China pledged herself not to allow unfair discrimination "throughout the whole of the railways in China," and Article 6 was to prevent violations of Chinese neutrality. As stated, the question of the Board of Reference was disposed of in a resolution adopted by the Conference, which read as follows:[23]

The representatives of the Powers assembled at the present Conference at Washington, to-wit, the United States of America, Belgium, the British Empire, China, France, Italy, Japan, the Netherlands, and Portugal:

Desiring to provide a procedure for dealing with questions that may arise in connection with the execution of the provisions of Articles III and V of the Treaty to be signed at Washington on February 6th, 1922, with reference to their general policy designed to stabilize conditions in the Far East, to safeguard the rights and interests of China, and to promote intercourse between China and the other Powers upon the basis of equality of opportunity;

Resolve that there shall be established in China a Board of Reference to which any questions arising in connection with the execution of the aforesaid articles may be referred for investigation and report.

The Special Conference provided for in Article II of the Treaty to be signed at Washington on February 6th, 1922, with reference to the Chinese Customs Tariff, shall formulate for the approval of the Powers concerned a detailed plan for the constitution of the Board.

Adopted by the Conference on the Limitation of Armament at the Sixth Plenary Sessions, February 4th, 1922.

Certain points stand out as distinctly new in the "Open Door" doctrine of 1922. Mr. Hughes was cor-

---

[23] *Ibid.*, 1642.

rect when he stated that it was a more definite and precise statement. He failed, however, to acknowledge a factor of importance. The acquisition of so-called spheres of influence is now incompatible with the "Open Door" doctrine. Theoretically the spheres of influence in China have ceased to exist, although so long as the interests of any Power predominate in a fixed region of China, and the Central Government pursues its present shallow policy, it is difficult to see how there can be any practical application of the theory. Nevertheless it is to be noted that by outlawing the acquisition of spheres of influence a new element was infused into the doctrine. So far as his doctrine was concerned, Secretary Hay recognized informally at least the spheres of influence and foresaw that further spheres might be established. If such a policy were carried to the extreme and if discrimination were widely practiced, the industry and commerce of the United States in China were most certainly threatened. Hay, therefore, was primarily concerned with limiting and defining the action of the Powers within their spheres of influence, believing that by so doing he would provide ample protection for American interests.

The status of the "Open Door" doctrine from 1899 to 1922 may perhaps best be described as a *modus vivendi*. The policy of the United States was expressed in the Hay Notes and to this policy various Powers assented in their replies. There was, however, no contract in the form of treaty between the Powers. Morally they were bound to adhere to the doctrine as they understood it, although on technical grounds their obligations might be interpreted differently. But with the signing of the "Open Door" Treaty of 1922 the Powers bound themselves by a document, the binding power of which cannot be questioned in international law, and what is more significant, China herself is bound by the same treaty to adhere to the new "Open Door" principle. In the original "Open Door," of course, China had no part. But granting this it does not follow that China is to reap exceptional benefits because of the obligation she now assumes, for to characterize in a sentence the new "Open Door" is to say that *it is an efficient means by which the Powers can protect themselves and their interests in China.* It is hardly necessary to add that the nations represented at Washington in 1921-1922 are not primarily concerned with protecting China. Destroy China's economic value to the outside world; make impossible the acquisition of vested rights, and special privileges there, and the solicitude of the nations for China's welfare will cease and such high sounding phrases as "sovereignty" and "territorial integrity" will be heard no more. Most of the leaseholds with their concessions and privileges and other indignities to Chinese sovereignty remained unchanged after the Conference. They exist side by side with the famous "Open Door." True the action of the Powers as to the future is restricted. But the *status quo* of 1921 was maintained. At times it has been questioned whether that *status quo* was compatible with the "Open Door" as defined by John Hay. How much more is it incompatible with the "Open Door" of 1922? The negotiators foresaw many dangers and the treaty carefully specified that it relates merely to principles and policies concerning China. Its purpose is an unattainable goal: equality of commercial opportunity in China. It is another example of the failure of the world to settle the Far Eastern question. It seems that it will remain unsolved until China is willing and able to be the master of her own house.

Another Manchurian problem to which the Conference gave its attention, to be sure most ineffectively, was that of the Chinese Eastern Railway, which stretches across Northern Manchuria and connects the South Manchuria line with Harbin. Prior to the World War this railway was under Russian control but in 1919 an Interallied Commission was established to control the transportation system of Siberia and it still exercised supervisory powers over the Chinese Eastern Railway at the time of the Conference. This agreement concerning the Commission had been reached in January between the United States and Japan and subsequently other Powers, including China, France, Great Britain, and Italy, co-operated. But the arrangement was purely temporary and at the time of the Washington Conference there were three problems of major importance: finance, operation, and police, which confronted the line.[24]

In an attempt, therefore, to save the road from falling still further into confusion, the Conference, on January 18, 1922, appointed a subcommittee of experts to consider what action might be taken, Secretary Hughes at the time pointing out that so far as the United States was concerned, there was but one interest, and that was that the railroad should be maintained as an artery of commerce, with free opportunity to all and unfair

---

[24] *Conference on the Limitation of Armament,* 1376-1378.

During the allied military advance in Siberia and afterward it was claimed that the Japanese military command made a definite attempt to secure control of the Chinese Eastern Railway with a view to extending Japanese influence into Northern Manchuria, making possible the diversion of trade from Vladivostok to Dairen in the Japanese Leased Territory. The management of the Chinese Eastern Railway was thrown into great confusion by the outbreak of the Russian Revolution and the establishment of the Interallied Commission in 1919 was stated to be an attempt to prevent the Japanese from gaining control of the line. (Buell, *op. cit.,* 12-13.)

See also Buell, *op. cit.,* 34-35, with respect to alleged Franco-Japanese pact of March, 1921, *re* Siberia and North Manchuria.

discrimination against none.[25] On January 23rd this Committee reported on the three problems already mentioned. It appeared that funds for financing the road could not be secured without foreign supervision of the railway and the recommendation was therefore made that a permanent finance committee, composed of representatives of the Powers at the Conference, take the place of the Interallied Commission, and act as trustee for the road until the recognition of a Russian Government.[26] It was suggested that the operation of the road be left in the hands of the Chinese Eastern Railway Company and that a dependable and effective police force be maintained. This body might be composed of Chinese but was to be paid and controlled by the Finance Committee.[27]

Mr. Hawkling Yen, the Chinese representative, objected to these recommendations, largely on the ground that international control of the Chinese Eastern Railway would constitute a violation of the administrative integrity of China. Further progress, therefore seemed impossible and the question was referred to a subcommittee of delegates, headed by Senator Root, and on February 2nd agreement was reached on two resolutions, which were adopted by the Conference on February 4th.

Resolved that the preservation of the Chinese Eastern Railway for those in interest requires that better protection be given

---

[25] *Conference on the Limitation of Armament*, 1270. The whole problem had been complicated in 1919-1920 when the Chinese Government attempted to establish its control over the road. It had replaced the Russian General Manager by three Chinese directors, action which brought forth a protest from the Russo-Asiatic Bank supported by the French Government. This led to an agreement of October 2, 1920, between the Bank and the Chinese Government by which the latter resumed temporary control of the road. Chinese troops were supposed to have replaced the Russian guards which had been withdrawn in the spring of 1918. (Buell, *op. cit.*, 12-13, and China *Year Book*, 1921-1922, 650-654.)

[26] Conference on the limitation of armament, 1378.

[27] *Ibid.*, 1378.

to the Railway and the persons engaged in its operation and use; a more careful selection of personnel to secure efficiency of service, and a more economical use of funds to prevent waste of the property.

That the subject should immediately be dealt with through the proper diplomatic channels.

The above resolution was approved by all the Powers including China; that which follows by the Powers other than China.

The Powers other than China, in agreeing to the resolution regarding the Chinese Eastern Railway, reserve the right to insist hereafter upon the responsibility of China for performance or nonperformance of the obligations toward the foreign stockholders, bondholders, and creditors of the Chinese Eastern Railway Company which the Powers deem to result from the contracts under which the Railroad was built and the action of China thereunder and the obligations which they deem to be in the nature of a trust resulting from the exercise of power by the Chinese Government over the possession and administration of the Railroad.[28]

Thus the sovereignty of China over the road was given a half-hearted recognition, and it was implied that the control of the Interallied Commission would continue. "That the subject should immediately be dealt with through the proper diplomatic channels" could hardly be interpreted otherwise than as a convenient means of side-stepping a problem which the Conference was not prepared to handle. The political turmoil which has surrounded the Chinese Eastern Railway since 1922 is sufficient proof that the actions of the Washington Conference on this subject were entirely inadequate.

Another major problem before the Conference, affecting the interests of the Great Powers in the Far East and consequently bearing at least indirectly on Manchuria, was the future of the famous Anglo-Japanese Alliance. This alliance originally negotiated in

---

[28] *Conference on the Limitation of Armament*, 1658.

1902, renewed in 1905, and again in 1911, has been the cause of much unfavorable criticism, especially on the part of the United States, where it was claimed that it served as a protection to Japanese imperialism and would some day be used to combine the forces of Great Britain and Japan against those of the United States in war. There is not the space here, nor is it the purpose of this paper to analyze the merits of such a thesis. So far as the specialized study of international interests in Manchuria is concerned, the reader will recall that the alliance served, during the years immediately preceding the Russo-Japanese War, as a necessary part of Japan's international equipment in asserting her objections to the Russian advance in Manchuria and Korea, and made possible her declaration of war in 1904. In the years following the war, the Alliance restrained the British Government from lending support to its nationals who were attempting to secure railway concessions in Manchuria contrary to the Chino-Japanese Agreements of December, 1905, a circumstance which aroused opposition to the Alliance not only in the United States, because of her financial interests in the proposed railways, but also in England.

When the Alliance was renewed for the second time in 1911, Great Britain secured the insertion of the arbitration clause, believing that her arbitartion treaty negotiated with the United States in the summer of the same year would be ratified by the American Senate, and thus the danger to Anglo-American cordiality would be removed. But the general arbitration treaty was not ratified by the Senate and it has been maintained therefore that Great Britain remained bound technically to go to war in defense of Japan and against the United States in case the latter country attempted to challenge Japan's position in the Orient.[29] The Alli-

[29] Buell, *op. cit.*, 120.

ance was to expire on July 13, 1921, and as a result of the American attitude Great Britain found herself in a most perplexing situation. She could neither afford to lose the friendship of Japan, which desired the renewal of the Alliance, nor alienate further the sympathies of the American Government, which was firmly opposed to its continuance. Consequently, six days before the Alliance would have expired a communication was presented to the League of Nations nullifying the military obligation of Great Britain under it should such obligation prove inconsistent with the procedure prescribed by the Covenant of the League.[30] This was the status of the Alliance at the time of the Washington Conference.

From the American point of view certain objections to the Alliance still remained, most of which owed their existence to the fact that the United States was not a member of the League of Nations and could properly refuse to conform to its procedure. It is not necessary for the present purpose or possible at this time to enter into a full discussion of the negotiations at Washington relative to the Alliance. The fact of importance is that through the Four-Power Treaty, adopted by the Conference, "the agreement between Great Britain and Japan, which was concluded at London on July 13,[31]

---

[30] *Ibid.*, 133. See also *League of Nations*, Treaty Series, September, 1920, i, No. 1.

[31] *Conference on the Limitation of Armament*, 1612-1616.

The parties to the treaty were the United States, Great Britain, Japan, and France. Article 1 provided that in case of controversy arising between them out of any Pacific question all the High Contracting Powers should be invited to a joint conference to which the whole subject will be referred. By Article 2, if the rights of the signatory Powers are threatened by aggressive action of any other power the former are to communicate fully together to determine what action, whether joint or separate, shall be taken to protect said rights. The termination of the Alliance was not to take place until the treaty was ratified.

1911, shall terminate." The preamble of the treaty states that it is negotiated "with a view to the preservation of the general peace and the maintenance of their (the four Powers') rights in relation to their insular possessions and insular dominions in the region of the Pacific Ocean." As regards the Anglo-Japanese Alliance the treaty was a pledge that Great Britain, United States, France, and Japan would not, without joint consultation, take action with respect to their Pacific insular possessions. Viscount Grey declared on December 14, 1921, that the Anglo-Japanese Alliance was to be merged into a quadruple agreement, which although it related only to the islands of the Pacific, would have an effect in spirit that would go far beyond the letter of the agreement.[32]

In how far the Four-Power Treaty, interpreted in its broadest aspects, will affect the entire Far Eastern question it is impossible to state. But there can be no doubt that it stands in marked contrast to the Anglo-Japanese Alliance. For under the new Treaty there is no obligation to go to war. The Powers signatory to the treaty merely accept an obligation to "confer." The treaty, therefore, may be said to have removed the so-called menace of the Anglo-Japanese Alliance to the United States, although it is claimed that it does not destroy entirely the moral encouragement which that Alliance gave to Japan's continental imperialism.[33]

It is now necessary to retrace our steps somewhat and resume the story of Manchurian affairs from the

---

[32] Quoted by Senator Robinson, *Congressional Record*, March 11, 1922, 4179.

[33] Buell, *op. cit.*, 196. In this connection Buell says: "There is no longer any possibility that the British and Japanese fleets will serve as a unit against us. . . . . Great Britain no longer guarantees Japan's special interests in the Far East. Nevertheless, her diplomatic freedom is still restricted by the Four-Power Treaty and by her interests in the Orient which Japan may imperil. In addition, the former freedom of action on the part of the United States has also probably been curtailed."

signing of the Treaty and Notes of May 25, 1915. Japan it will be recalled had reinforced her position in the "Three Eastern Provinces," but her goal had been attained at the expense of what little friendship China still retained for her, while the suspicion, if not the animosities of the Western Powers, were aroused against her. None of these circumstances gave promise of smooth sailing in Far Eastern affairs and the problem became still more perplexing with the entry of China into the World War in 1917. However, in May, 1918, after the collapse of the Russian Government and the signature of the Brest-Litovsk Treaty, Japan and China signed a military and naval agreement for cooperation against the common enemy.[34] It was alleged at the time that these agreements would permit the Japanese to construct forts on Chinese territory (presumably in certain parts of Manchuria as a precaution against a Russian advance) and that Japan would assume control of China's railways, shipyards, arsenals, and the national finances. These rumors were denied by the Japanese Government and the publication of the texts of the agreements themselves proved that the rumors were groundless.[35]

On the basis of these agreements a loan of 20,000,000 yen gold was advanced by Tokyo to China for war purposes as the result of a contract signed on September 28, 1918. On the same date a preliminary agreement for a loan to finance the construction of four railways in Manchuria and Mongolia was concluded. This agreement followed an exchange of notes of September 24th in which China approached Japan with a view to se-

[34] Treat, op. cit., 226. See also MacMurray, Treaties, vol. 2, 1407-1412.

[35] See statement of the Japanese Minister for Foreign Affairs of May 30, 1918, in MacMurray, Treaties, vol. 2, 1407-1449.

curing a loan,[36] for the construction of railways. From our point of view this agreement was of importance because of its effect on the railway development of Manchuria, but as regards the general status of the treaties of 1915 another agreement of 1918 was more significant. The Japanese Government consented, at the request of China, to induce Japanese bankers to loan the Peking Government funds for the construction of two railways in Shantung Province. The preliminary advance was 20,000,000 yen. Options on these loans had been granted to Germany in December, 1913. At the time the loan was made Japan announced she would withdraw most of her troops along the Kiaochow-Tsinan Railway, that the railway would be worked as a joint Chino-Japanese enterprise and that the civil administration established by the Japanese in Shantung would be abolished. China heartily assented to these proposals. Apparently the significance of these arrangements did not appear at the time but when China sought the restoration of the German rights in Shantung at the Versailles Peace Conference she discovered that the secret agreements of 1918 had greatly weakened her legal case,[37] not merely regarding the Shantung but also regarding the Manchurian Treaty.

At Paris in 1919, China was not able to establish her claim that the 1915 treaties had arisen out of the war and were thus a proper subject for discussion at the Peace Conference. Because of the fact that the Manchurian phases of the Twenty-one Demands did not

---

[36] MacMurray, *Treaties*, 1448-1449. The railways to be constructed included lines between: Jehol and Taonan, Changchun and Taonan, Kirin and Kaiyuan by way of Hailung, a point on the Jehol-Taonan Railway to a certain seaport. The negotiation of this preliminary agreement found its origin in the exchange of notes regarding the construction of certain railways in Manchuria between Japan and China of October 5, 1913. (See MacMurray, *Treaties*, vol. 2, 1054.)

[37] Treat, *op. cit.*, 226-227.

figure in the Paris discussions only the mere results of the Conference action will be mentioned here. China's claim for the direct restitution of Shantung rested on two assumptions: the first that the Shantung Treaty of 1915 was signed under duress; and the Agreements of 1918 were only temporary arrangements; secondly, that all treaties between China and Germany had been abrogated when China entered the war. The argument, however, was of no avail. China made the railway agreement of 1918 after she entered the war and clearly indicated thereby that the Treaty of 1915 was valid. This fact is one which cannot be ignored. Then, too, to argue that the Agreement was only temporary, in face of the acceptance of an advance of 20,000,000 yen, only added to the absurd position in which China found herself. Furthermore, Japan was supported in her claims at Paris by treaty agreements with the Allied Powers with the result that in the settlement Germany renounced in favor of Japan all her rights, titles, and privileges which she had acquired in Shantung in March, 1898.[38]   Then in a supplementary understanding given at Paris, Japan declared that her policy was to return the Shantung Peninsula to China retaining only the economic privileges granted to Germany and the right to establish a settlement at Tsingtao under the usual conditions.[39]   And it is significant to note that regardless of the guarded pronouncements of the Powers, particularly the United States, with respect to the 1915 and 1918 agreements, the Far Eastern settlement at the Paris Conference implied a definite recognition of those engagements and thus served to strengthen Japan's position in Manchuria.[40]

---

[38] *The Treaties of Peace*, 1919-1923, vol. 1, 93.

[39] Baker, *Woodrow Wilson and World Settlement*, vol. 2, 263.

[40] Hornbeck, "Shantung at the Peace Conference," in Temperley, *A History of the Peace Conference of Paris*, vol. 6, 375.

There can be no question that after the unhappy events of 1915, culminating in the signing of the Treaties of May 25th, Japan adopted a new policy toward China. It is not too much to say that the Tokyo Government was aroused to the folly of the recent negotiations, and fearing for the whole future of Japan's interests in China now sought by means of a more moderate policy to make amends for grave mistakes. China, of course, was in urgent need of funds immediately upon her entry into the war, and during the ministry of Count Terauchi, 1916-1918, large sums were loaned to both the Central and Provincial Governments of China by Japanese bankers. These loans had the support of the Japanese Government and not a few of them were for the development of the Manchurian Provinces. Several of these agreements were of considerable importance. On October 12, 1917, in accordance with Article 7 of the Treaty of May 25, 1915, concerning South Manchuria and Eastern Inner Mongolia, the loan agreement of the Kirin-Changchun Railway was revised. It was by Article 3 of this agreement that the South Manchuria Railway Company assumed the management of the line as already mentioned in chapter ten.[41] For the readjustment of the reserves of the Provincial Bank of Manchuria, Japanese capitalists concluded a loan agreement for 3,-000,000 gold yen on April 22, 1918.[42]

---

[41] MacMurray, op. cit., vol. 2, 1390-1391.

The term of the revised loan is thirty years, and it may not be redeemed in full before the expiration of that period. But when the loan is redeemed in full the South Manchuria Railway Company will hand over the railway to the Chinese Government, which has simply for the time being entrusted the management to the Japanese Company.

[42] MacMurray, op. cit., vol. 2, 1416. It is understood that three loans for the same purpose, two of them dated June 9, 1916, and one dated August 1, 1916, had previously been concluded between the same parties, namely the Bank of Chosen and the Fengtien Provincial Government.

A preliminary loan agreement for the construction of a railway from Kirin to Hueining through the southern part of Yenchi (Chientao) was concluded between China and the Industrial Bank of Japan on June 18, 1918.[43]   This loan was made consequent to Article 3 of the Sino-Japanese Agreement of April 15, 1907, which stipulated that should the Kirin-Changchun Railway be extended it should be constructed with Chinese funds, but if Chinese capital could not be secured China was to consult with the Tokyo Government concerning a loan.   This stipulation was also mentioned in the Sino-Japanese Treaty of 1909.   The agreement concluded on June 18, 1918, provided for the immediate advance of $10,000,000 to the Chinese Government and this sum was paid into the Tokyo Office of the Sino-Japanese Exchange Bank on June 19th, to the credit of the Peking Government.[44]

Then on August 2, an agreement for a loan of 30,-000,000 yen in Japanese gold was concluded for the development of gold mining and forestry in the Provinces of Heilungkiang and Kirin, both of which properties were pledged as security for the loan.[45]   Then on September 28th was concluded the preliminary agreement for a loan for the four railways of Manchuria and Mongolia already mentioned in this chapter.[46]   These agreements served to increase Japan's

---

[43] *Ibid.*, vol. 2, 1430.

[44] The Peking *Times* of July 2, 1918, printed a statement concerning the report of the Minister of Communications in regard to this agreement, which is reprinted in MacMurray, *Treaties*, vol. 2, 1432.

[45] The nature of these proceedings was explained in a note from the Exchange Bank of China to the Chinese Ministers on August 2, 1918. The sole purpose as there stated was to render assistance to the Chinese Government in its financial readjustment. The banks participating in the loan declared that they had no intention to monopolize special interests regarding forests and mining or to obstruct the occupations of the local residents. (MacMurray, *Treaties*, vol. 2, 1439.)

[46] *Ibid.*, vol. 2, 1448-1449. It should be noted that on December 27, 1915,

interests on the mainland of Asia and to strengthen her position there. And the development was natural enough. Financially China was in a hopeless condition. Furthermore, Japan for the first time had the funds available and could make what terms she desired, independent of competition of the European financiers. The effects of this freedom of action which was Japan's during these years, were soon to be evident in the negotiations which attended the Four-Power Consortium of 1920.

The China Consortium Agreement signed on October 15, 1920, indicated two things regarding Japan's policy toward Manchuria. In the first place it was evident that the Tokyo Government was prepared to safeguard and to extend as far as possible its interests in South Manchuria and Eastern Inner Mongolia; and in the second that this policy would not be pushed beyond the point of friendly compromise with such powers as Great Britain and the United States. On October 8, 1918, the American State Department dispatched a note to the British, French, and Japanese Embassies at Washington enclosing a memorandum outlining the American plan for a new international group to render financial assistance to China.[47] This new Consortium was to consist of representative financial institutions of Great Britain, France, Japan, and the United States.

The first intimation of serious difficulty in harmonizing the interests of the four powers in the proposed Consortium came on June 18, 1919 (the British Government had already accepted the American plan on

---

China concluded a loan agreement with the Yokohama Specie Bank *re* the Ssupingkai-Chengchiatun line.

[47] Carnegie Endowment for International Peace, Division of international law, *The Consortium*, 10-15.

March 17)[48] in a letter from Mr. M. Odagiri of the Yokohama Specie Bank in London to Mr. Thomas W. Lamont of Messrs. Morgan, Grenfell and Company stating that the Japanese group had been instructed by its principals "that all rights and options held by Japan in the regions of Manchuria and Mongolia, where Japan has special interests, should be excluded from the arrangements for pooling provided for in the proposed agreement. This is based on the very special relations which Japan enjoys geographically, and historically, with the regions referred to, and which have been recognized by Great Britain, the United States, France, and Russia on many occasions."[49]   Mr. Lamont's reply of June 23, 1919, regretted the existence of a misunderstanding, pointing out that Manchuria and Mongolia being important parts of the Chinese Empire, any attempt to exclude them from the scope of the Consortium must be inadmissable.[50]   The grave import of the question was such that Mr. Lamont brought it to the attention of the American State Department.

Therefore, on July 30, 1919, the American Government protested to the Japanese Embassy at Washington against the views of the Japanese Group in seeking to exclude Manchuria and Mongolia from the Consortium.[51]   This was followed by similar action on the part of the British Foreign Office on August 11, 1919.

---

[48] *The Consortium*, 15.

[49] *Ibid.*, 19-20. The reference to the pooling arrangement had to do with the clause providing that the groups pool all existing and future options, except such concessions as were already in operation. (*Ibid.*, 16.)

[50] *Ibid.*, 21.

[51] *Ibid.*, 26-28. "The Imperial Japanese Government has not indicated that it shares the opinion expressed by the Japanese bankers; but inasmuch as the question raised by the latter has been referred to this Government by the American representative it is felt to be appropriate to bring the latter to the notice of the Imperial Government."

The British memorandum stated that "One of the fundamental objects of the American proposals as accepted by the British, Japanese, and French Governments, is to eliminate special claims in particular spheres of interest and to throw open the whole of China without reserve to the combined activities of an International Consortium.   This object cannot be achieved unless all the parties to the scheme agree to sacrifice all claim to enjoy any industrial preference within the boundaries of any political sphere of influence."[52]   The atmosphere was not cleared, however, when on August 27th the American Government received a memorandum from the Japanese Embassy in Washington accepting resolutions adopted at the Paris meeting of Bankers, but excluding Manchuria and Mongolia from the Consortium.[53]   The American and British Governments refused to accept the Japanese reservation in memoranda of October 28 and November 19, respectively.[54]

Japan was now faced with the task of defending her position or withdrawing the reservation.   Silence would have at least implied acquiescence in the pointed suggestions of both the British and American notes.   On March 2, 1920, therefore, Japan stated her reasons for wishing to exclude South Manchuria and Eastern Inner Mongolia from the scope of the Four-Power Group.[55]   Summarized these reasons were: (1)   the regions of South Manchuria and Eastern Inner Mongolia stand in close relation to Japan's political and economic existence and enterprises launched in these regions often involve questions vital to the national

---

[52] *Ibid.*, 28-30.
[53] *Ibid.* 30-31.
[54] *Ibid.*, 31-34.
[55] *Ibid.*, 34-38.

safety; (2) Japan's interest in Manchuria and Mongolia is vital because it is through these regions that Russian influences may effect their pentration into Japan; (3) Japan therefore has vital interests in South Manchuria and Eastern Inner Mongolia as distinct from other powers.   Japan also protested that her *pro*posal "was prompted by no desire of making any territorial demarkation involving the idea of economic monopoly or of asserting any exclusive political pretentions or of affirming a doctrine of any far-reaching sphere of interest in disregard of the legitimate national aspirations of China, as well as of the interests possessed there by the powers concerned."[56]   The particular concerns which Japan reserved as outside of the scope of the Consortium included: (1) The South Manchuria Railway and its branches, together with the mines which are subsidiary to the railway; (2) the construction of the Kirin-Changchun Railway, Shinminfu-Mukden Railway, and Ssupingkai-Chengchiatun Railway having been completed and their operation commenced were according to Article 2 of the proposed intergroup arrangement in a stage of substantial progress and therefore beyond the common activities of the new Consortium; (3) the Kirin-Hueining Railway, the Chengchiatun-Taonanfu Railway, the Changchun-Taonanfu Railway, the Kaiyuan-Kirin Railway, the Taonanfu-Jehol Railway, and the railway connecting a point on the Taonanfu-Jehol Railway with a seaport were stated to be branch or feeding lines of the South Manchuria Railway, to bear an important relation to national defense of Japan and were therefore to be con-

---

[56] The previous note of the Washington authorities indicated that the United States Government was decidedly of the opinion that the proposal of the Japanese Government in regard to South Manchuria and Eastern Inner Mongolia amounted either to exclusive political pretensions or to the establishment of a so-called sphere of interest.

sidered outside the common activities of the new Consortium.[57]

Both Great Britain and the United States found the formula proposed by Japan to be unsatisfactory. The British Government in its memorandum of March 19, 1920, declared that it "is so ambiguous and general in character that it might be held to indicate on the part of the Japanese Government a continued desire to exclude the co-operation of the other three banking groups from participating in the development . . . . of important parts of the Chinese Republic . . . ."[58] The American Government in its memorandum of March 16th expressed "grave disappointment" that the Japanese formula should be in terms "so exceedingly ambiguous and in character so irrevocable that it might be held to indicate a continued desire on the part of the Japanese Government to exclude the American, British, and French banking groups from participation in the development, for the benefit of China, of important parts of that Republic . . ."[59] Replying to these statements the Japanese Government abandoned its claim for acceptance of the formula,[60] asking at the same time, however, for assurances from the British and American Governments with respect to certain railways to be constructed. The points on which Japan asked assurances were: (1) in the event of the new Consortium projecting in future a scheme of extending the Taonanfu-Jehol Railway to the north with a view to connecting with the Eastern Chinese Railway, the assent of the Japanese Government thereto must be obtained beforehand through the Japanese

---

[57] *The Consortium*, 38.
[58] *Ibid.*, 45, Earl Curzon to Viscount Chinda.
[59] *Ibid.*, 39.
[60] *Ibid.*, 46-48, 48-51.

Group, inasmuch as such an extension—being tantamount to a renewal of the Chinchow-Aigun Railway scheme—is calculated to have a serious effect on the South Manchurian Railway; (2) in view of Japan's particular desire that the Taonanfu-Jehol Railway and a line connecting it with a seaport be constructed speedily, the Japanese group may be permitted to undertake their construction alone in the event of the other three powers being reluctant to finance it.[61]   In the replies of the British and American Governments Japan was reminded that she was asking for the right to veto the construction by the Consortium of a line from Taonanfu to join the Chinese Eastern Railway, and that this was entirely unnecessary after the assurances which had been given by both governments. Both powers declared that the establishment of the Consortium should mark the beginning of a new era in which the nations should work together in harmony in China.[62]

By May 8th, the Japanese Government had decided to waive further discussion of the points raised,[63] and three days later the Japanese Banking Group notified Mr. Lamont "that certain points in the agreement and in operations of the proposed Consortium, hitherto somewhat obscure, having been cleared up to the satisfaction of our government and of ourselves, we are

---

[61] *The Consortium*, 50-51.   In her reply to the British Government Japan stated that she relied upon the promise of the British Foreign Office to give Japan a written assurance to the effect that Britain fully recognizes the fundamental principle of safeguarding the integrity of the national defense and the economic existence of Japan, as proposed by Japan, so that the Japanese Government have no occasion to apprehend that the new Consortium would embark upon any activities affecting the national defense and the economic existence of Japan. *(Ibid.,* 49-50.)

[62] *Ibid.,* 52-55.   The British reply was dated April 28, 1920 ; the American, April 29, 1920.

[63] *Ibid.,* 57-60.

now able . . . to . . . announce that . . . we will accept the Consortium agreement."[64]   Mr. Lamont's reply of May 11th stated that inasmuch as some questions had arisen as to the status of specific railway enterprises contemplated or actually begun in Manchuria and Mongolia, he would state what had actually been agreed upon:

1. That the South Manchuria Railway and its present branches, together with the mines which are subsidiary to the railway, do not come within the scope of the Consortium;

2. That the projected Taonanfu-Jehol Railway and the projected railway connecting a point on the Taonanfu-Jehol Railway with a seaport are to be included within the terms of the Consortium Agreement;

3. That the Kirin-Hueining, the Chengchiatun-Taonanfu, the Changchun-Taonanfu, the Kaiyuan-Kirin (via Hailung), the Kirin-Changchun, the Sinminfu-Mukden, and the Ssupingkai-Chengchiatun Railways are outside the scope of the joint activities of the Consortium.[65]

Thus while no specific clause was inserted in the agreement the Tokyo Government had the practical assurance of the remaining three powers that they would not countenance operations inimical to Japanese interests in Manchuria and Mongolia.[66]   China was informed of the scope and objects of the proposed Consortium on September 28 and the actual agreement was concluded, as already mentioned, on October 15.[67]   In this manner, then, was Japan's position in Manchuria defined when the Washington Conference was called in August, 1921.

At the Washington Conference China had three main objects to gain: (1) tariff autonomy, (2) the return of Shantung and (3) the cancellation of the Twenty-One Demands. It is only with the last of these that

---

[64] *Ibid.*, 60-61.
[65] *Ibid.*, 62.
[66] *Ibid.*, 62-64.
[67] *Ibid.*, 65-72.

we are concerned, and it may be noted that the question of the Twenty-One Demands was now largely a Manchurian question since Shantung was considered a subject for separate negotiations. In a word, China's object was to secure the termination of the leases of Port Arthur, Dairen, and the South Manchuria Railway in 1923, the date on which they would originally have expired. Neither Manchuria nor the Twenty-One Demands were on the Conference agenda and China was forced to introduce the subject indirectly. Accordingly, on November 29th, Dr. Sze, Chinese Minister at Washington and a Chinese Delegate, asked the Committee on Pacific and Far Eastern Questions that all unauthorized foreign troops,[68] police, foreign telegraph and wireless systems be withdrawn from Chinese soil. Mr. Hanihara replied by stating that while Japan was willing to withdraw her troops from China proper as soon as actual conditions warranted, it was impossible for Japan to forego the right and duty of maintaining railway guards in Manchuria.[69] It is probably a correct interpretation to say that Mr. Hanihara's statement was a declaration to the Powers that Japan did not propose to have her position in Manchuria questioned. The Chinese delegation might have realized this, but as on former occasions the Peking representatives were blind to all matters save the attainment of their object.

China then attempted a new attack and on December 3rd Mr. Koo asked the annulment and early termina-

---

[68] *Conference on the Limitation of Armament*, 986-998. According to the information submitted by the Chinese one full division of troops is usually maintained in Manchuria by Japan. The Japanese police in Manchuria at the time consisted of: (a) those stationed within the leased territory of the Liaotung Peninsula; (b) those stationed along the South Manchuria Railway and within the railway zone; (c) those established within the Japanese consulates, and (d) those stationed in nonopen ports.

[69] *Ibid.*, 1004.

tion of the foreign leaseholds.[70]   There could be no question, in view of the time of its introduction, that in this proposal China's main object was the destruction of Japanese power in Manchuria and Mr. Koo explained that the elimination of both the German and Russian menace in the Far East had removed the cause which might justify such leaseholds.   Mr. Hanihara's reply made it clear that Japan had no intention of relinquishing "the important rights she had lawfully acquired and at no small sacrifice.[71]   Three days later the Twenty-One Demands were thrust boldly into the discussions of the Conference when Mr. Koo again attacking the Manchurian leaseholds declared that the extension of the Kwantung leasehold "was obtained in such circumstances that the dispute about its validity remains one of the most grave outstanding questions between China and Japan."[72]   Carrying the subject further Dr. Wang on December 14th asked the cancellation of the 1915 Treaties and Notes.[73]   It appeared that China was determined to press the question of the Demands to a definite issue while Japan was equally determined to oppose any discussion of their validity. A critical situation was avoided, however, when Mr. Hughes on January 16th suggested that the subject of the Twenty-One Demands and the spheres of influence be postponed until after the settlement of the Shantung

---

[70] *Ibid.*, 1062.

[71] *Ibid.* 1064.   The point was made by the Japanese delegate that Japan's leased territories had been obtained not directly from China but as successor to other Powers.   The strategical importance of the Manchurian leasehold was also mentioned.   "The territory in question," said Hanihara, "forms a part of Manchuria—a region where, by reason of its close proximity to Japan's territory, more than anything else, she has vital interests in that which relates to her economic life and national safety."

[72] *Ibid.*, 1084.

[73] *Ibid.*, 1160.

Question.[74] This settlement was announced on February 1st, and the following day Mr. Hughes announced that Japan wished to make a statement on the subject of the 1915 Treaties and Notes. This statement was made by Baron Shidehara in the form of a declaration.

1. Japan is ready to throw open to the joint activity of the International Consortium recently organized, the right of option granted exclusively in favor of Japanese capital, with regard, first, to loans for the construction of railways in South Manchuria and Eastern Inner Mongolia, and, second, to loans to be secured on taxes in that region; it being understood that nothing in the present declaration shall be held to imply any modification or annulment of the understanding recorded in the officially announced notes and memoranda which were exchanged among the governments of the countries represented in the Consortium and also among the national financial groups composing the Consortium, in relation to the scope of the joint activity of that organization.

2. Japan has no intention of insisting on her preferential right under the Sino-Japanese arrangements in question concerning the engagement by China of Japanese advisers or instructors on political, financial, military, or police matters in South Manchuria.

3. Japan is further ready to withdraw the reservation which she made, in proceeding to the signature of the Sino-Japanese treaties and notes of 1915, to the effect that Group V of the original proposals of the Japanese Government would be postponed for future negotiations.[75]

The first Japanese concession in this declaration was largely a confirmation of the Consortium Agreement. The second point was of more immediate importance; in the case of Group V, it was largely a recognition of a situation which Japan was unable to avoid. Tokyo realized that the demands of this group could not be pressed while the Powers were free to interfere. She was therefore content to waive the reservation.

China's reply delivered the following day while ex-

---

[74] *Ibid.*, 1212.
[75] *Ibid.*, 1510-1512.

pressing satisfaction that Japan had made certain concessions, voiced the regret of the Peking Government that Japan had not been led to renounce the other claims predicated upon the Treaties and Notes of 1915.[76]

Making clear the position of the American Government, Mr. Hughes read the note dispatched by it to Tokyo and Peking of May 13, 1915, stating that Washington could not recognize any agreement between China and Japan impairing the treaty rights of the United States or its citizens in China.[77] Mr. Hughes added that doubtless loans for railway construction in South Manchuria and Eastern Inner Mongolia, if requiring foreign capital, would be undertaken by the Consortium. But it should be observed that existing treaties would leave the opportunity for such enterprises open on terms of equality to the citizens of all nations. For it could scarcely be assumed that this general right of the treaty Powers in China could be restricted to the nationals of those countries which are participants in the work of the Consortium. Mr. Hughes hoped it was in this sense that the Conference might interpret the declaration of the Japanese Government. The question of the Twenty-One Demands, so far as the Washington Conference is concerned, was thus concluded, with China reserving the right at any time in the future to seek a solution of those portions of the 1915 Treaties and Notes which had not been relinquished by the Japanese Government.[78] How much this reservation will mean to China only the future can disclose. For the present at least Japan's position in Manchuria is secure and the validity of the Treaties and Notes of 1915 has not been successfully challenged.

---

[76] *Ibid.*, 1556.
[77] *Ibid.*, 1560.
[78] *Ibid.*, 1564.

BIBLIOGRAPHY

BIBLIOGRAPHY

No attempt has been made by the writer to present here a critical bibliography for such a one could be given satisfactorily only at great lenth. There are many general works of reference dealing with Manchuria which will not be found in the following list and these omissions are explained by limitations of space. The writer has aimed to present here a fairly complete list, however, of those works which are of the greatest value to the student of Manchurian affairs. In some cases these are books which deal primarily with the history of China "proper" and devote perhaps a few pages or a chapter to Manchuria. Yet in some of these works is contained much material of importance. The appended list of titles, of course, contains some which are not cited in the text but all of these have been examined and, whether cited or not, have been employed by the author in building the background of INTERNATIONAL RIVALRIES IN MANCHURIA.

The following bibliography is classed under four main headings: (1) Government documents; (2) Collections of treaties; (3) Books, including specialized studies on Manchuria and general work on the Far East; (4) Newspapers, periodicals, and miscellaneous pamphlets. Each major division is arranged alphabetically.

So far as government documents are concerned, the writer has relied largely upon the British Parliamentary Papers, the Parliamentary Debates, and the Diplomatic and Consular Reports. The Foreign Relations Series of the United States also contains very valuable material which has been used throughout. Although, generally speaking, they are not so satisfactory as the corresponding British series, the American Consular and Trade Reports have afforded substantial contributions to the subject. The French diplomatic documents covering affairs in China have also contributed but for a study of this nature have not been so valuable as the memoirs of M. Gérard. The most important German source is contained in the series just published, *Die Grosse Politik der Europaischen Kabinette, 1871-1914.* Volume 19 contains valuable documents concerning the Russo-Japanese War.

A number of collections of treaties are of value to the student of Manchurian affairs. The most important of these are *Treaties and Conventions, etc., between China and Foreign States,* published by the Imperial Maritime Customs; Chung, *Korean Treaties;* and MacMurray's *Treaties and Agreements with and Concerning China.*

In the third division the reader will find both primary and secondary sources, the most important of which have all been cited in the text. Outstanding in this material are the memoirs of such statesmen and diplomats as Witte, Rosen, Iswolsky, Kuropatkin, and Gérard. Many of the secondary sources which will be found in this list must, however, be used with great care. In some cases the writers have had inadequate facilities for research, while in many others they have been interested in vindicating or condemning policies followed by one or another of the powers interested in the Far East. The result is that their works have relatively little historical value. At the same time, it has been necessary to use some of these works in marshaling the facts of the narrative.

As regards the periodical literature, only a comparatively few titles will be given. There is an immense amount of material of varying quality, but only the most significant articles have been included.

1. GOVERNMENT DOCUMENTS

China. *The Chino-Japanese Negotiations. Chinese official statement with documents and treaties with annextures.* Peking, 1915.

The Maritime Customs. Returns of trade and trade reports, 1913-1916. Shanghai, 1914-1917. Filed in Conference on Limitation of Armament. (Chinese delegation.)

France. *Documents Diplomatiques, Affaires de Chine 1898-1903.*

Germany. *Die Grosse Politik der Europaischen Kabinette 1871-1914.* Sammlung der Diplomatischen Akten des Auswärtigen Amtes im Auftrage des Auswärtiges Amtes Herausgegeben von Johannes Lepsius, A. M. Bartholdy, Friedrich Thimme, 1925. Deutsche Verlagsgesellschaft fur Politik und Geschichte. M.B.H. in Berlin W 8. Vol. 19, Der Russisch-Japanische Krieg.

Great Britain. *Parliamentary Papers*—Lords. 1861, vol. 18. Correspondence respecting affairs in China, 1859-1860.

Parliamentary Papers, vol. XCI, 1887. H. C. Fulford, "Journey in Manchuria."

Parliamentary Papers. Despatch from. H. M. Minister at Tokyo—Treaty of 1895 CIX. III. 1895.

Parliamentary Papers. Despatch from H. M. Minister at Paris. (Chino-French treaties—1895, signed at Peking, 1896.) XCV. 23. June 20, 1895.

Parliamentary Papers. Correspondence between H. M. Government and the Russian Government with regard to their respective railway interests in China. China No. 2, 1899. CIX.

Parliamentary Papers. China (1899) No. 1. Correspondence respecting the Affairs of China. No. 459, inclosure 2, 1899, CIX.

Parliamentary Papers. Correspondence respecting the Anglo-German Agreement of October 16th, 1900. 1900, CV.

Parliamentary Papers. China No. 3, Further Correspondence respecting events at Peking (in continuation of China No. 4, 1900), 1901, XCI.

Parliamentary Papers, China No. 2. Despatch from H. M. Ambassador at St. Petersburg respecting the Russo-Chinese Agreement as to Manchuria. 1901, XCI.

Diplomatic and Consular Reports. China, Report for the year 1901 on the Trade of Newchwang. In Accounts and Papers, vol. CVI. London, 1902.

Parliamentary Papers, China No. 2. Correspondence respecting the Russian Occupation of Manchuria and Newchwang. 1904, CX.

Diplomatic and Consular Reports, China. Report for the year 1903 on the Trade of Newchwang. In Accounts and Papers, vol. XCVII. London, 1904.

Diplomatic and Consular Reports, China. Report for the year 1904 on the Trade of Newchwang. In Accounts and Papers, vol. LXXXVIII. London, 1905.

Diplomatic and Consular Reports, China. Report for the year 1905 on the Trade of Newchwang. In Accounts and Papers, vol. CXXIII. London, 1906.

Diplomatic and Consular Reports, China. Report for the year 1906 on the Trade of Newchwang. In Accounts and Papers, LXXXVIII. London, 1907.

Diplomatic and Consular Reports. Foreign Trade of China for the year 1906. Foreign Office, 1907. In Accounts and Papers, 1908, CX.

Diplomatic and Consular Reports, China. Report for the year 1909 on the Trade of Newchwang. In Accounts and Papers, 1910, XCVII.

Diplomatic and Consular Reports, China. Report for the year 1909 on Foreign Trade of China. Commercial Reports (annual), No. 4556. In Accounts and Papers, vol. XCVII, 1910.

Manchuria. *Handbooks prepared under the direction of the Historical Section of the Foreign Office.* London, 1920.

Japan. *Correspondence regarding the negotiations between Japan and Russia, 1903-1904.* Presented to the Imperial Diet, March, 1904.

An Official Guide to Eastern Asia, vol. 1. Manchuria and Chosen. Imperial Japanese Government Railways. Tokyo.

United States. *Executive Documents.* First Session, 35th Congress, 1857-1858, vol. 12, Serial 958, Ex. Doc. No. 98. Explorations of Amoor River, by Perry McD. Collins.

Foreign Relations, 1894.

Naval Intelligence Office, General Information Series 14. Preliminary notes on China-Japan War. Report of Witzel, H. M., and Karmany, Lincoln.

Foreign Relations, 1894. Appendix I.

Foreign Relations, 1902. Convention and arrangement between Russia and China respecting Manchuria.

Foreign Relations, 1903-1904. Manchuria correspondence concerning open ports, evacuation by Russia, etc.

Foreign Relations, 1906. Part I. The Open Door Policy in Manchuria, Establishment of Custom-Houses and Opening of Ports to International Trade.

Foreign Relations, 1907. Part I. The Open Door Policy in Manchuria, Establishment of Custom-Houses and Opening of Ports to International Trade.

Foreign Relations, 1910. Proposal for Neutralization of Railways in Manchuria.

Conference on the Limitation of Armament, Washington, November 12, 1921, to February 6, 1922, Washington, 1922.

Daily Consular and Trade Reports. Department of Commerce and Labor, Bureau of Manufactures. Washington.

Monthly Consular and Trade Reports. Department of Commerce and Labor, Bureau of Manufactures. Washington.

Consular and Trade Reports (Monthly), December, 1906, No. 315. Trade Conditions in Manchuria.

Consular and Trade Reports (monthly), February, 1907, No. 317.

Consular and Trade Reports (monthly), March, 1907, No. 318, Open Door in Manchuria.

Consular and Trade Reports (monthly), June, 1907, No. 321.

Consular and Trade Reports (monthly), June, 1908, No. 333.

Consular and Trade Reports (monthly), January, 1909, No. 340.

Consular and Trade Reports (monthly), June, 1909, No. 345. Financial Condition of South Manchuria Railway.

Consular and Trade Reports (monthly), December, 1909, No. 351.

Consular and Trade Reports (daily), November 8, 1910.

Arnold, Julean, *Commercial Handbook of China*, in two volumes, Washington, 1919 and 1920.

Arnold, Julean, Changes in the Economic Life of the Chinese People. United States Department of Commerce. *Trade Information Bulletin*, No. 5, March 23, 1922.

Palen, *Memorandum on Present and Potential Food Producing Possibilities of Manchuria*. Department of Commerce, Washington, prepared for Conference on Limitation of Armament. 1921.

2. COLLECTIONS OF TREATIES, ETC.

China. *History of the Peace Negotiations between China and Japan, March-April, 1895*. Tientsin, 1895.

Treaties, Conventions, etc., between China and Foreign States. Vol. 1, 2nd ed. The Maritime Customs. Shanghai, 1917.

Chung, Henry. *Korean Treaties*. New York, 1919.

The Consortium. *The official text of the Four-Power Agreement for a Loan to China and Relevant Documents.* (Carnegie Endowment for International Peace, Division of International Law.) Washington, 1921.

Korea. *Treaties and Agreements.* (Carnegie Endowment for International Peace. Pamphlet 43), Washington, 1921.

MacMurray, G. V. A. *Treaties and Agreements with and Concerning China.* (In two volumes, vol. 2, 1894-1919.), New York, 1921.

Manchuria. *Treaties and Agreements.* (Carnegie Endowment for International Peace, Division of International Law.), Washington, 1921.

Map of Manchuria and Korea. Edited by the Investigation Bureau attached to the President of the South Manchuria Railway.

Outer Mongolia. *Treaties and Agreements.* (Carnegie Endowment for International Peace. Pamphlet 41.) Washington, 1921.

Sino-Japanese Negotiations of 1915. *Japanese and Chinese Documents and Chinese Official Statement.* (Carnegie Endowment for International Peace, Division of International Law. Pamphlet 45.), Washington, 1921.

The Treaties of Peace, 1919-1923. Two volumes. New York, 1924.

3. BOOKS

Abbott, James F. *The Sino-Japanese Convention of 1909 and Its Significance.* Bulletin of Washington University.

Japanese Expansion and American Policies. New York, 1916.

Alexinsky, Gregor. *Modern Russia.* Translated by Bernard Miall. London, 1914.

Adachi, Kinnosuke. *Manchuria, A Survey.* New York, 1925.

Ariga, Nagao. *La Guerre Sino-Japonaise.* Paris, 1896.

La Guerre Russo-Japonaise. Paris, 1908.

La Chine et la Grande Guerre Européene. Paris, 1920.

Asakawa, K. *Japan's Relation to China.* In Clark University Lectures, "China and the Far East." New York, 1910.

The Russo-Japanese Conflict. Boston, 1904.

Atkinson, Thos. W. *Travels in the regions of the Upper and Lower Amoor and the Russian acquisitions on the confines of India and China.* London, 1860.

A Literary and Historical Atlas of Asia. Everyman's Library.

Auber, Peter. *China, an Outline of its Government, Laws, and Policy, and of the British and Foreign Embassies to, and intercourse with, that Empire.* London, 1834.

Baker, Ray Stannard. *Woodrow Wilson and World Settlement.* (Written from his unpublished and personal material.) In three volumes. New York, 1922.

Ball, J. Dyer. *Things Chinese.* London, 1904.

Ballard, G. A. *The Influence of the Sea on the Political History of Japan.* New York, 1921.

Bau, M. J. *Foreign Relations of China.* New York, 1921.
The Open Door Doctrine. New York, 1923.

Bell, John, of Antermony. *Travels from St. Petersburg in Russia, to Various Parts of Asia, in 1716, 1719, 1722, etc.* (In "A general collection of the best and most interesting voyages and travels in all parts of the world." Ed. by John Pinkerton.) London, 1811.

Bernstein, Herman. *The Willy-Nicky correspondence, being the secret and intimate telegrams between the Kaiser and the Tsar.* New York, 1918.

Bigham, Clive. *A Year in China, 1899-1900.* London, 1901.

Bishop, Joseph Bucklin. *Theodore Roosevelt and his Time, shown in his own letters.* Two volumes. New York, 1920.

Blakeslee, George H. *Japan and Japanese-American Relations.* New York, 1912.

Bland, J. O. P. *Recent Events and Present Policies in China.* Philadelphia, 1912.
Li Hung Chang. New York, 1917.

Boulger, D. C. *History of China.* Two volumes. London, 1898.
Central Asian Questions. London, 1885.

Brand, Adam. *A Journal of the Embassy from Their Majesties John and Peter Alexievitz, Emperors of Muscovy, etc. Overland into China. By Everard Isbrand, Their Ambassador, 1693-1695.* London, 1698.

Brinkley, Captain F. *China, Its History, Arts, and Literature.* Boston, 1902.

Brown, Arthur Judson. *The Mastery of the Far East.* London, 1919.

Brunnert, H. S. and Hagelstrom, V. V. *Present-day Political Organization of China.* Shanghai, 1912.

Bryce, James. *International Relations.* New York, 1922.

Buell, Raymond L. *The Washington Conference.* New York, 1922.

Bülow, Prince von. *Imperial Germany* (foreword by J. W. Headlam, translated by M. A. Lewenz). New York, 1917.

Challaye, Felicien. *La Chine et le Japon Politique.* Paris, 1921.

Cambridge History of British Foreign Policy. Vol. III, 1866-1919. Edited by A. M. Ward, and G. P. Gooch. Chapter III, Dawson, Wm. H., "Foreign Encroachments in China 1885-1898." Cambridge, 1923.

Cheng, S. G. *Modern China: a political study.* Oxford, 1919.

Chih Hsu, Mongton. *Railway Problems in China.* Columbia University series of studies in "History, Economics, and Public Law." New York, 1915.

China Year Book, 1916. Edited by H. T. Montague Bell and H. G. W. Woodhead. London.

China Year Book, 1921-1922. Edited by H. G. W. Woodhead. Peking and Tientsin.

China Year Book, 1923. Edited by H. G. W. Woodhead. Tientsin.

China. *Chinese Repository.* Vol. 1 to 20. May, 1832-December, 1851, Vol. XX. Canton, 1833-51.

Chirol, Valentine. *The Far Eastern Question.* London, 1896.

Christie, Dugald. *Thirty Years in the Manchu Capital.* New York, 1914.

Clement, Ernest W. *A Handbook of Modern Japan.* Chicago, 1907.

Colquhoun, A. R. *The "Overland" to China.* London, 1900.

Cordier, Henri. *Histoire des Relations de la Chine avec les puissances occidentales, 1860-1902.* Three volumes. Paris, 1902.

Historie Général de la Chine, et de ses relations avec les pays estrangers, depuis les temps les plus anciens jusqu'a la chute de la dynastie Mandchoue. Four volumes, Paris, 1920.

Bibliotheca sinica. Paris, 1904-1908.

Cowen, Thomas. *The Russo-Japanese War.* From the outbreak of hostilities to the battle of Liaoyang. London, 1904.

Coxe, William. *Account of the Russian discoveries between Asia and America.* London, MDCCLXXXVII.

Crandall, Samuel B. *Treaties, their making and enforcement.* Washington, 1916, 2nd ed.

Croly, Herbert. *Willard Straight.* New York, 1924.

Curzon, G. N. *Problems of the Far East.* Westminster, 1896.

Denby, Charles. *China and Her People.* Two volumes. Boston, 1906.

Dennett, Tyler. *Americans in Eastern Asia.* New York, 1922.

Roosevelt and the Russo-Japanese War. New York, 1925.

Dennis, Alfred L. P. *The Anglo-Japanese Alliance.* University of California Press, 1923.

The Foreign Policies of Soviet Russia. New York, 1924.

Dillon, E. J. *The Eclipse of Russia.* New York, 1918.

D'Orléans, Père P. J. *History of the Two Tartar Conquests of China.* London, 1854.

Du Halde, J. B. *Description, Geographique, Historique, Chronologique, Politique, et Physique de l'Empire de la Chine, et de la Tartarie Chinoise.* Four volumes. A la Haye. MDCCXXXVI.

Eckardstein, Baron von. *Ten Years at the Court of St. James, 1895-1905.* Translated and edited by Professor George Young. London, 1921.

Florenz, Karl. *Deutsche Vortrage Hamburgisher Professoren. Deutschland und Japan.* Hamburg, 1914.

Foster, John W. *American Diplomacy in the Orient.* Boston, 1903.

Diplomatic Memoirs. Two volumes. Boston, 1909.

Franke, V. *Die Grossmachte in Ostasien von 1894 bis 1914: ein Beitrag zur Vorgeschichte des Krieges.* Brunswick and Hamburg, 1923.

Gérard, A. *Ma Mission en Chine, 1893-1897.* Paris, 1918.

Ma Mission au Japon, 1907-1914. Paris, 1919.

Giles, Herbert A. *A History of Chinese Literature.* New York. 1901.

The Civilization of China. New York, 1911.

China and the Manchus. Cambridge, 1912.

Golder, F. A. *Russian Expansion on the Pacific, 1641-1850.* Cleveland, 1914.

Gowen, Herbert H. *An Outline History of China.* Boston, 1913.

Grosier, J. B. G. A. *A general description of China.* Two volumes. London. MDCCLXXXVIII.

Gubbins, G. H. *The Making of Modern Japan.* Philadelphia, 1922.

Harrison, E. J. *Peace or War East of Baikal?* Yokohama, 1910.

Hashagen, Jultus. *England unt Japan seit Schimonoseki. Essen,* 1915.

Heawood, Edward. *A History of Geographical Discoveries in the 17th and 18th Centuries.* Cambridge, 1912.

Hershey, Amos S. *The International Law and Diplomacy of the Russo-Japanese War.* New York, 1906.

Hishida, S. G. *The International Position of Japan as a Great Power.* New York, 1905.

Hornbeck, Stanley K. *Contemporary Politics in the Far East.* New York, 1919.

Shantung at the Peace Conference. In Temperley's "A History of the Peace Conference of Paris," vol. 6, 1924, 368-390.

Hoshino, T. *Economic History of Manchuria.* Seoul, 1920.

Hosie, Alexander. *Manchuria, Its People, Resources, and Recent History.* London, 1904.

Hsü, Shuhsi. *China and Her Political Entity,* New York, 1926.

Howe, M. A. De Wolfe. *George von Lengerke Meyer, His Life and Public Services.* New York, 1920.

Huang, Feng-Hua. *Public Debts in China.* Columbia University series of studies in "History, Economics, and Public Law." New York, 1919.

Ichihashi, Y. *Washington Naval Treaty and the Pacific Problem.* (Unpublished memorandum.)

Iswolsky, Alexander. *Recollections of a Foreign Minister.* Translated by Chas. L. Seeger. Garden City, N. Y., 1921.

James, H. E. M. *The Long White Mountain, or a Journey in Manchuria.* London, 1888.

Japan Times Publishing Company. *Economic Development of Korea and Manchuria.* Tokyo, 1923.

Japan. *The Japan Year Book, 1921-1922.* By Y. Takenob. Tokyo.

Japan and the Japanese People. (Nations of the War series.) London, 1915.

Kawakami, K. K. *American-Japanese Relations.* New York, 1912.

Japan in World Politics. New York, 1917.

Japan and World Peace. New York, 1919

Japan's Pacific Policy. New York, 1922.

Kennan, George. *E. H. Harriman, a biography.* Two volumes. Boston, 1922.

Kent, Percy Horace. *Railway Enterprise in China.* London, 1907.

The Passing of the Manchus. London, 1912.

Koo, V. K. Wellington. *The Status of Aliens in China.* Columbia University, 1912.

Korff, S. A. *Russia's Foreign Relations during the last half century.* New York, 1922.

Kuropatkin, General. *The Russian Army and the Japanese War.* Translated by Captain A. B. Lindsay. Edited by Major E. D. Swinton. Two volumes. New York, 1909.

Latourette, Kenneth Scott. *The Development of China.* Boston and New York, 1917.

The Development of Japan. New York, 1918.

Lawton, Lancelot. *Empires of the Far East.* Two volumes. London, 1912.

Leroy-Beaulieu, Pierre. *The Awakening of the East.* New York, 1900.

Manchuria, Land of Opportunities. Published by the South Manchuria Railway Company. New York, 1922.

Manchuria. *A Voice of the People of Manchuria.* Paris, 1919.

Martin, R. Montgomery. *China: political, commercial, and social; in an official report to Her Majesty's Government.* Two volumes. London, MDCCCXLVII.

McCormick, Frederic. *The Tragedy of Russia in Pacific Asia.* Two volumes. New York, 1907.

McLaren, Walter W. *A Political History of Japan during the Meiji Era, 1867-1912.* New York, 1916.

"M.E.S." His Book. A tribute and a souvenir of the twenty-five years, 1893-1918, of the service of Melville E. Stone as General Manager of the Associated Press. New York, 1918.

Michie, Alexander. *The Englishman in China.* Two volumes. Edinburgh and London. MDCCCC.

Miliukov, P. N. *Russia, Today and Tomorrow.* New York, 1922.

Millard, Thos. F. *America and the Far Eastern Question.* New York, 1909.

Our Eastern Question. America's contact with the Orient and the Trend of Relations with China and Japan. New York, 1916.

Moore, J. B., *A Digest of International Law, 1906.*

Morse, H. B. *The Trade and Administration of the Chinese Empire.* London, 1908.

The International Relations of the Chinese Empire. Three volumes. London, 1910, 1918.

Murray, Hugh. *Historical Account of discoveries and travels in Asia.* Three volumes. Edinburgh, 1820.

Okakura. *Les Ideaux de l'orient le Reveil Du Japon.* Paris, 1917.

Okuma, Count S. *Fifty Years of New Japan.* Two volumes. New York, 1919.

Oppenheim, L. *International Law, a Treatise.* Two volumes. London, 1905.

Overlach, T. W. *Foreign Financial Control in China.* New York, 1919.

Parker, E. H. *China's Intercourse with Europe.* Shanghai, *China, her history, diplomacy, and commerce from the earliest times to the present day.* London, 1917.

Pasvolsky, Leo. *Russia in the Far East.* New York, 1922.

Pooley, A. M. (edited by). *The Secret Memoirs of Count Tadasu Hayashi.* New York, 1915.

Japan's Foreign Policies. London, 1920.

Popowski, Josef. *The Rival Powers in Central Asia.* Westminster, 1893. (Translated from the German by Arthur Baring Brabant and edited by Charles E. D. Black.)

Rambaud. Alfred. *The Expansion of Russia.* In "The Case of Russia." New York, 1905.

Ravenstein, E. G. *The Russians on the Amur.* London, 1861.

Reboul, Lieutenant-Colonel. *Le Conflict du Pacifique et notre Marine de Guerre.* Paris, 1922.

Reinsch, Paul S. *World Politics, at the End of the 19th Century.* New York, 1916.

An American Diplomat in China. Garden City, N. Y., 1922.

Richard, L. *Comprehensive Geography of the Chinese Empire and Dependencies.* Shanghai, 1908.

Rockhill, W. W. *China's intercourse with Korea from the 15th century to 1895.* London, 1905.

Theodore Roosevelt, an Autobiography. New York, 1922.

Rosen, Baron. *Forty Years of Diplomacy.* Two volumes. New York, 1922.

Ross, Rev. John. *The Manchus, or the Reigning Dynasty of China.* London, 1880.

Quadflieg, Franz. *Russische Expansions-Politik von 1774 bis 1914.* Berlin, 1914.

Schmitt, B. E. *England and Germany 1740-1914.* Princeton Universtiy Press.

Smidt, Dr. H. *Japan in Weltkriege und das China Problem.* Bremen, 1915.

South Manchuria Railway. *Abstract of the Twenty-second Report of the South Manchuria Railway Company of the year ended March 31, 1923.* Dairen.

Stead, Alfred. *Japan by the Japanese.* New York, 1904.

Straight, Willard. *The Present Situation in Manchuria.* (Published in "China and the Far East" Clark University lectures. Edited by G. H. Blakeslee.) New York, 1910.

Stuart, Graham H. *French Foreign Policy from Fashoda to Serajevo, 1898-1914.* New York, 1921.

Takahashi, Sakuyé. *International Law applied to the Russo-Japanese War.* New York, 1908.

Thayer, Wm. Roscoe. *The Life and Letters of John Hay.* Two volumes. Boston and New York, 1915.

Timkowski, George. *Travels of the Russian Mission through Mongolia to China, and residence in Peking, in the years 1820-1821.* Two volumes. London, 1827.

Tomimas, Shutaro. *The Open Door Policy and the Territorial Integrity of China.* New York, 1919.

T'oung Pao. *Archives pour servir à l'ètude de l'histoire, des langues, de la Géographie et de l'ethnographie de l'Asie orientale.* Rédigées par MM. Gustave Schlegel et Henri Cordier. 1890.

Treat, Payson J. *Japan and the United States, 1853-1921.* Boston and New York, 1921.

Ular, Alexandre. *A Russo-Chinese Empire.* English version of "Un Empire Russo-Chinois," by Alexandre Ular. Westminster, 1904.

Vladimir (Volpicelli, Zenove). *The China-Japan War.* London, 1896.

Russia on the Pacific and the Siberian Railway. London, 1899.

Weale, B. L. P. (Simpson, B. L.). *Manchu and Muscovite, being Letters from Manchuria written during the Autumn of 1903.* London, 1904.

The Reshaping of the Far East. Two volumes. New York, 1905.

The Truce in the Far East and Its Aftermath. New York, 1907.

The Fight for the Republic in China. New York, 1917.

The Truth about China and Japan. New York, 1919.

An Indiscreet Chronicle from the Pacific. New York, 1922.

Wenckstern, Friedrich von. *A bibliography of the Japanese Empire.* Two volumes. Leiden, 1894; Tokyo, 1907.

Whigham, H. J. *Manchuria and Korea.* London, 1904.

Williams, F. W. *The Manchu Conquest of China.* Clark University addresses, November, 1912. New York, 1913.

Williams, S. Wells. *The Middle Kingdom.* A survey of the geography, government, literature, social life, arts, and history of the Chinese Empire and its inhabitants. Two volumes. New York, 1913.

Williamson, Alexander. *Journeys in North China.* Two volumes. London, 1870.

Willoughby, W. W. *Foreign Rights and Interests in China.* Baltimore, 1920.

China at the Conference; a report. Baltimore, 1922.

The Memoirs of Count Witte. Translated from the original Russian Manuscript and edited by Abraham Yarmolinsky. Garden City, N. Y., 1921.

Wright, George Frederick. *Asiatic Russia.* London and New York, 1903.

Wood, G. Zay. *The Chino-Japanese Treaties of May 25, 1915.* New York, 1921.

Yen, En Tsung. *The Open Door Policy.* Boston, 1923.

Younghusband, Captain Francis. *Among the Celestials.* London, 1898.

The Heart of a Continent. London, 1904.

4. NEWSPAPERS, PERIODICALS, ETC.

Asakawa, K. Korea and Manchuria under the New Treaty. *Atlantic Monthly,* November, 1905. Boston.

Japan in Manchuria, I. *Yale Review,* August, 1908.

Japan in Manchuria, II. *Yale Review,* November, 1908.

The Manchurian Conventions. *Yale Review,* November, 1909.

Bland, J. O. P. The Washington Conference and the Far East. *Edinburgh Review or Critical Journal.* October, 1922. London.

Cahen, Gaston. Les relations de la Russie avec la Chine et les peuplades limitrophes, a la fin du XVIIᵉ siècle et dans le premier quart du XVIIIᵉ. *Revue Historique,* Paris, 1907.

Chino-Russian Treaty, June 17, 1924. *Current History,* September, 1924.

The Chinese Social and Political Science Review. Peking, 1916-1920.

Denby, Charles. How Peace was made between China and Japan. *Forum,* March-August, 1900.

Dennett, Tyler. President Roosevelt's Secret Pact with Japan. *Current History,* October, 1924.

Dillon, E. J. Russia and Manchuria, Contemporary Review, June 1903, London.

The story of the peace negotiations. *Contemporary Review*, October, 1905. London.

Japan and Russia—the story of how peace was brought about. *Contemporary Review*, February, 1907. London.

Far Eastern Review. Manila, Shanghai, and Yokohama.

Fay, Sidney B. The Kaiser's Secret Negotiations with the Tsar, 1904-1905. *American Historical Review*, October, 1918.

The Geographical Journal, vol. XI, 1898, London. Russian explorations in Manchuria, abridged from a paper by E. E. Anert, in the Izvestia of the Russian Geographical Society, 1897, and the Yearly Report for 1896. By P. Kropotkin.

Vol. XIV, 1899, London, 1899. Through the Hun Kiang Gorges; or, Notes on a tour in "No Man's Land," Manchuria, by Robert T. Turley.

Graves, Louis. An American in Asia. VI. Willard Straight in Far Eastern Finance. *Asia*, February, 1921.

La Guerre et la Situation Financière de la Russie pendant les Sept Premiers mois de 1904. *Revue Économique Internationale*. September-December, 1904. Paris.

Guichen, Viscomte de. La Politique Extèrieure du Japon, depuis quinze ans. *Revue d'Historie diplomatique*, 1909. Paris.

Iyenaga, T. Manchuria's Strategic Railroad. *The World's Work*, June, 1910. New York.

Japan. *Japan Chronicle*, May-June, 1915. Kobe.
The Japan Weekly Mail. Yokohama, 1909.

Jenks, Jeremiah W. The Japanese in Manchuria. *The Outlook*, March 11, 1911.

Journal of the Royal Geographical Society, vol. 39, 1869. London. Williamson, Alex., Notes on Manchuria, Observations made on visits.

Vol. 42, 1872. London. An expedition through Manchuria from Peking to Blagovestchensk in 1870. By the Archimandrite Palladius, Chief of the Russo-Greek Church Mission at Peking. Compiled from the Journal of the Archimandrite and translated by E. Delmar Morgan.

Kawakami, K. K. The New Manchuria. *The Forum*. October-December, 1906.

Russia's Move to Treat China as an Equal. *Current History*, September, 1924.

The Policy of Secretary Knox. An editorial in *The Outlook*, February 12, 1910.

Kuropatkin, General. The Military and Political Memoirs of. Translated by G. Kennan in *McClure's Magazine*, Vol. XXXI, No. 5, September, 1908.

Japan's Strength in the War. Translated by Geo. Kennan in *McClure's Magazine*, Vol. XXXI, October, 1908.

The Causes of Russia's Defeat by Japan. Translated by Geo. Kennan in *McClure's Magazine*, December, 1908.

The Treaty at Portsmouth. Translated by Geo. Kennan in *McClure's Magazine*, January, 1909.

Langer, Wm. L., *The Origin of the Russo-Japanese War in Europäische Gespräche*, Hamburg, 1926.

Leroy-Beaulieu, Pierre. Le Probleme Chinois, *Revue des Deux Mondes*. November 1, 1900. Paris.

Makino, N., *Interview with Baron Makino*, April 2, 1919. (In files of Hoover War Library.) Paris, 1919.

The Manchurian Question. In *The London Times*, Weekly Edition. January 29, 1904, February 5, 1904. London.

Marvin, George. Willard Straight. *Japan*, December, 1924. See also November issue.

Matusorski, Z. Sketch of the Chinese Empire, translated by Lt. Colonel W. E. Gowan. *Imperial and Asiatic Quarterly Review*. Vol. IX, 1895.

Millard, Thos. F. America in China. *The Forum*, vol. 44, July-December, 1910.

Murakoshi, S. Periodicity of Manchurian Climatic Factors in relation to Agriculture. *Manchuria Daily News* (Dairen) monthly supplement, November 1, 1924.

New York Times. March-May, 1915.

North China Herald and Supreme Court and Consular Gazette. 1915. Shanghai.

Ozaki, Y. Misunderstood Japan. *North American Review*, October, 1900.

Parker, E. H. Russia's sphere of influence, or a thousand years of Manchuria. *The Imperial and Asiatic Quarterly Review*, April, 1900. Third Series, vol. 9.

Pinon, René. La Chine et les Puissances Européenes, 1894-1904. *Revue des Deux Mondes*. August 1, 1904.

Rea, George Bronson. Daylight in Manchuria. Reprinted from *Far Eastern Review*, November, 1920. Shanghai and Tokyo.

Read, Sheridan P. Russia in North China. *Independent*. February 28, 1901.

Reinsch, Paul S. Secret Diplomacy and the Twenty-one Demands. *Asia*, November, 1921.

The Literature of the Russo-Japanese War, I and II. By a British Officer. *American Historical Review*, April, 1911, and July, 1911.

Seibold, Louis. Japan, Her Vast Military Undertakings and World Expansion. *New York Herald*.

Sowerley, Arthur De C. The Exploration of Manchuria. Annual Report of the *Smithsonian Institute*, 1919. Washington, 1921.

Stead, Alfred. Conquest by Bank and Railways, with examples from Russia in Manchuria. *The Nineteenth Century,* June, 1903. New York.

Swift, J. T. Philander C. Knox. *America-Japan,* October, 1921. Published by the American-Japan Society of Tokyo.

The Times, Weekly Edition, London, February 5, 1904.

The Truth about the Sino-Japanese "Conversations." *Japanese Student's Union,* London, April, 1915.

Tsukunaga, K. Manchurian Soil. *Manchuria Daily News* (Dairen) monthly supplement, November 11, 1924.

Yamagata, Prince Isaburo. South Manchuria under Japanese Control. *The Transpacific Magazine,* Tokyo, October, 1922.

INDEX

INDEX

Abaza: 80; 118

Adviser: foreign, 28

Aigun: treaty of, 18-19

Albasin: 11-12

Alexander III: 46; 63

Alexieff: 87; 114

Alexieff-Tseng Agreement: 87

American policy: see United States

American trade: in Manchuria 176 et seq

Amur region: occupation by Russia, 17-18; annexation by Russia, 86

Amur river: 1; 3; economic value of, 8; seizure by Russia, 14

Anglo-German Convention: 91; 96

Anglo-Japanese Alliance: 98; renewal of, 146; 185; 262; second renewal, 275

Anglo-Russian railway agreement: 76

Antung: 32

Antung-Mukden Railway: 143; 207 et seq; 241

Area: of Manchuria, 2-3; 6

Armies: Japanese and Chinese in Korea, 26-27; Russian in Manchuria, 83 et seq.

Asakawa: 37

Baikal: 46

Bay: Yedo, 22

Bezobrazoff: 80; 113

Bismarck, Prince von: 36

Blagovestchensk: massacre at, 83-84

Bland, J. O. P: 180

Board of Reference: (Washington Conference) 269

Borden, Sir Robert: 268

Boundaries: of Manchuria, 3-4

Boxer Rebellion: 82; 140

Briner, Mr.: 113

British-American Tobacco Company: 163

Buck, Mr.: 159

Cables: see telegraphs

Canton: 18

Cassini, Count: 40; 51; statement of in New York Tribune, 107; 132

Cassini Concention: 55 et seq.

Changchun: 139

Changpai: mountains, 5

Charter Oath: 23

Chefoo: 42

Chientao: 215 et seq; 282

Chili: 3

China: Great Wall of, 7; 76; revolution in, 7; Mongols in, 8; sovereignity of, 102; integrity of, 161; leaseholds, 251; tariff autonomy, 289

China Consortium: 283 et seq; attitude of powers toward, 287

Chinchow: 44

Chinchow-Aigun Railway: 191

DATE DUE

DATE DUE			
APR 15 1968			
MAY 12 0 1969			
GAYLORD			PRINTED IN U.S.A.